The

URBAN
VEGAN

The
URBAN VEGAN

250 Simple, Sumptuous Recipes
from Street Cart Favorites to Haute Cuisine

Dynise Balcavage

ThreeForks

Guilford, Connecticut
Helena, Montana
An imprint of The Globe Pequot Press

For John

ThreeForks®

A ThreeForks Book

ThreeForks is a registered trademark of Morris Book Publishing, LLC.

Text design: Sheryl P. Kober
Project editor: Julie Marsh
Layout artist: Casey Shain

Library of Congress Cataloging-in-Publication Data

Balcavage, Dynise.
The urban vegan : 250 simple, sumptuous recipes, from street cart favorites to haute cuisine / Dynise Balcavage.
p. cm.
Includes index.
ISBN 978-0-7627-5281-2
1. Vegan cookery. I. Title.
TX837.B257 2009
641.5'636—dc22

2009022430

Printed in the United States of America

10 9 8 7 6 5 4 3 2 1

CONTENTS

INTRODUCTION

Remember the children's fable about the city mouse and the country mouse?
I'm a city mouse.

Some people are understandably uncomfortable with the crowds, traffic, and cultural differences found in a large urban center. But to me, they're as essential as food and water. Even though I was born and raised in a small, boondockian coal-mining town, I've always been drawn to the ethnic diversity and ever-changing rhythm of cities, both at home and abroad. The differences in food, dress, and cultures make me feel more connected to humanity. The hustle and bustle of urban life energizes and inspires me, and of course, inspires my cooking.

Finding vegan food in an urban environment, for me, is an endless treasure hunt. Since I live in Philadelphia—a city of three million, I'm lucky enough to have access to countless farmer's markets, health food stores, food festivals, and gourmet shops. I'm constantly on the lookout for exotic products to sample. One of my favorite past-times, for example, is exploring ethnic food markets. We have some very large ones here in Philly, and I literally spend hours wandering the aisles, dazzled by the colorful labels, the unfamiliar alphabets, and the delicious tension of navigating uncharted, vegan-possible territory.

Philly is a restaurant town, and I take advantage of the full spectrum of culinary choices my city has to offer. Luckily for me, Ethiopian, Japanese, Malaysian, Laotian, Burmese, Indian, Vietnamese, soul food, upscale herbivore, and pinch-penny vegan are all just a short walk or subway ride away. I always bring home a doggy bag and a container of inspiration for my recipes.

Since I'm an avid traveler—thirty countries and counting—my cooking is also informed by trips to cities like New Delhi, Shanghai, Paris, Rio de Janeiro, Tangiers, Istanbul, and Katmandu. Forget traditional souvenirs. I bring home suitcases full of ingredients to expand my cooking repertoire, like saffron from Spain, yerba mate from Argentina, and guava cheese from Barbados (yes, it's vegan).

When people learn I'm vegan, their most common, knee-jerk response is "But what do you eat?" I can't help but giggle when they ask, because I have such a hard time keeping up with all the foods I want to try and recipes I want to try to create. I wrote this cookbook, in part, as a very long answer to their short question. I also wrote it because I want you to find inspiration in your own city, in the cities you visit, and most importantly, in your own kitchen.

COOKING NOTES

"The Tyranny of the Recipe"

London food writer and cook Nigella Lawson often writes about overcoming "the tyranny of the recipe." Learning to cook and developing your own style in the kitchen does not mean following recipes religiously. Cooking should be fun and creative. And some substitutions need to be made from necessity; there's nothing I hate more than running out to the store at the last minute to buy a missing ingredient. I usually don't.

People often write and ask questions like "Can I substitute agave nectar for molasses?" The short answer? Of course. The slightly long answer: . . . It won't taste exactly the same. You have to understand the rules before you can break them. Ingredients with similar tastes and textures are naturally interchangeable: pears and apples, for example, chocolate and carob, and tempeh and seitan.

My advice is to try recipes—mine or anyone else's—exactly as written the first time, and then improvise to your heart's content. This is especially important when baking. Baking requires precise measurements, so changing ratios can be disastrous, not to mention wasteful.

Kitchen Equipment
That Makes My Life Easier

Since I live in a city apartment, space is a precious resource. Like most foodies, I can spend endless hours browsing in cookware shops and online, salivating over the latest gadgets, pans, and knives. But reality always sets in when I stop and realistically ask myself, "Where would I store it?"

So, I've learned to make do without the bagel slicer and the apple corer. But I've found that the following items are worth the space and money. They are timesavers and have helped make my cooking life much happier and more efficient.

Garlic press: Since I eat a lot of garlic, that adds up to a lot of chopping. With a garlic press, you simply place a whole clove inside the chamber, squeeze, and you have a nice pat of uniformly minced garlic. The peel stays inside the chamber; you simply remove it and toss it.

Good knives: For years, I struggled through my culinary adventures with crappy Ikea knives. Although I coveted better knives, I thought buying them was living beyond my means. Eventually, I broke down and bought a set of Henckels chef's knives, complete with butcher block storage unit, at a discounted price. I'm so glad I did. Unlike silly impulse purchase gadgets that clog up my drawers, these knives see daily use and make chopping so much easier. Get the best knives you can afford, and make sure they feel good in your hand.

Immersion blender: One day, I made red beet soup and decided to puree it in my blender. I filled the pitcher too full and the soup splattered all over my white walls, counters, and appliances. My kitchen looked like a murder scene. The following week, I bought an immersion blender. I haven't looked back.

Potato ricer: I'm surprised at how many people have never used a ricer; once you buy one, you'll find yourself making mashed potatoes at least once a week. Simply place a hot, cooked potato (or any root vegetable, really) inside, with skin intact. Give it a gentle squeeze and voilà! It extracts the insides and leaves the skin inside the ricing chamber, which you then pull out and compost or throw down the disposal. Ricers are also great for making spaetzle.

Silpat mats: Silpats prevent foods from sticking when baking. I resisted buying these for years, and then I found some discounted at Marshalls. After one use, I knew they were worth the money, and then some.

I have three, two small and one large, which is imprinted with a ruler and several circular guides that are helpful when making pie crusts. I especially love using my large, Pepto Bismol pink silpat when rolling out dough and making pasta. Cleanup is so much easier now than in my pre-silpat life.

Stand mixer: If you bake at least twice a week, I'd say this is a must. Although I occasionally pull out my electric mixer, I constantly use my fire engine red KitchenAid mixer for making cakes, cookies, and breads. Just turn it on your chosen speed, and you're free to roam the kitchen and do other things. You can also buy fun attachments, like a pasta maker. Plus, stand mixers look ultra-cool and are available in virtually every color of the rainbow. I love my KitchenAid, but many other great brands are available.

Food notes

All salt is sea salt.

All sugar is vegan sugar.

Milk is either soy or rice unless otherwise noted.

Chocolate is dark chocolate; I recommend it contain at least 65 percent cocoa.

Flour: Half whole-wheat, half spelt, unless specified.

Vegan butter: Earth Balance is the only brand I use.

Vegenaise is the only brand of vegan mayonnaise I use.

VEGANIZING 101

Just because you decided to go vegan or incorporate more vegan recipes into your diet doesn't mean that you have to now give away all of your non-vegan cookbooks and stop watching cooking shows on the Food Network. Some people—mostly non-vegans—are surprised to learn that I'm a self-professed cooking show and cookbook junkie. In fact, most of the 150 cookbooks I own are not vegan. Over the years, I've developed an innate sense of how to veganize recipes. You will, too.

But before we go on, let me tell you why I hate the verb "veganize." To say you are going to "veganize" a traditionally non-vegan food, in my eyes, diminishes the inherent splendor of vegan cooking. To "veganize" a recipe somehow implies that you are holding up non-vegan food as the "gold standard," that vegan cooking is not quite as good as the non-vegan recipe that you are modifying. (And I have yet to hear of an omnivore "omnivizing" a non-vegan recipe.) But since the verb "veganize" is pretty well-accepted in vegan circles, I'll use it here—somewhat grudgingly—and will try not to get all PC on you.

ZEN PALATE, BEGINNER'S PALATE

Being vegan certainly takes some dietary adjustments. It takes a bit of a mental adjustment, too. So a little bit of Zen wisdom is pertinent here. It's important to stay in the present.

You don't expect an apple to taste like a mushroom, do you? Nor do you expect a cup of coffee to taste like a cup of tea. So why, I wonder, would anyone look back and expect ingredients commonly used in vegan cuisine, like seitan, tofu, and tempeh, to taste like meats? They are not meats. They are unique foods, just like apples and mushrooms, with unique histories, tastes, textures, and properties. The same goes for nutritional yeast-based sauces and soy- and nut-based cheeses. They might look like dairy-based cheese and cheese sauces, but they are not.

My point, in short, is that all tastes, other than our innate love of sweetness, are acquired. Imagine how glum food would be if we never moved beyond our affinity for sugar. We all somehow learned how to like and identify the unique flavors of olives, coffee, wine, chili, and pickles, to name just a few. So try to appreciate new foods for what they are. Approach them with the open mind of a beginner and with an innocence, rather than with a preconceived notion of what they are supposed to taste like. Accept them for what they are, just as you accept people for who they are.

Learning to veganize recipes will certainly help you expand your repertoire and will help you get the most out of your cookbook collection—and Food Network addiction. Never take a recipe, including mine, too literally. Don't be afraid to experiment and to make each dish your own. That said, I've included variations on many recipes so you can play around a bit.

Mock Meats

Many vegans and vegetarians shun mock meats on principle. I've never been a huge mock meat consumer. But since it's now widely available and tasty and it persuades some people to eschew meat, then I say, why not indulge? Mock meats provide high quality protein—plus fiber and important minerals—without all the nasty side effects of animal flesh, like saturated fat, cholesterol, and hormonal residues, to name just a few. My only issue with mock meat is one of semantics: I detest when companies or restaurants give vegan foods non-vegan names. This implies—incorrectly, of course—that the vegan version is a less-than-perfect substitute, and not a perfectly wonderful food on its own. I think it's time to start calling foods by their rightful names: seitan strips instead of chicken strips, and Tofu Marsala instead of Vegan Veal Marsala for example.

Since mock meats are costly, I try to buy only those that I find too difficult or cumbersome to make at home. For this reason, I enjoy vegan chorizo and sausages. I am also partial to vegan hot dogs during the summer, split in half and grilled, with plenty of relish, ketchup, and mustard. There's nothing like the smoky, crumbly texture of tempeh bacon, which I use in many recipes in this cookbook. And anyone who reads my blog knows that Riblets have prevented me from ordering takeout after many a busy workday.

A dizzying array of mock meats lines the supermarket shelves these days, especially thanks to the larger box health-food stores like Whole Foods. I even found gluten chunks in meat-loving Lima, Peru, and Barbados. Try a few and discover the brands and kinds you like. Some are better than others.

You can generally swap equal amounts of vegan meats for meats in most recipes.

Useful mock meats:
  Ground seitan
  Seitan chunks
  Soy burgers
  Tempeh
  Tofu
  Textured vegetable protein (TVP)

Vegan cheeses

For many people, this is the ultimate "I could never be vegan" bugaboo, and I can empathize to a point.

Although I did not grow up eating much cheese, I developed an affinity for it in my twenties. For ages, I was one of those vegetarians who declared loudly, "I could never give up cheese!" It was almost a knee-jerk reaction. Going without was actually easier than thinking about it. One day, and I no longer missed it.

As is the case with mock meats, an astonishing spectrum of vegan cheeses is now available, from slices and blocks to grated cheeses and sauces. Again, how much and what you decide to use depends on your taste, lifestyle, and budget (they're not cheap). Just make sure the products you buy do not contain casein or whey, which are actually milk products.

I buy the occasional block of vegan cheese and always have vegan slices in the fridge, for those nights when I hear the call of the wild grilled cheese sandwich. I used to also buy vegan parmesan, but have come to prefer nutritional yeast.

Useful vegan cheeses:
Slices in American, mozzarella, and jack (Vegan Slices are great for grilled cheese sandwiches and come in both soy and rice varieties)
Chunk cheese in mozzarella and cheddar
Vegan Parmesan (lately, I've been using nutritional yeast in place of Parmesan)

Eggs

It's a myth that eggs are needed for baking, as evidenced by the countless successful vegan bakeries and vegan baking cookbooks out there. Eggs are one way to give lift and moisture to baked goods, but they come at a high cost—especially to the chickens, who typically live in appalling conditions, rarely seeing the light of day or moving outside their cages. They also come at a high cost to the humans who consume them. Besides being pricey, eggs are linked to high cholesterol and salmonella, not to mention the fact that many are hormone- and antibiotic-laden. If you're worried about lift, a little more baking powder ($1/2$ to 1 teaspoon) can act as "Viagra" for your cakes and cookies.

For baking, I've used 1 heaping tablespoon soy flour plus 1 tablespoon of water for many, many years, even long before I went vegan. I find it results in very moist baked goods, plus it's easy to remember. Some people claim that they can taste the soy, but despite my ultra-sensitive palate, I've never found this to be

the case. Think about it: Soy is neutral-tasting and bland (think tofu!). I've listed other egg substitutes below, equal to one egg. Find the ones that work for you.

1 heaping tablespoon soy flour plus 1 tablespoon water

$1/2$ mashed banana: Obviously, only use this in sweet baked goods. It won't exactly make the tastiest quiche.

3–4 tablespoons applesauce: Again, only use this substitute in sweet baked goods.

$1/4$ cup soft, pureed tofu: For best results, whir in the blender before adding to your batter.

3 tablespoons flax seeds plus 2 tablespoons water: Whiz around in the blender before using. This is my least favorite method; I don't like the flaxy taste in baked goods, but some people do. Plus they do provide important omega-3 fatty acids.

Store-bought egg substitute: follow package instructions (you can find it in most health food stores).

Milk

Soy, rice, hemp, coconut, and almond milks occupy several shelves and half the so-called dairy aisle in my Whole Foods market. There are vegan half and halves, vegan creamers, vegan whipped creams, vegan yogurts, sour creams, and puddings. I've even seen soy milk in grocery stores in most developing countries, so I doubt you will have any problems in this department.

Butter

Earth Balance is the best vegan margarine I've found; I never use anything else. My other favorite butter substitute is a mashed avocado. Try it on toast. Sublime! You can also substitute oils for butter in most dishes.

Honey

I find that spoon for spoon, agave nectar is a stupendous honey stand-in. Plus, it has a lower glycemic index, so it gives you a more even shot of energy; you won't crash and burn after eating it. Maple syrup, brown rice syrup, and corn syrup will also do the trick.

THE URBAN VEGAN PANTRY

For the most part, the vegan pantry is more remarkable for what it does not contain than for what it includes. By and large, I stock my cupboards with the same types of basics that most people stock: flour, grains, beans, baking sundries, etc. But being an urban vegan, I have access to some esoteric ethnic and gourmet ingredients, so a few items deserve elaboration.

Whole grains
Whole wheat couscous
Brown rice
Quinoa
Amaranth
Barley
Millet
Steel cut oats
Spelt
Wheat berries

Flours/pastas
Whole-wheat pastry flour (a good substitute for white flour in baking)
Spelt flour
Teff flour
Soy flour
Chickpea flour (also known as gram flour, available in health food stores and Indian markets)
Pastas in assorted shapes, both regular and whole grain
Rice noodles
Soba noodles

Soy and other non-dairy milks, plus non-dairy milk products
Soy (Plain, vanilla)
Rice
Almond
Hemp
Soy yogurt
Soy sour cream
Soy cream cheese
Hard soy cheeses and/or slices (without casein)
Earth Balance (tubs and sticks)
Earth Balance shortening (sticks)

Nut butters
Peanut
Tahini
Cashew
Almond (expensive, but so worth the money)
Soy

Legumes (dried are wonderful, but canned are a timesaver, especially if you are busy)
Chickpeas
Cannellini beans (white beans)
Pinto beans
Kidney beans
Lentils (brown, red)
Black beans
Pigeon peas
Black-eyed peas
Dried peas (green or yellow)

Sweeteners
- Vegan white sugar
- Vegan brown sugar
- Vegan confectioners' sugar (also called powdered sugar)
- Agave nectar
- Brown rice syrup
- Maple syrup

Oils
- Extra-virgin olive oil. Get a fruity version, if possible.
- Olive oil, for sautéing
- Canola oil
- Flax oil for salad dressings; excellent source of omega-3 fatty acids
- Walnut oil for salad dressings; adds interesting flavor and omega-3 fatty acids
- Black sesame oil: A little goes a long way; strong, smoky-nutty flavoring for Asian-inspired dishes
- Coconut oil: A healthful oil that's gotten some bad press; hard at room temperature; wonderful for baking

Chocolate
- Best-quality dark chocolate buttons and chips; I recommend 65 percent cocoa or higher like Guittard and El Rey
- Cacao nibs (unprocessed chocolate; pleasantly bitter; do not melt—good addition to baked goods and to some savory dishes)
- Vegan white chocolate chips (available in health food stores and through online vegan shops)

Nuts and seeds
- Walnuts
- Pecans
- Almonds
- Sunflower seeds
- Pine nuts
- Pumpkin seeds
- Nigella seeds
- Seeds and beans for sprouting (mung beans, alfalfa seeds, etc.)
- Poppy seeds
- Sesame seeds

Alcohol
- Cointreau or Triple Sec
- Marsala
- Sherry (Amontillado)
- Brandy
- Cognac
- Armangac (pairs extremely well with prunes)
- Calvados
- Poire William
- Rum

Ethnic ingredients
- Tapioca pearls
- Miso
- Shoyu/Soy sauce
- Thai curry paste

Herbs and spices
- Smoked Spanish paprika
- Hungarian paprika (sweet and hot)
- Sumac
- Chipotle pepper
- Chili pepper
- Cumin
- Garlic powder
- Oregano
- Tarragon
- Basil
- Thyme
- Sage
- Bay leaves
- Cinnamon
- Nutmeg
- Allspice
- Cloves
- Ground ginger
- Fresh herbs, as needed (Grow your favorites in a small pot on a sunny windowsill, so you never run out.)

THE ICONS

 Low-fat
These recipes won't blow your diet—provided you eat only one serving!

 Fast
Cooks of average experience can generally pull together these recipes in less than 30 minutes.

 Omnivore Friendly
Choose these recipes when trying to impress an omnivore. Generally speaking, they resemble the taste and texture of traditional non-vegan recipes.

 Frugal
These recipes won't bust your budget since they are built on a foundation of cheap-and-cheerful pantry staples.

 Kid-Friendly
These foods tend to appeal to little fingers and still-developing palates.

CAFE CULTURE

Cafes are a mainstay of city life. These urban sanctuaries serve as homes away from home, where you can kick back and comfortably enjoy a snack and a hot drink. You can go alone and become instantly anonymous, burying your head in a newspaper or book. Or you can meet your friends for a quick gossip session. Part of cafes' charm and enduring longevity is the fact that they force you to slow down and remain in the moment and focus on the task at hand, if only for a while—a necessity when you live in a bustling city.

Cafes somehow manage to evolve with the times. Once upon a time, Ernest Hemingway, Pablo Picasso, and Gertrude Stein argued about art and culture over endless cups of espresso in Paris' grand Left Bank cafes. These days (in the United States anyway), you are more likely to see wannabe writers slouched over their laptops. In fact, I wrote a good bit of this book at a cafe near my loft.

CAPPUCCINO

Espresso coffee, to taste (you must use coffee specifically ground and roasted for espresso in this recipe)
1 cup plain, full-fat soy milk
Best quality cocoa powder, for dusting
Vegan sugar, to taste

I first fell in love with cappuccino during my pre-vegan days—in a quaint little cafe in Torino, Italy. Luckily, vegan cappuccino is simple to make at home—even without an expensive, counter-hogging espresso machine. All you need is a blender and a "caffetiera," a small, inexpensive Italian stovetop coffee pot available at most kitchenware shops for under $20.

1. Fill the caffetiera with water and coffee, according to the caffetiera's instructions. Be careful not to overfill. Put the coffeepot on low and check occasionally. Make sure it doesn't boil. Your nose will probably let you know when the coffee's coming up.
2. When the coffee's up, turn the heat down as far as it will go. Pour your soy milk into a Pyrex container and nuke in the microwave for about 2½ minutes, or until warmed through (times will vary, depending on your microwave).
3. Pour the warm milk into your blender. Cover it and, keeping your hand on the lid, blend the milk for about 10 seconds. Pour your coffee into a tall, heat-resistant glass or mug. Using a spatula, hold back the foam, and pour the milk into the glass. Then crown your cappuccino with the remaining foam. Dust with cocoa powder and add sugar, if desired.

Yield: 1 serving

Variations

For a caffe latte, skip the blender step. For a mocha, drizzle some chocolate syrup inside the cup before pouring in the coffee.

FAIR-TRADE COFFEE

We all want to earn a fair wage for our work, right? Many coffee farmers, despite backbreakingly hard work, cannot earn a decent living growing and harvesting one of the world's favorite brews. Buying and demanding fair trade coffee helps ensure that coffee is sold at a fair price and that these workers earn sustainable wages, via organized cooperatives. Ideally, the higher coffee prices are also invested in health care, education, and other local benefits to the coffee farming communities.

PECAN STREUSEL COFFEE CAKE

I often work and write in wireless cafes in various city neighborhoods. Unfortunately, only a handful offer vegan baked goods. This moist breakfast cake tastes just as decadent as any non-vegan version, but it's lower in fat and contains zero cholesterol. It's my morning coffee's new best friend.

This cake doesn't take long to put together, but it does take awhile to bake. So make it the night before, and then impress your family and friends with this crowd-pleasing treat.

1. Preheat oven to 350°F and grease a Bundt pan.
2. In a medium bowl, beat together Earth Balance, tofu, and sugar until extremely well blended—about 5 minutes. Add salt, vanilla, and soy flour and blend until mixed. The batter should be thick, with no lumps.
3. In another medium bowl, gently mix in remaining dry ingredients and add to the sugar mixture. Finally, add the sour cream and beat on low until blended.
4. Combine all the streusel ingredients in a small bowl, including optional additions, if using. Mix well.
5. Spoon half the cake batter into the Bundt pan. Sprinkle the streusel evenly across the top, and then finish with the remaining batter.
6. Bake for 40 to 50 minutes, or until a knife inserted in center comes out clean. Let cake cool at least 30 minutes before carefully turning out onto a display dish.

Yield: 16 slices

Cake

3 tablespoons Earth Balance
6 tablespoons full-fat silken tofu
1 cup vegan sugar
1 teaspoon sea salt
2 teaspoons vanilla
3 heaping tablespoons soy flour
1 ½ teaspoons cinnamon
½ teaspoon ground ginger
¼ teaspoon nutmeg
2 ¼ cups flour (I use part whole wheat pastry flour and part spelt)
1 tablespoon baking powder
½ teaspoon baking soda
1 cup vegan sour cream or vanilla or plain vegan yogurt

Streusel

½ cup chopped pecans
½ cup vegan brown sugar
1 teaspoon cinnamon
1 teaspoon flour
3 tablespoons Earth Balance, melted

Optional streusel additions

Up to ½ cup of any of the following:
Vegan chocolate chips
Carob chips
Cinnamon chips
Pre-soaked raisins
Dried cranberries

Variation

Substitute walnuts, almonds, or any combination for the pecans.

CITRUS-SCENTED BLUEBERRY MUFFINS

2 cups of flour (I use half whole-wheat pastry flour and half spelt flour)

½ cup plus 2 tablespoons vegan sugar

I tablespoon soy flour

I tablespoon baking powder

Healthy pinch of sea salt

I tablespoon organic lemon zest or ¼ teaspoon lemon oil

I cup soy or rice milk

I teaspoon vanilla

¼ cup coconut or canola oil

I cup blueberries (fresh or frozen but not defrosted)

Almost every city cafe has a glass case filled with muffins. Most of them are oversize, fat-laden, and of course, not vegan. These muffins are a snap to prepare. Thanks to the small amount of coconut oil, they taste richer and more sinful than they actually are.

1. Preheat oven to 400°F. Line muffin tins with baking cups or spray lightly with cooking spray.
2. Mix dry ingredients in a large bowl.
3. Mix wet ingredients in a separate large bowl. Add wet ingredients to dry. Add blueberries. Stir until just moistened. Do not overstir.
4. Spoon batter into cups. Fill each cup about ⅔ full. Bake for 15–20 minutes or until knife inserted in the muffins' centers comes out clean. Cool for at least 5 minutes before eating.

Yield: 12 muffins

Variations

Substitute orange zest or oil for the lemon zest or oil.
Or substitute ½ teaspoon Fiori di Sicilia.

DOUBLE APPLE CAKE

This moist cake is sort of like city meets country. It gives you a double dose of apple—one shot from jarred applesauce (city) and the other from a tart Granny Smith (country). Served warm—and drizzled with agave nectar, if you have a sweet tooth—this easy cake pairs nicely with both tea and coffee. It's best eaten in a day or two, but you probably won't have any problems finishing it quickly.

1. Preheat oven to 350°F. Grease a 9 x 9-inch cake pan.
2. Toss apple with ginger, cinnamon, 1 tablespoon of the sugar, and the lemon juice. Set aside. In a large bowl, mix all dry ingredients except sugar. Set aside.
3. With mixer on low, blend ¾ cup sugar, oil, applesauce, soy milk, and vanilla until smooth. Add the dry ingredients in batches, scraping down the sides of the mixing bowl as needed. Turn mixer to medium and mix until combined.
4. Fold in the apple mixture and stir well. Pour into prepared pan and bake for 25 to 30 minutes, or until cake tester placed in center comes out clean.

Yield: 9 servings

1 large Granny Smith or other tart apple, peeled and cut into ¼-inch pieces
1 tablespoon powdered ginger
1 teaspoon cinnamon
¾ cup plus 1 tablespoon unrefined sugar
1 teaspoon lemon juice
1 cup whole-wheat pastry flour
½ cup unbleached white flour or unbleached spelt flour
2 tablespoons soy flour
1 teaspoon baking powder
1 teaspoon baking soda
5 tablespoons cold-pressed canola oil
1 cup applesauce, preferably organic
¼ cup soy milk
1½ teaspoons vanilla

Variation

Use pear sauce and pears in place of the apples.

CREPES WITH ALMOND SAUCE AND FRESH RASPBERRIES

Almond Sauce

½ cup soy creamer

½ teaspoon almond extract

2 tablespoons sugar

1 teaspoon Earth Balance

1 teaspoon cornstarch

Crepes

1 cup flour (whole-wheat pastry flour is fine)

1 cup plain soy milk

½ cup pure water

2 tablespoons soy flour

1 teaspoon vanilla or almond extract

2 tablespoons Earth Balance, melted

Cooking spray

Fresh, organic raspberries, to taste

Toasted slivered almonds for garnish

On Sunday, if I don't go out to brunch, I like to take the time to cook extra-special breakfasts to remind myself that it's my day off. These crepes are very light, yet intensely satisfying. The almond sauce is similar to a British hard sauce. Luckily, you don't have to travel all the way to London to enjoy it.

1. Whisk all sauce ingredients together in a saucepan. Bring to a slow boil, whisking constantly. Turn down heat and cook until thickened, again whisking constantly. Remove from heat.

2. Whisk flour, soy milk, water, soy flour, extract, and Earth Balance together in a medium bowl until smooth and no lumps remain. Batter should be thin—add a bit more soy milk, if necessary.

3. Heat pan over medium high and spray with cooking oil spray. Pour about 2 tablespoons of batter onto pan and immediately twist the pan in one direction so that a thin layer of batter evenly coats the pan. Cook until bottom is golden. Set aside on a plate while you make the rest of the crepes.

4. Fold each crepe in quarters. Drizzle almond sauce over crepes, and top with a healthy serving of raspberries. Garnish with toasted slivered almonds, if desired.

Yield: 6 servings

CHERRY-CHOCOLATE CHUNK SCONES

These days, it seems like every cafe in every U.S. city offers a huge basket of scones. My breakfast scones are a snap to make. The juxtaposition of earthy, dark chocolate chunks against the sour-sweet dried cherries somehow exudes a certain sophistication. You feel more cultured while eating them, especially with fresh-brewed tea, your morning paper, and an extended pinky. You can substitute chocolate chips for the chunks, but I prefer the intensity of biting into a huge chunks of best-quality chocolate.

1. Heat oven to 425°F. Grease a cookie sheet.
2. In a large bowl, mix flour, sugar, soy flour, baking powder, and salt. Add the Earth Balance chunks to this mixture, and using your fingers, rub well into the flour. The mixture should resemble damp sand. Stir in the cherries and chocolate chunks.
3. In another bowl, mix all the wet ingredients. Add to the flour mixture and mix until just wet. Do not overmix. The dough should be wet, but not too wet, and will stick to your hands a bit. If it's too dry, add more milk, 1 tablespoon at a time.
4. Form into a doughball and place onto the cookie sheet. Use your fingers to press and form into a 7- to 8-inch round. Cut into 8 wedges.
5. Bake for 16 to 18 minutes or until crust is golden brown and a knife inserted into the thickest part of the scones comes out clean.
6. Remove from oven, retrace your cut lines with a knife, and allow to cool on a rack. Serve plain, with Earth Balance, or with jam.

Yield: 8 scones

1½ cups flour (I use half spelt and half whole-wheat pastry flour)
½ cup sugar
2 heaping tablespoons soy flour
1 tablespoon baking powder
½ teaspoon sea salt
4 tablespoons cold Earth Balance, cut into pea-size pieces
½ cup dried cherries
¼–½ cup dark chocolate buttons, crushed into chunks
½ cup rice milk
1 teaspoon apple cider vinegar
1 teaspoon almond extract
½ teaspoon vanilla extract

Variations

Substitute dried blueberries or raspberries for the cherries.
Add ½ cup toasted nuts of your choice.

DEF-JAM BARS

Crust

1 batch All-Purpose Sugar Cookie dough (see page 174)

Spread

1 10-ounce jar your favorite jam (raspberry, orange marmalade) or spread (chestnut, chocolate-hazlenut, nut butter)

Topping

¼ cup dark or white (vegan) chocolate chips—or create a batch of each

Optional additions

½ cup chopped nuts (toasting them beforehand really coaxes out the flavor)

½ cup dried fruit (cranberries, chopped cherries, chopped apricots)

½ cup mini dark or white (vegan) chocolate chips

These bars are the quintessential urban cookie. Like hip-hop music, they are unapologetically individualistic. They lean heavily on improvisation. Use whatever jams or spreads you have on hand; flavor the cookie dough however you like, and top them with chocolate, white chocolate, nuts—or just let them go naked. Did I mention how gorgeous they are, drizzled with Jackson-Pollack-esque splatters of chocolate? They are little bars of pure poetry.

1. Preheat the oven to 300°F.
2. Press the cookie dough into a greased medium cookie sheet. Bake for 15 to 20 minutes, or until set. Be careful not to let the edges brown.
3. Let cool on a rack for 30 minutes. When cool, spread your topping of choice onto the dough. If you're adding nuts or mini chocolate chips, sprinkle them onto the jam (the jam acts like a "glue" of sorts).
4. Pour chocolate chips in a glass dish. Microwave at 50 percent power in 30-second intervals, until chips are melted. Stir well, then using a spoon or spatula, splatter onto the cookies in a random fashion.
5. Let cool, then cut into bars.

Yield: 30 large bars

Variations

Flavor combination ideas—the possibilities are endless!

*   Flavor cookie dough with almond extract; use raspberry jam, ½ cup toasted almonds, and top with white chocolate drizzle.
*   Flavor cookie dough with orange extract; use orange marmalade, and top with dark chocolate drizzle.
*   Use chestnut cream (buy in gourmet shops); top with dark chocolate drizzle.
*   S'mores: Use vegan marshmallow crème; top with dark chocolate drizzle and crumbled vegan graham crackers.
*   Flavor cookie dough with coconut extract; use pineapple jam, ½ cup toasted pecans, top with half white chocolate drizzle, half dark chocolate drizzle, and a dusting of dried coconut.

PUMPKIN SPICE BABY BUNDTS

Living in the city means you often have to share. You share seats in the sub-way, for example, and drivers share the road with bikers. You share public places. And many cities even have environmentally friendly car shares and bike shares. It's nice to know, though, that when you make these single-serving mini cakes, you'll never have to share your Bundt cake. This pumpkin spice cake is moist and surprisingly light. The espresso powder adds a masculine shot of gravitas.

1. Grease a baby Bundt pan. Heat oven to 400°F.
2. In a large bowl, mix brown sugar, applesauce, oil, vanilla, orange oil, pumpkin, and maple syrup until smooth and well blended.
3. Using low speed, mix in flours, about ½ cup at a time, and then add espresso powder, baking powder, spices, soda, and salt. Fold in nuts and raisins and pour into the pan, filling each cavity ¾ full.
4. Bake for 40 to 45 minutes until a knife inserted in the center comes out clean. (If Bundts start to brown too quickly, cover with foil.) Allow to cool completely before glazing.
5. Using a fork, whisk all glaze ingredients together until smooth. Drizzle glaze on cakes.

Yield: 6 baby bundts

Cake

¾ cup brown sugar, packed
½ cup applesauce
5 tablespoons canola oil
1 teaspoon vanilla
Drop or two of orange oil
1 15-ounce can unsweetened pumpkin puree
¼ cup maple syrup
1½ cups flour (half spelt, half whole-wheat pastry flour)
2 heaping tablespoons soy flour
1 tablespoon espresso powder (optional, but excellent)
1 tablespoon baking powder
2 teaspoons cinnamon
¾ teaspoon ground ginger
½ teaspoon nutmeg
¼ teaspoon baking soda
¼ teaspoon salt
½ cup chopped nuts (toasting them beforehand really coaxes out the flavor)
½ cup raisins

Glaze

1 cup powdered sugar
1 teaspoon vanilla
1 tablespoon plus 1 teaspoon soy or rice milk

JACKFRUIT-BANANA SMOOTHIE

I 20-ounce can jackfruit in syrup, drained
I cup coconut milk (light is fine)
½ frozen banana
I tablespoon sugar (optional)
3 ice cubes

We normally associate the word "cafe" with baristas and Starbucks. But when you live in the city, cafes can range from the big chains to ethnic, family-run holes in the wall.

Chinese and Vietnamese cafes serve an astonishing array of teas, coffees, juices, and smoothies. One of my favorites is made with jackfruit—a succulent yellow-orange fruit that tastes like a cross between a peach and a mango. Besides being tasty, it's surprisingly high in calcium; you can find it in most Asian groceries. When coupled with a banana and coconut milk, this decadent smoothie exudes a sinful creaminess that's reminiscent of a custard cream.

Process everything in a blender until smooth.

Yield: 2 large smoothies

BUBBLE DRINKS

⅓ cup black tapioca pearls (available in the refrigerated section of most Asian markets)
Pulp I avocado or I cup fresh, chopped fruit (mango, jackfruit, durian, kiwi, watermelon, honeydew melon, or strawberry)
½ cup coconut milk
3 cups vanilla soy milk
½ cup sugar or other sweetener (for avocado only; most other ripe fruits need only one tablespoon or so of sugar)
6 ice cubes

Here's another drink inspired by Asian cafes. These refreshing, smoothie-esque fruit shakes are usually made with some combination of sugar, sweetened condensed milk, and/or fruit. (But you can ask for soy milk or tea, instead.) You can't help but smile at the cheerful polka dots of gummy tapioca pearls.

1. Cook tapioca pearls in boiling water for 3 to 4 minutes. Drain, then cover with cold water so they don't stick together. Drain once again just before using.
2. Whip the remaining ingredients in the blender until smooth. Spoon the tapioca pearls into glasses, then pour the shake over the pearls.

Yield: 2 large or 4 small servings

BERRY TART

Since my days are usually crazed with work and activity, my idea of the ultimate treat is to disappear in the corner of my favorite cafe and spend a few blissful hours there, perusing guilty-pleasure magazines and Web surfing, while nursing a strong cup of tea and a slice of tart. This recipe means you can indulge in these guilty pleasures in the privacy of your own home—wearing slippers, for added comfort.

1. Preheat oven to 375°F.
2. Mix everything for crust but syrup and water in a food processor until it forms a ball. Mix the maple syrup and water together and set aside. Put the ball of dough on a sheet of floured wax paper. Roll until very thin then place in your tart tin. Place pie weights in tart. Bake for 15 minutes. Remove pie weights and brush entire tart with the maple syrup water. Bake for 5 more minutes, then let cool.
3. In blender or food processor, mix filling ingredients until smooth and creamy. When the tart is cool, spread the creamy tofu filling into the tart shell.
4. Decorate the top with clean raspberries or any other combination of fruit. Concentric circles look especially nice.
5. Put ¼ cup of apricot or peach jam in the microwave on high for about 20 seconds to thin. Or heat it on low in a saucepan. Then use a pastry brush to gently spread this glaze on top of the fruit. This keeps the fruit from drying out and turning color.

Yield: 8 servings

Variations

Kiwis, apricots, and organic oranges all work nicely, either alone or in combination with other fruits listed.

Crust

1½ cups flour (I use half whole-wheat pastry flour, half spelt)
¼ cup sugar
6 tablespoons canola oil
2–4 tablespoons water or soy milk (add as much as you need to make the crust form a ball)
½ teaspoon cinnamon (optional)
1 tablespoon maple syrup
¼ cup water

Filling

1 12-ounce box firm silken tofu (Do not use the kind in the refrigerated section—too grainy. Use the kind that comes in aseptic boxes.)
1 cup powdered sugar
1 teaspoon vanilla or ½ teaspoon almond or lemon extract
2 tablespoons flour

Fruit and glaze

About 1–2 cups fresh raspberries, blueberries, huckleberries, blackberries, or strawberries
¼–½ cup apricot or peach jam

RAW-KLAVA

1¼ cups nuts of your choice
(good choices: walnuts, almonds,
pecans, pistachios, or a mixture)
4 tablespoons agave nectar
2 teaspoons fresh-squeezed
lemon juice
1 teaspoon cinnamon
Pinch of sea salt
Splash of orange flower water
(optional, but lovely)
Optional: 2 tablespoons almond
flour for rolled version

I am, by no means, a raw foodist, though I do love it and know I should eat more of it—especially when it tastes as good as these tasty little baklava alternatives. Besides the obvious health factor, you'll also enjoy this recipe because you get all the flavors of traditional baklava without added, non-nutritious fat—and more importantly, without having to wrestle with that hateful phyllo dough.

1. Process the nuts in a food processor until they reach a floury consistency. Add the other ingredients until you can't process any further.
2. Spread in a greased pie tin, cut into pieces, and refrigerate. Decorate with slivered almonds if desired. Or roll into 10–12 balls, and coat in almond flour.
3. Refrigerate for at least an hour. Remember: Raw desserts can be more fragile than their belly-busting counterparts, so treat the squares gently and remove them with the tines of a fork.

Yield: 10–12 baklava

GO-TO ZUCCHINI BREAD

2 cups zucchini, shredded
3 heaping tablespoons soy flour
2 cups sugar
¾ cup canola oil
1 tablespoon vanilla
3 cups flour
1½ tablespoons baking powder
2 teaspoons cinnamon
1 teaspoon baking soda
1 teaspoon salt
½ cup raisins (optional)
½ cup walnuts, chopped (optional)

In late August, city farmer's markets swarm with baseball-bat-size zucchini, and cafes and bakeries across the United States offer innumerable interpretations of zucchini bread. This is my go-to recipe—a veganized version of my mother-in-law Clara's famous zucchini bread. You can make it with or without nuts and/or raisins. Try it with yellow squash should you be faced with a surplus. But those tiny green confetti flecks are really what it's all about.

1. Preheat oven to 350°F. Grease and flour 2 small loaf pans.
2. Place zucchini in colander for 30 minutes to drain excess water. In a large bowl, mix zucchini, soy flour, sugar, oil, and vanilla until blended. Add flour and other dry ingredients and mix until blended. Fold in the raisins and nuts, if using. Pour into pans and bake for 40 to 60 minutes, or until a knife inserted in the center comes out clean. If top browns too quickly, "tent" with a piece of aluminum foil.
3. Allow to cool completely (about an hour) before attempting to remove from loaf pans.

Yield: 2 loaves

Variation

To lower the fat, use ½ cup oil and ¼ cup applesauce.

VIETNAMESE-INSPIRED TAPIOCA PUDDING

Since I'm a coconut freak, I often hang out in Vietnamese cafes, where coconut milk flows from the taps like water. I typically order a Rainbow Ice to drink, a colorful concoction of coconut milk, sweet red beans, and green agar jelly, along with a simple tapioca and coconut pudding for dessert. The slightly chewy texture of these pea-size cassava balls always seems so much more exotic than the tapioca pudding I grew up with. Perhaps it's the fact that they're almost as big as small marbles! This recipe is by no means authentic, as you can tell from the rum extract, which I added to play off the bananas. But it's a good example of how you can successfully mix your childhood influences with those you encounter during your travels.

1. Bring water and soy milk to a boil. Add tapioca and reduce heat to a brisk simmer (medium-low). Simmer uncovered, stirring occasionally, for about 40 minutes, or until tapioca balls are slightly chewy and exude a translucent "halo."
2. Add remaining ingredients and reduce heat to low. Cook for 15 more minutes, stirring occasionally. Chill in refrigerator for a few hours before serving,

Yield: 4 servings

2 cups water
1 cup soy or rice milk
⅔ cup medium-size tapioca pearls
3–4 ripe bananas, sliced thinly
½ cup corn
½ cup coconut milk (light is fine)
½ cup sugar
1 teaspoon lemon juice
1 teaspoon vanilla
½ teaspoon rum extract (or substitute ½ teaspoon more vanilla)
1 teaspoon sesame seeds
Pinch sea salt

Variations

Substitute diced mango or sweet red beans for the corn
or in addition to the corn.

BROWNIE BITES

8 tablespoons Earth Balance, softened

1 cup brown sugar, packed

6 tablespoons cocoa powder

1 teaspoon espresso powder

2 heaping tablespoons soy flour

1 cup flour (I use half whole-wheat pastry flour and half spelt)

¼ teaspoon salt

1 teaspoon baking powder

¾ cup soy milk

6 tablespoons dark chocolate chips (mini if available)

It's a fact: City dwellers are thinner than their suburban peers. This is not surprising, since, compared to those who live in rural and suburban areas, we urbanites tend to walk more (to work, to the store, to appointments) and have more healthy food choices at our fingertips.

Soft and fudgy, these preportioned, decadent little nuggets will satisfy your sweet tooth while still allowing you to keep your city-skinny figure—assuming, of course, that you stop at just one! Sprinkle them with powdered sugar for a magical fairy dust finish.

On the other hand, if you are a total hedonist and find these brownies to be too tame, there's a solution for you, too. Top them with your decadence of choice: a spoonful of vanilla, dulce de leche or chocolate soy ice cream, raspberry jam, soy whipped cream, or chocolate-hazelnut spread.

1. Preheat oven to 350°F. Grease a 24-count mini-muffin pan.
2. Cream together Earth Balance and sugar until fluffy.
3. In a medium bowl, mix together remaining dry ingredients. Little by little, stir into wet mixture, alternating with about ¼ cup of soy milk each time.
4. Mix until smooth, scraping down the sides of the bowl as needed. Stir in the chocolate chips. Lick spoon and beaters. (Cook's reward!)
5. Divide among mini-muffin tins, pouring about 1 heaping teaspoon or so of batter into each cup. Bake for 8 to 10 minutes, or until cake tester comes out clean.
6. Cool on racks for at least 15 minutes before serving.

Yield: 24–34 bites

LIKE BUTTAH—BUT BETTAH

Vegan margarines are available in most major supermarkets. But be careful: some contain hydrogenated oils (aka "transfats") and are not very healthy. My favorite brand is Earth Balance; it comes in tubs and sticks, and its flavor and texture is unsurpassed.

REAL HOT CHOCOLATE

First, let's get one thing straight: Heated chocolate soy milk is NOT hot chocolate. You haven't tasted hot chocolate until you've made it from scratch, without so much as a smidgen of cocoa powder or chocolate syrup.

This decadent version harkens back to the thick, creamy hot chocolate you'll find in a Madrid cafe on a cold December morning. It's comfort in a cup, but if you need a little extra, add a glug of spirits, just before removing from the stove.

For most recipes, soy and rice milks are interchangeable. But this is one instance you need the fat and creaminess of the soy milk to help this steaming winter drink achieve its fully decadent potential.

I cup full-fat plain soy milk
3 tablespoons best-quality dark chocolate buttons or chips (at least 65 percent cocoa solids)
I teaspoon vanilla
½–I teaspoon agave nectar
I teaspoon to I tablespoon rum, brandy, or Kahlua (optional)
Whipped cream or vegan marshmallows for garnish

1. In a small saucepan, gently heat milk, chocolate, vanilla, and agave nectar over low heat until the chocolate is completely melted. If you're using the alcohol, stir it in just before removing from the stove.
2. Serve plain, with a dollop of vegan whipped cream, or better yet, topped with vegan marshmallows.

Yield: I cup

Variations

For a mocha hot chocolate, add I teaspoon instant espresso powder while heating the other ingredients on the stove. For peppermint hot chocolate, add I or 2 drops of peppermint extract while heating the other ingredients on the stove.

CHAI

4–5 cups water or amount required to fill a small teapot

1 cinnamon stick

5 whole peppercorns

4 cardamom pods

2–3 black tea bags, depending on how strong you prefer your tea, or equivalent of loose-leaf tea

Soy or rice milk, warmed

Sugar or agave nectar

One of my favorite escapes from the hustle and bustle of city life involves curling up on a funky old cafe couch with a good book and a tall soy chai. After a few sips and a few pages, somehow the world seems like a better place.

Don't feel like going out? Make your own chai at home, then snuggle up with it in your comfiest chair under the afghan your grandma crocheted for you. (You can wear your fuzzy bunny slippers. No one will know.)

1. Bring water and spices to a boil. Pour into teapot and add tea bags. Allow to steep for about 5 minutes, or to your taste.
2. Add milk and sweetener to taste.

Yield: 1 small pot, enough for 2 people

COCONUT-LIME BARS

½ cup plus 3 tablespoons flour

1 cup sugar, divided into ⅓ and ⅔ cup

Pinch of salt

¼ cup coconut oil

⅓ cup nuts, ground to a flour in food processor

2 teaspoons lime zest (zest from about 2 organic limes)

3½ to 4 tablespoons lime juice (from about 2 limes)

1 tablespoon soy or rice milk

1 teaspoon coconut extract

1 cup shredded coconut

Most city cafes feature one or two gooey bar cookies for dunking in coffees. These lime-scented bars would go nicely with an herbal citrus tea. The rich, sweet coconut flavors provide a nice balance to the tang of the lime.

1. Preheat oven to 350°F. Grease an 8 x 8-inch or 9 x 9-inch pan.
2. In a medium bowl, cut together ½ cup flour, ⅓ cup sugar, salt, and coconut oil until crumbly. Stir in nuts, then press into prepared pan.
3. Bake for about 20 to 25 minutes or until golden. Remove and let cool slightly.
4. In a medium bowl, using a fork, stir together ⅔ cup sugar, lime zest and juice, milk, 3 tablespoons flour, and extract until smooth. Mix in shredded coconut.
5. Spread over baked crust and bake for 20 to 27 minutes or until set and just starting to turn golden.
6. Let cool on a wire rack for one hour, then chill in refrigerator for 30 minutes before cutting into bars.

Yield: 16 bars

Variation

Use another organic citrus fruit (e.g., lemon, oranges, blood oranges) instead of the lime zest and juice.

PUNK ROCK CAKES

Although I'm not positive, I'm fairly certain that rock cakes get their name from their dry, craggy appearance. They originated in England, but I fell for them in Barbados, where I looked forward to them every day for breakfast. After learning that they are inherently vegan, I named my version "Punk Rock Cakes," in honor of all the rough and craggy-looking punk rockers who—gentle souls—embraced and popularized veganism.

These humble little biscuits are quite dry, with just a hint of sweetness from the currants and zest, and pair more nicely with tea than coffee.

1. Preheat oven to 325°F. Grease a cookie sheet.
2. In a large bowl, add flours and baking powder. Using a pastry cutter or two knives, cut in Earth Balance and work until the mixture forms large crumbs. Add sugar, dried fruits, milk, zest, lemon juice, and vanilla. Mix with a heavy spatula until well combined.
3. Drop golf-ball-size amounts of batter onto cookie sheet. Bake for 15 to 20 minutes or until golden.

Yield: 10–12 cakes

1½ cups plus 3 tablespoons flour
1 tablespoon soy flour
2 teaspoons baking powder
5 tablespoons Earth Balance
½ cup sugar
½ cup currants, raisins, or sultanas
¼ cup candied cherries (optional, but pretty)
4–6 tablespoons soy or rice milk
2 teaspoons organic lemon zest, minced as finely as you can manage
1 tablespoon lemon juice
1 teaspoon vanilla

QUICK BERRY JAM

Back when I lived in the 'burbs, I used to make jams and jellies all the time. At that time, I had enough room to store all the necessary canning paraphernalia. But in my small city kitchen, space is limited, so when I make jam, I do it in small batches.

This berry jam is a snap to make, even for preserve-making neophytes. It's much better and fresher than the jarred stuff that they give you in cafes. You'll find yourself making it often.

1. Combine all ingredients in a large saucepan and cook over low heat, stirring occasionally, until all the sugar dissolves, about 10 minutes.
2. Slowly bring to a gentle boil and cook until jam has thickened, about another 10 minutes.
3. Cover and refrigerate. (Should keep for about 1 week in the fridge. You can also freeze all or a portion for a few months.)

Yield: about 3 cups

2 pints strawberries, hulled and sliced
1 pint raspberries
¾ cup sugar
1 tablespoon lemon juice

POLITICAL BISCOTTI

2 cups flour

½ cup cocoa powder

⅔ cup sugar

2 teaspoons baking powder

½ teaspoon salt

½ cup canola oil

6–10 tablespoons soy or rice milk

1 teaspoon vanilla

½ cup carob chips

½ cup dates, chopped into small pieces (about 6 large)

Every city cafe prominently displays a large apothecary jar brimming with delectable biscotti. This makes sense since they seem meant to be dipped in coffee. And the slightly dry texture ensures that more cookie will end up in your mouth than at the bottom of your cup.

Political banter is also a mainstay of cafe culture. Which leads me to the seemingly disparate ingredients included in these biscotti. When it comes to carob and chocolate, people tend to be very "either/or." They are always considered separately, as two distinctive flavors that were never meant to come together, sort of like Palestine and Israel. But the fact is that the sweet bitterness of dark chocolate and the earthy mustiness of carob are inherently complementary. The dates act as a sort of sticky-sweet peacemaker, a culinary UN if you will.

1. Preheat oven to 350°F. Grease a large cookie sheet or line it with a silpat.
2. Mix dry ingredients in a large bowl. Mix wet ingredients in a medium bowl or pitcher, starting with just 6 tablespoons of milk. Mix wet ingredients into dry. Mix well and switch to your hands when the dough becomes too difficult to handle with a spoon. If dough is too dry to stick together, add more milk, in 1-tablespoon increments.
3. When dough sticks together, knead in the carob chips and dates. Form into 2 approximately 9 x 3-inch logs. Bake for 25 minutes, or until a cake tester inserted in the center comes out clean.
4. Allow to cool for an hour. Using a serrated knife, cut into ½-inch biscotti. Turn them flat side down and bake for an additional 15 to 25 minutes, depending on how crispy you prefer your biscotti, turning once about halfway through. Allow to cool completely on a rack.

Yield: 24–28 biscotti

BLUE MOSQUE AYRAN

6 ounces plain, full-fat soy yogurt

1⅓ cups water

1–2 tablespoons dried mint

Salt to taste (up to 1 teaspoon)

Fresh mint for garnish

You can find this yogurt-based drink at any cafe or from any street vendor in Istanbul. Unfortunately, it's not vegan. This creamy vegan version uses soy yogurt; it's so refreshingly good that the imam would definitely approve.

Mix yogurt, water, mint, and salt in a blender until frothy. Serve in a tall glass with a sprig of mint.

Yield: 2 drinks

ALL-NIGHT BREAKFAST
AT THE DINER

Nothing could be finer than eating at the diner. Part trashy, part comfort, cheap and cheerful—and usually grossly unhealthy—diners always seem welcoming and consistent. You don't encounter too many surprises there, and that's exactly what you're craving: familiarity. They harken back to simpler times, when cell phones and video games were just a twinkle in some future genius's eyes.

Diner breakfasts are an institution in most American cities. One special perk of city life is that many diners serve breakfast 24/7.

Now, even vegan breakfast lovers can get their 3:00 a.m. pancake fix after a night on the town.

BETTER THAN BUTTERMILK-PANCAKES

I cup flour
I cup soy milk, plus 1–4
  tablespoons more
I heaping tablespoon soy flour
1½ teaspoons baking powder
½ teaspoon vinegar
Pinch salt

Optional additions

½–1 cup any of the following:
  carob chips, chocolate chips,
  blueberries, or raisins
2 mashed, ripe bananas and ¼ cup
  chopped walnuts
½ cup chopped apples and 1
  teaspoon cinnamon

Eating Saturday breakfast out is one of urban life's greatest pleasures. But on Sunday, my idea of heaven is to sleep in, and then eat these spongy pancakes while I sip on cappuccino and attempt—unsuccessfully—to finish the *New York Times* crossword puzzle.

1. Whisk first 6 ingredients together in a large bowl until no lumps remain. Gently fold in optional ingredients, if using. Batter will be thick. If it is too thick to handle (this will vary depending on the humidity where you live), add more soy milk, in 1-tablespoon increments.
2. Cook on an oiled griddle or nonstick pan over medium-high heat until you start to see bubbles appearing. At this point, flip the pancake and cook the other side until golden brown.

Yield: 4 extra-large or 6 medium pancakes

CHOCOHOLIC WAFFLES

Cacao nibs are the cleaned, roasted, and crushed pods of the cacao bean. In other words—pure chocolate. Since no sugar is added, cacao nubs are earthily bitter. Use them whenever you want to impart a pleasant, nutty crunch. You can find them in most gourmet shops. Sure, they're costly, but a little goes a long way.

Here, I've paired cacao nibs with Dutch-process cocoa to create these decadent breakfast waffles.

1 cup flour (I use ½ white spelt and ½ whole-wheat pastry flour)
3 tablespoons Dutch-process cocoa
1 tablespoon vegan sugar
1 heaping tablespoon soy flour
2 teaspoons baking powder
Pinch salt
1¼ cups soy milk
1 teaspoon vanilla
2 tablespoons canola oil
3 tablespoons cacao nibs

1. Mix first six ingredients in a medium bowl. Mix wet ingredients in a separate bowl and add to dry ingredients. Mix until just combined (do not overmix). Batter should be a bit lumpy. Gently stir in the cacao nibs just before cooking the waffles.
2. Drop batter onto waffle iron (¼ cup is the usual measure) and cook according to manufacturer's instructions. Try not to peek until the light tells you they are done, or they will tear apart.
3. Serve with Earth Balance and maple syrup, or toast waffles and use to make a soy ice cream sandwich.

Yield: 4 large or 16 small waffles

Variations

Use mini dark chocolate chips instead of cacao nibs.
Finish with raspberry sauce instead of maple syrup.
You can also use this batter to make pancakes instead of waffles.
(Yield: About 8 medium pancakes)

ORANGE-POPPY SEED WAFFLES

1¼ cups white spelt flour

1 heaping tablespoon soy flour

3 tablespoons sugar

1½ teaspoons baking powder

1½ tablespoons poppy seeds

⅛ teaspoon salt

1 cup soy yogurt

½ cup rice milk or soy milk (I prefer rice milk here)

4 tablespoons canola oil

1 teaspoon orange extract

¼ teaspoon orange oil or 2 tablespoons organic orange zest

Pimp your diner waffles! A refreshing hint of orange and tiny Seurrat-like dots of poppy seeds help transform your breakfast from "ho-hum" to "oh, yum!" A cup of soy yogurt makes these waffles extra moist, but balanced by the citrus, they taste feather light. Slather them with Earth Balance and maple syrup, and enjoy them with a strong cup of Earl Grey tea.

1. In a large bowl, stir together all dry ingredients.
2. In another bowl, whisk together wet ingredients, then whisk them into the dry ingredients, stirring very well until smooth. Batter will be thick; this is normal.
3. Using a spatula, spread batter onto the center of your waffle iron and cook according to the manufacturer's directions.

Yield: 4–6 large waffles, depending on the size of your waffle iron

Variation

For a really good, basic waffle, skip the poppy seeds and orange oil, and replace the orange extract with vanilla extract.

DECONSTRUCTED MONKEY BREAD

With all the rolling and rising, traditional Monkey Bread is a pain to make. And let's face it, even if you're a city dweller, finding a bakery vegan version is not always easy. This recipe uses only one dish to make a breakfast cake that provides the same cinnamon-chewy-gooeyness of Monkey Bread in about 40 minutes, counting baking time. Since it isn't really Monkey Bread, I added a nut topping that adds crunch, fiber, and important omega-3s. It's the perfect sugar fix. Serve warm with a glop of Earth Balance, or as a dessert, warmed with a scoop of vanilla soy ice cream.

1. Preheat oven to 350°F.
2. Mix batter ingredients in a medium bowl and spread evenly in a pie plate sprayed with cooking spray. Mix together all topping ingredients except nuts in a separate bowl. When the liquid ingredients are combined, stir in the nuts.
3. Mix sugar and cinnamon together, and sprinkle mixture evenly over the batter. Spread the nut topping evenly over the cinnamon-sugar and batter.
4. Bake for 30 to 40 minutes or until browned and knife inserted in center comes out clean. Cool for about 5 minutes. Serve warm with a glop of Earth Balance, or as a dessert, warmed with a scoop of vanilla soy ice cream.

Yield: 8 servings

Batter

2 cups whole-wheat pastry flour
2 tablespoons yeast
1 cup sugar
1/4–1/2 teaspoon sea salt
3 tablespoons Earth Balance, melted
3/4 cup very warm (but not hot!) water

Topping

1/3 cup dark corn syrup
1/3 cup brown sugar
2 tablespoons Earth Balance, melted
1/2 cup chopped walnuts

Cinnamon-Sugar

1/4 cup sugar
1 teaspoon cinnamon

BLUEBERRY-BANANA BREAD

2 heaping tablespoons soy flour
2 teaspoons baking powder
½ teaspoon baking soda
1¾ cups flour (I use 1 cup whole-
  wheat flour and ¾ cup spelt)
¾ cup sugar
Scant ½ teaspoon salt
Dash cinnamon
1½ teaspoons rum extract
½ teaspoon vanilla extract
6 tablespoons canola oil
3 large ripe bananas, mashed in a
  medium bowl
6–8 tablespoons soy or rice milk
1¼ cup fresh blueberries

City living means smaller appliances and closet-like kitchens. I usually make this bread in late July and early August, when my fridge overflows with $1-a-pint blueberries, and my freezer door won't shut because of all the frozen bananas I've accumulated. (I save overripe bananas in plastic ziplock bags for smoothies and baking.)

1. Preheat oven to 350°F. Spray a medium loaf pan with cooking spray.
2. Mix dry ingredients in a large bowl.
3. Add extracts and oil to mashed bananas, and then stir in 6 tablespoons of milk. Add more milk in 1-tablespoon increments, if necessary; batter should be thick and just moistened. Do not overmix.
4. Gently fold in the blueberries and pour into prepared loaf pan. Bake for 60 to 80 minutes, or until knife inserted in center comes out clean. If edges start to brown too quickly, "tent" with aluminum foil for the remainder of the baking.
5. Let cool for at least 30 minutes before slicing.

Yield: 1 loaf

SHIITAKE ON A SHINGLE

1 tablespoon Earth Balance
¼ teaspoon sea salt
Lots of freshly ground black
  pepper
¼ pound shiitake mushrooms,
  chopped fine
½ pound cremini mushrooms
  (baby 'bellas), chopped fine
1 tablespoon nutritional yeast
1 tablespoon flour
½ cup plain soy or rice milk
1 teaspoon soy sauce
½ teaspoon Dijon mustard
Splash liquid smoke
1 teaspoon dried tarragon
½ teaspoon dried sage
4 slices whole-grain bread

Shiitake mushrooms and tarragon—and the absence of dried chipped beef—transform this lowbrow diner classic from trashy to classy.

1. In a large saucepan, preferably nonstick or cast-iron, melt Earth Balance over medium heat. Add salt and pepper and cook the mushrooms over medium heat, stirring occasionally, until soft, about 10 minutes.
2. Sprinkle the yeast and flour over the mushrooms and let it cook undisturbed for about 1 minute. Turn heat to low.
3. In a separate bowl, whisk together milk, soy sauce, mustard, liquid smoke, and herbs.
4. Slowly pour the liquid over the mushrooms, stirring well. Cook until thickened, about 3 minutes. Mixture should be very thick. If you prefer a thinner consistency, simply add more soy milk, a tablespoon at a time.
5. Toast 4 slices of bread, preferably whole grain (these are the "shingles"). Spread with Earth Balance and then divide mushroom mixture over top.

Yield: 4 servings

COCO-MANDA MUFFINS

Labra-doodles. Chi-weenies. Jugs. Walking around the city, I've seen practically every incarnation of the so-called designer dogs—mixes of popular canine breeds. If you're thinking about adopting a pet, please visit your local animal shelter first. So many abandoned and neglected animals are in desperate need of loving homes. Adopting a shelter dog is infinitely rewarding and costs much less than buying a purebred (The notion of "pure breeds" actually creeps me out). And you'll save two lives for the price of one: By adopting one shelter pet, you will free up much needed space for another animal in need.

I say, designer muffins, not designer dogs! My "designer" Coco-Manda Muffin combines formidable, sumo wrestler-heavy coconut with ballerina-light and graceful mandarin oranges. Together, they meet in a balanced breakfast muffin that pairs nicely with hot tea.

2½ cups flour (I use half whole-wheat pastry, half spelt)
¾ cup sugar
⅓ cup coconut flakes
2 heaping tablespoons soy flour
2 teaspoons baking powder
¼ teaspoon baking soda
Pinch sea salt
1 cup coconut milk (light is fine)
½ cup sugar-free applesauce
3 tablespoons coconut oil
1½ teaspoons coconut extract
¼ teaspoon orange oil
1 cup mandarin orange sections, drained and cut in twos

1. Preheat oven to 400°F. Line muffin tins with baking cups or spray with cooking spray.
2. In a large bowl, mix the dry ingredients.
3. In a medium bowl, mix the wet ingredients, except for mandarin sections. Add the wet to the dry ingredients, stirring until just mixed. (Do not overstir. This will make your muffins tough.) Gingerly mix in the delicate mandarin sections.
4. Divide batter between muffin tins. Take care to cover any exposed mandarin section with batter, to prevent them from drying out.
5. Bake for 15 to 20 minutes or until knife inserted in center comes out clean. Cool at least 10 minutes before enjoying.

Yield: 12 large muffins

ENGLISH MUFFINS

Starter

¾ cup whole-wheat pastry flour
¾ cup white unbleached flour
¾ cup water
1 teaspoon yeast

Dough

¾ cup soy milk
2 tablespoons Earth Balance
¼ cup water
¾ cup whole-wheat pastry flour
¾ cup white unbleached flour
1 teaspoon yeast
2 tablespoons cornstarch
1 teaspoon salt
2 tablespoons sugar
2 healthy teaspoons baking
  powder

They have nooks. They have crannies. And they're vegan. Making English Muffins is only slightly more complicated than making pancakes. But on a sleep-in Sunday morning, making them is much easier than getting dressed to go out for brunch. Put the starter together the night before. These taste even better after drying out for a few days.

1. In a medium bowl, mix starter ingredients well. Cover and let sit overnight at room temperature—up to 12 hours. When ready, the starter will be spongy and with holes.
2. Heat soy milk, Earth Balance, and water in microwave on high for about 1 minute. It should be warm, not hot. In a large bowl, mix the starter dough, soy milk mixture, and the remaining ingredients until very smooth—about 5 minutes on medium-low. (Using a stand mixer makes this much easier.) The dough will be very sticky. This is normal. Cover and let sit for about 90 minutes.
3. At this point, the dough should double in size and resemble a fluffy beige cloud. Drop dough by ¼ cupfuls onto dry medium-hot skillet. Dough will be sticky. With a greased spatula—and your fingers, if necessary—carefully pat dough into circles. (You can also use English muffin rings for this purpose.) Cook for 4 minutes, until dirty blonde. Flip, flatten with spatula, and cook flip-side for 2 more minutes.
4. Let muffins cool for about 10 minutes. Using the tines of a fork, separate the muffins, then toast, top with Earth Balance and/or jelly, and enjoy with tea and your morning paper.

Yield: 12–15 muffins

CHICAGO DINER

In most city diners, dry English muffins, bagels, toast, and oatmeal are the only vegan options you'll find on the menu. That's why we're all extra-jealous of Chicago vegans. At the Chicago Diner, you can chow down on kinder, gentler versions of American classics, including scrambled tofu, soy bacon, and veggie sausages for breakfast, and Dagwood sandwiches, barbecue wings, and meat(less) loaf for lunch. www.Veggiediner.com

RASPBERRY SWIRL POUND CAKE WITH LIMONCELLO GLAZE

Have a pound cake craving? You can find a slice at just about every all-night diner. You cannot, however, always find a vegan version. This very American rendition gets a dash of European sophistication from fiori di Sicilia, the citrus essence used in Italian pannetone. Fresh lemon juice, lemon zest, and a Limoncello glaze reach across the aisles to tease out the raspberries' tart, slightly cloying flavor.

1. Preheat oven to 375°F. Grease and flour an average loaf pan.
2. In a large bowl, sift together flours, baking powder and salt.
3. In another large bowl, cream together the Earth Balance and sugar. Add the vanilla, fiori di Sicilia, and soy milk, and mix until smooth. Stir in the flour mixture, about ½ cup at a time, and mix until blended.
4. Pour half the batter into the pan. Add half the jam in heaping tablespoons, and swirl into the batter. Be sure to swirl all the way down to the bottom and to the edges of the pan. Repeat with the rest of the batter and jam.
5. Bake for 50 to 55 minutes, or until a knife inserted in the center comes out clean. If crust begins to brown, add a foil "tent."
6. In a medium bowl, mix glaze ingredients with a fork until smooth. If the glaze seems too dry, add more milk by the teaspoon until it reaches your desired consistency.
7. Allow cake to cool completely before icing it with the glaze.

Yield: 1 12-slice pound cake

Cake

1¾ cups flour
2 heaping tablespoons soy flour
1 tablespoon baking powder
¼ teaspoon salt
8 tablespoons (1 stick) Earth Balance, at room temperature
1 cup sugar
1 teaspoon vanilla
1 teaspoon fiori di Sicilia (or substitute ½ teaspoon each organic lemon and orange zest)
½ cup soy or rice milk
¼–½ cup raspberry jam
2 tablespoons sugar

Limoncello Glaze

1 cup powdered sugar
2 tablespoons Limoncello (store-bought, or make your own—see page 204)
1 tablespoon soy or rice milk

BLUEBERRY GRUNT

Filling

4 cups blueberries (or other fruit like rhubarb, raspberries, or strawberries)

½ cup packed brown sugar

¼ cup molasses

¼ cup water

3 tablespoons lemon juice

Zest 1 organic lemon, chopped

¼ teaspoon nutmeg

¼ teaspoon cinnamon

Dumplings

1 cup all-purpose flour

½ cup whole-wheat flour

2 tablespoons sugar

2 teaspoons baking powder

½ teaspoon salt

3 tablespoons Earth Balance, cut into tiny cubes

¾ cup vanilla soy milk

Soy creamer, soy whipped cream, or vanilla soy ice cream, for topping

You hear a lot of strange sounds living in the city. Usually, the only time I hear grunting—thank goodness—is when I'm working out at the gym. (And I must say, it's a pet peeve.) So how did this kinder, gentler grunt get its name?

Grunt is traditionally cooked in a cast-iron skillet, and when the fruit and dumplings cook and bubble, they make a noise that resembles the grunting of an animal. (Hopefully, this fact has already endeared this recipe to 99 percent of vegans.)

1. Mix all the filling ingredients in a large skillet. Over medium-high heat, bring to a boil—stir about 5 minutes. Reduce heat to medium. Simmer until the fruit gets soft and velvety. The mixture should thicken a bit after about 10 minutes.

2. Meanwhile, whisk together the flours, sugar, baking powder, and salt in a medium bowl. Add the Earth Balance and cut in until the mixture resembles cornmeal (you could also use the food processor, but using your hands is more fun). Add the soy milk and mix until dough is just blended and sticky.

3. Drop the batter onto the berry concoction by spoonfuls. Reduce the heat to medium-low. Cover the pan and simmer until the dumplings are firm and a knife comes out clean—about 20 minutes.

4. Serve warm with a dollop of vegan whipped cream, a scoop of soy ice cream, a drizzle of soy creamer—or if you're having a really bad day, all of the above.

Yield: 8 servings

CHOCOLATE-PUMPKIN BREAD PUDDING

I know what you're thinking. Another odd combination. But chocolate and pumpkin have more in common than you might realize. Both flavors are characteristically deep and earthy. Both are shining stars in the baking world. And together, they pack a double-whammy antioxidant punch.

Bread pudding is, of course, a diner mainstay, but few serve exotic, let alone vegan, versions. This gooey autumnal rendition is especially wonderful with a dollop of vegan whipped cream or vanilla—or better yet, pumpkin soy ice cream.

1. Preheat oven to 350°F. Spray an 8 x 8- or 9 x 9-inch baking pan with cooking spray.
2. Using your hands, crumble bread into bite-size pieces and place in greased pan.
3. Mix pumpkin, rice milk, Earth Balance, sugar, spices, salt, and brandy in a large bowl. If mixture seems too thin, add more milk. Stir in the chocolate and then pour carefully over bread crumbs in pan, taking care not to let it spill over the edges.
4. Let sit for 5 minutes to allow the bread to absorb the liquid. Then, use a spatula to gently mix, ensuring that all bread is soaked with liquid and that chocolate is evenly distributed.
5. Bake for 60 to 75 minutes or until a knife inserted in center comes out clean. Let cool for at least 10 minutes before serving. Serve warm or cold.

Yield: 6 servings

8 slices stale bread (if you only have fresh, let it sit out overnight before using)

1 15-ounce can unsweetened pumpkin

1–1½ cups rice or soy milk

2 tablespoons Earth Balance, melted

¾ cup sugar

1½ teaspoons cinnamon

1 teaspoon powdered cardamom

¼ teaspoon nutmeg

1 teaspoon powdered ginger

¼ teaspoon salt

2 tablespoons brandy (optional, but nice!)

1 cup dark chocolate buttons, chunks, or chips

ALTERNATIVE GRANOLA

2 cups rolled oats
½ cup raw, hulled sunflower seeds
¼ cup pecan, almond, or walnut pieces
¼ cup dry quinoa
2 tablespoons dry amaranth
1 teaspoon cinnamon
Pinch salt
2 tablespoons coconut oil
⅓–¾ cup brown sugar
½ cup agave nectar
1 teaspoon vanilla
½ teaspoon orange extract
¼ cup flaked or shredded coconut
½ cup raisins *
½ cup cranberries *
* Or use 1 cup of either

Most diners serve breakfast cereals, and the better ones serve granola—with soy milk. But chances are you won't find this granola at your corner diner. That's because, in addition to the must-have nuts and oats, it also contains two alternative grains: amaranth and quinoa. I got the idea for this recipe after souvenir shopping in a Lima, Peru, supermarket. I bought a few packages of local granola and noticed that quinoa was one of the main ingredients. Eureka! Dry toasting it coaxes out its inherent nuttiness.

Most store-bought granola is sickeningly sweet. This granola is delicate, nutty, and subtly sweet. If you prefer a more cloying cereal, add the full amount of brown sugar. As a special added bonus, while this granola bakes, it infuses your kitchen with a lovely orange-nutty aroma.

1. Preheat oven to 375°F. Grease a medium cookie sheet and set aside.
2. In a large bowl, mix together oats, sunflower seeds, nuts, grains, cinnamon, and salt.
3. In a small saucepan, combine coconut oil, brown sugar, agave nectar, and extracts. Heat on low and cook gently until sugar is dissolved.
4. Remove from heat and pour into bowl with grains. Using a wooden spoon, stir well and make sure all grains are covered with the liquid. Spread onto the cookie sheet and bake for 5 to 7 minutes. Remove from oven and stir. Bake for 5 to 7 more minutes. Again, remove from oven and stir. Lower temperature to 350°F and bake for 5 to 15 more minutes, or until golden and crunchy.
5. Remove from oven and stir in coconut and dried fruit. Let sit at room temperature for about 8 hours.
6. Transfer to tightly sealed containers. Will keep for a few weeks. Serve with soy or rice milk or as a topping for soy yogurt or ice cream. Also delicious as a heated cereal.

Yield: 4 cups

CRAN-APPLE OATMEAL

Oatmeal is one breakfast dish vegans can always count on at diners. Unfortunately, they're almost always made with mushy instant rolled oats, which, to me, taste more like wallpaper paste than sustenance. My version relies on healthier, tastier steel-cut oats, which have a slightly chewy texture when cooked. And to flavor the oatmeal, I cook the oats in an apple juice "broth," much like you would use vegetable broth to flavor grains like rice and millet.

⅔ cup unsweetened apple juice
⅓ cup water
2 tablespoons dried cranberries
⅓ cup dry steel-cut oats
¼ teaspoon cinnamon
Dash salt

1. Pour apple juice and water into a small saucepan. Stir in cranberries and bring to a boil.
2. Add oats and cinnamon. Cover and lower to a simmer. Cook for 10 to 20 minutes, depending on how chewy you like your oatmeal.
3. Add salt, mix, and serve.

Yield: 2 servings

Variation

Substitute raisins for cranberries.

BREAKFAST BURRITO

Luckily, more urban diners are putting scrambled tofu on the menu. But scrambled tofu alone is not an exciting enough reason for me to crawl out of bed on a Sunday morning. But a breakfast burrito? Olé!

1½ tablespoons olive oil
1 shallot, chopped
3 garlic cloves, minced
1 red pepper, sliced very thinly
1½ teaspoons cumin
½ teaspoon chili powder
¼ teaspoon turmeric
1 pound extra-firm tofu, pressed for about 1 hour, then crumbled
1 cup black beans, rinsed and drained
6 tablespoons nutritional yeast
Salt and pepper, to taste
6–8 large tortillas (make your own—see page 46)
½ cup vegan sour cream
1–2 cups salsa (to taste)
1 tomato, diced
1 avocado, chopped
2 tablespoons fresh cilantro, chopped
Hot sauce (optional)

1. In a large frying pan, heat the oil over medium heat. Sauté the shallot, garlic, and peppers until shallots and pepper are soft. Add spices, stir well to mix, and then add crumbled tofu. Cook for another minute or so, to ensure spices and oil mixture evenly coat tofu.
2. Add black beans and nutritional yeast, and cook until warmed through, about 3 to 5 more minutes. Season with salt and pepper.
3. Spread each tortilla with a heaping tablespoon of both sour cream and salsa, then top this with one-sixth of the black bean–tofu mixture, a bit of tomato, and some avocado. Season, to taste, with hot sauce. Roll up burrito-style and top with cilantro. Serve with extra salsa and hot sauce, if desired.

Yield: 6 servings

EASY CORNMEAL SCRAPPLE

3½ cups vegetable stock
1 cup cornmeal
¼ cup flour
1 teaspoon sage
1 teaspoon fennel seeds
1¼ teaspoons salt
¼ teaspoon freshly ground pepper
14 ounces breakfast-style vegan
  sausage (a scant 2 cups)
Maple syrup or apple sauce
  (optional)

Scrapple is classic American peasant food that has become a mainstay in countless city diners. It's slightly sweet and slightly savory—and its texture resembles a cross between polenta and a terrine. It's usually pan-fried, drizzled with fresh maple syrup, and served with a side of greasy home fries and toast.

Unfortunately, as you might guess from the name, scrapple is made from all sorts of meaty unmentionables. Besides tasting much better, my version relies on ingredients you can easily find in the grocery store. Your arteries will thank you, and so will the animals.

1. In a large stockpot, bring stock to a boil. Grease a medium loaf pan.
2. In a medium bowl, mix together all dry ingredients, ensuring there are no lumps.
3. When stock is boiling, whisk in the dry ingredients, a tiny bit at a time, whisking well each time (mixture needs to be very smooth). Lower heat to medium-low and cook for 1 minute, whisking constantly.
4. Add sausage and use a heavy-handled wooden spoon to break it up while you continue to stir in the cornmeal mixture. You should try to break up the sausage into lentil-size pieces. This takes a lot of elbow grease, and your arm will be tired when you're done! This is normal and very good for your biceps, so be sure to switch arms halfway through to get an even workout.
5. Once all the sausage is incorporated, cook for about 10 more minutes, continuing to "chop" and stir with the spoon. The mixture will be very, very thick.
6. Using a large spatula, spoon the mixture into the prepared loaf pan. Smooth the top, cover, and refrigerate overnight, or at least 8 hours.
7. To serve, cut into slices, lightly dredge in flour and pan-fry. As it fries, press each side down slightly with spatula. Serve with maple syrup or applesauce.

Yield: 1 large loaf; serves 10–12

QUICHE DU JOUR

Let them eat quiche!

I was going to give you my recipe for Quiche Lorraine, but then I realized that a modular quiche recipe would be much more useful. Make your own Quiche du Jour by tailoring this quiche to suit your own personal preferences and to utilize whatever's in season or cheap. It's also a great way to reinvent leftover vegetables.

1. Preheat oven to 400°F. Grease a 10- or 11-inch quiche pan.
2. Roll out dough and press into quiche pan. Set aside.
3. In a food processor, blend together tofu, parsley, nutritional yeast, cornstarch, salt, and milk or cream until creamy and smooth, scraping down the sides as needed.
4. Pour tofu mixture into the prepared crust. Gently arrange filling on top and sprinkle with optional topping, if desired. Bake on third oven shelf from the top for 30 to 40 minutes, or until crust is golden brown and tofu is firm and no longer wobbly.
5. If your veggies are cooking too quickly, simply cover the quiche with aluminum foil until it's properly baked.
6. Cool on rack. Let sit for at least 10 minutes before slicing. Slice with a sharp knife and remove with a pie server.

Yield: 6 to 8 servings

Optional additions

2 additional tablespooons of any fresh herb of your choice
¼ cup sun-dried tomatoes
¼ cup sliced olives
½ cup vegan cheese (place in crust before you fold in the tofu mixture)

Optional toppings

Nutritional yeast
A sprinkling of nutmeg
Panko

1½ Flaky Pie Crust recipes (see page 160)
1 14-ounce aseptic box of extra-firm silken tofu (do not use refrigerated tofu here; it isn't creamy enough)
3 tablespoons fresh parsley, chopped
5 tablespoons nutritional yeast
2 teaspoons cornstarch
½ teaspoon salt
2 tablespoons soy cream or soy milk

Fillings

2 cups of filling. Feel free to mix, match, and extrapolate. Some ideas to get you started:

Spinach or kale, sautéed in olive oil, with raisins
Brussels sprouts, halved and parboiled
Sliced tomato and fresh basil
Shiitake, portobello, and cremini mushrooms, sautéed in sherry or Marsala
Onions and peppers, sliced thinly and sautéed in olive oil
Fresh corn with a dash of smoked paprika
Sautéed radicchio with 1 tablespoon agave nectar
1 package of tempeh bacon, steamed for 10 minutes, drained, and crumbled (Quiche Lorraine)
Roasted red peppers, marinated artichoke hearts, heart of palm, or any combination, drained very well before using

FINER-THAN-DINER CINNAMON-RAISIN BREAD

Dough

3 cups flour (I use half whole-wheat, half spelt)

¼ cup teff flour (if you don't have any, you may replace with regular flour)

I tablespoon instant yeast

I tablespoon soy flour

I ½ teaspoons cinnamon

⅓–½ cup brown sugar, packed

I teaspoon salt

¼ cup canola oil

I cup warm water (not hot, just warm enough to touch)

Filling

½ cup raisins

¼ cup brown sugar, packed

I teaspoon cinnamon

Dash salt

Topping

2 tablespoons Earth Balance, softened

2 tablespoons brown sugar, packed

I tablespoon flour

½ teaspoon cinnamon

2 tablespoons slivered almonds

Everyone loves cinnamon-raisin bread, especially toasted and swimming in Earth Balance. There's something instantly comforting about the taste and the smell, which is probably why so many diners serve it. Unfortunately, however, many diners rely on thin, mass-produced cinnamon-raisin bread that's closer to cardboard than carb.

My version packs a powerful cinnamon punch, encased in a sugary-nutty topping. The teff flour adds a little extra nuttiness and nutrition. Despite appearances, it's easy to make. You just need to be home for a few hours to supervise the dough rising. It's wonderful toasted and also makes a great base for Pain Perdu (see page 35). So make this bread. Your family will thank you and your kitchen will smell wonderful.

1. Grease a 4½ x 8½ x 2¼-inch loaf pan.
2. In a large bowl, mix all dough ingredients. Using the bread hook on your mixer, knead for 5 to 7 minutes, until dough is very smooth.
3. Place in an oiled bowl, cover tightly with a damp tea towel, foil, or plastic wrap, and let it rise until doubled, about 1 hour.
4. While the dough rises, combine the filling ingredients in a small bowl. Set aside.
5. Combine topping ingredients in a small bowl, using your fingers to rub the Earth Balance into the remaining ingredients. Set aside.
6. Form dough into an 8 x 12-inch shape. (Using a silpat, especially one with a printed-on ruler, is extremely helpful here.) Sprinkle the shape with the filling and then use your fingers to press it into the dough. Don't be afraid to press the raisins down. If you encounter raisin clusters, simply use your fingers to rearrange them. Make sure raisins cover entire slab of dough fairly evenly.
7. Roll the dough, jellyroll style, from the short end, tucking ends under slightly and pinching seams shut. Place in the loaf pan. Again, cover and let rise for about an hour to an hour and a half. When properly risen, dough should extend beyond the edge of the pan.
8. Preheat the oven to 350°F.
9. Once the dough is risen, pat the topping mixture onto the top of the loaf, being careful not to deflate it. Don't worry about it falling off; baking will "fire" most of the sugary topping onto the loaf.
10. Bake for about 35 to 45 minutes, or until loaf sounds hollow when tapped. If you find the topping browning too quickly, cover the loaf with aluminum foil.
11. Remove from oven and cool on a rack for 5 minutes. Run a knife along the edges and gently turn the loaf upside down and remove. Let cool for at least 15 minutes before slicing. (This is the hardest part!)

Yield: I loaf

(A LA RECHERCHE DU) PAIN PERDU

If Proust were alive today, the narrator in his autobiographical novel *A La Recherche du Temps Perdu* would have experienced his epic epiphany over my veganized version of Pain Perdu instead of those cholesterol-laden madeleines.

Pain Perdu is essentially French French Toast—except that it's more like a breakfasty bread pudding. Serve it warm, drenched in Earth Balance and maple syrup, and topped with a dusting of confectioner's sugar.

To save time, I suggest assembling this recipe the night before, and then baking it the next morning.

1. Grease an 8 x 8-inch or 9 x 9-inch brownie pan. Preheat the oven to 350°F.
2. Arrange 4 slices of bread in the pan.
3. In a medium bowl, whisk together cream cheese, jam, sugar, spices, salt, and vanilla until smooth. Spread this mixture across the 4 bread slices, then top with the other 4 slices, sandwich style.
4. Sift the chickpea flour and cornstarch into a large bowl. Whisk in a tiny bit of the rice milk to form a slurry. Try to whisk out any lumps that may appear. Add the remaining rice milk, whisking continually, to form a smooth liquid. Whisk in the sugar, salt, and the vanilla.
5. Pour the custard base over the bread slices and let it sit at least an hour (or as long as overnight).
6. Bake for 30 minutes. Remove from oven and carefully flip each of the sandwiches. Don't worry if they break apart; they probably will, and this will not affect the finished product.
7. Return to oven and bake an additional 20 to 30 minutes or until most of the liquid has cooked away and Pain Perdu is firm but wobbly.
8. Let cool for at least 5 minutes before serving.

Yield: 4 servings

Bread layer

8 slices stale bread (try it with Finer-Than-Diner Cinnamon-Raisin Bread, see page 34)

2 heaping tablespoons vegan cream cheese, softened

2 heaping tablespoons your favorite jam (good flavors to try include raspberry, orange marmalade, strawberry, or blackberry)

2 teaspoons sugar

Dash nutmeg

¼ teaspoon cinnamon

¼ teaspoon salt

1 teaspoon vanilla

Custard

4 tablespoons chickpea flour (also called gram flour)

1 tablespoon cornstarch

3 cups plain or vanilla rice milk

¼ cup sugar

¼ teaspoon salt

2 teaspoons vanilla

ROASTED RED PEPPER AND ONION FRITTATA

1 tablespoon plus ½ teaspoon
    olive oil
1 medium onion, chopped
3 garlic cloves, minced
½ cup plus ¼ cup roasted red
    peppers, chopped
1 12.3-ounce aseptic box
    extra-firm tofu (do not use
    refrigerated)
6 tablespoons nutritional yeast
3 tablespoons flour
1 teaspoon baking powder
2 tablespoons fresh basil, chopped,
    or 2 teaspoons dried
½ teaspoon salt or more, to taste
Freshly ground pepper to taste

A frittata is a baked Italian omelet; half-cooked on the stovetop and half-cooked in the oven—much fancier and healthier than any generic diner omelet. Tofu lends itself nicely to this vegan version. I recommend making it in a 9-inch, cast-iron pan and serving it with Earth-Balance-slathered toast.

1. Preheat oven to 400°F. Heat 1 tablespoon oil in a large saucepan over medium heat. Sauté the onions and garlic until soft.
2. In food processor, process ½ cup red peppers, tofu, yeast, flour, baking powder, basil, and salt until very smooth and creamy.
3. Rub remaining ½ teaspoon oil into cast-iron skillet. Arrange onion mixture evenly on bottom then spread tofu mixture over top, flattening out with a spatula. Strew the remaining ¼ cup peppers on top and gently press them into the tofu. Season with freshly ground pepper. Cook over medium heat until bottom starts to set, about 15 to 20 minutes.
4. Put in oven and bake for an additional 20 to 25 minutes, or until firm.
5. Cool for at least an hour before cutting. Serve at room temperature. Placing the frittata in the refrigerator for a few hours before cutting is helpful.

Yield: 4 servings

LUNCH CART

Vegan urban dwellers are lucky to enjoy countless lunch options—from good-and-greasy cart food and fancy restaurant meals to bagged lunches in the park. Eating lunch out every day is certainly fun, but it can get expensive. By packing my lunch each day instead of eating out, I save the equivalent of almost $350 a year.

Besides the cost factor, making your own lunch means you have greater control over what you are putting into your body. For the same price of a fat- and sodium-laden cart sandwich on white bread, you can make yourself a well-rounded lunch, complete with whole grains, veggies, and a piece of fruit or two. And then there's the flavor factor!

Packing your own lunch is a snap, once you get the hang of it. You can use all the money you save to go on vacation.

SLOPPY JOES

2 tablespoons canola oil
2 onions, chopped
3 garlic cloves, minced
1 red pepper, chopped
2 cups tomato sauce
1⅓ cups textured vegetable
  protein (TVP)
1–2½ teaspoons chili powder (to
  taste)
1 tablespoon red wine vinegar
1 tablespoon vegan
  Worcestershire sauce (or soy
  sauce)
2 tablespoons brown sugar
2 tablespoons barbeque sauce
Salt and pepper to taste
Dash of hot pepper flakes
  (optional)

I'm a sucker for these messy, deconstructed burgers during my lunch break. Serve them on a whole-grain bun or piled atop any rice or any grain.

Be sure to pack the buns and filling separately. Just nuke the Sloppy Joe mixture for a minute before dumping it onto your bun. All of your office-mates will eye your lunch with envy. Hey, why not share? Sloppy Joes are classic comfort food. And if you work in a busy city office or cube farm, you'll need these to get you through to 5:00 p.m.!

1. Heat oil in large saucepan over medium heat. Sauté the onions until translucent and then add the garlic and red pepper and sauté for an additional minute.
2. Add the remaining ingredients and turn heat to low. Stir well, cover, and simmer for 15 minutes, or until most of the liquid is absorbed and peppers and TVP are soft.

Yield: 4 servings

SMOKED PAPRIKA HUMMUS

1 can chickpeas, drained
4 tablespoons olive oil
5 tablespoons tahini
3 tablespoons fresh squeezed
  lemon juice
2 teaspoons Spanish smoked
  paprika
1 teaspoon cumin
2 garlic cloves
Up to ⅓ cup water, or amount
  needed to achieve desired
  consistency

Hummus is stereotypical vegan fare. There are as many recipes for this humble chickpea spread as there are vegans and vegetarians. In my version, the Spanish smoked paprika deepens the flavor and enhances the tahini's earthiness. It infuses the hummus with a sultry, smoky sophistication reminiscent of a wood-burning fireplace in a Madrid tapas bar. I love this hummus slathered on crispbread, or spread thickly on whole-grain bread, with crisp mung bean sprouts for crunch. But frankly, my favorite way to eat it is with a spoon—right from the bowl.

1. Mix all ingredients, except water, in a food processor until they reach a creamy, smooth consistency.
2. Add water as needed, 1 tablespoon at a time, until you get the desired texture.

Yield: 2 cups

Variation

Use a can of white beans instead of chickpeas.

RAPINI PANINI

"Rapini" is Italian for "broccoli rabe." This bitter green vegetable is a popular condiment on Philadelphia cheese steaks. But who needs meat when the vegetable alone is packed with so much flavor? Although you can use any kind of baguette or hard roll in this recipe, the gentle sweetness of whole-wheat bread and garlic contrasts nicely against the subtle bitterness of the greens.

1. Slice garlic evenly and sauté in olive oil, along with red pepper flakes, if using, over medium-low until softened. Be careful not to brown the garlic. (Your nose will tell you when it's ready.) Toss in blanched greens and cook until warmed through. Salt to taste.
2. Cut the baguette into fourths and pull out the soft middle. (Save and use for breadcrumbs.) Line with vegan cheese slices or yeast and then fill with hot broccoli rabe mixture.

Yield: 4 servings

10 cloves of garlic (Yes. You read correctly. 10 cloves)

5 tablespoons olive oil

Red pepper flakes (optional)

2 bunches broccoli rabe, blanched and chopped (To blanch, fill a large pan with about 2 inches of water and bring to a boil. Cook broccoli rabe about 5 minutes until tender.)

1 whole-wheat baguette, preferably organic

4 vegan cheese slices, or 4 tablespoons nutritional yeast

Salt, to taste

Suggested Sides

Corn on the cob; sliced tomatoes with best-quality olive oil and freshly chopped basil.

SEITAN SANDWICH SPREAD

1 cup "chicken"-style seitan
3 tablespoons Vegenaise
3 tablespoons shredded carrots
2 teaspoons relish
1 scallion, chopped
1 capful apple cider vinegar
¼ teaspoon agave nectar, maple syrup, or brown rice syrup
Salt and pepper to taste
Squirt of mustard (optional)

There's a certain vegan chicken salad sandwich spread that I love—at a certain oversize, box-shop, health food grocery in my neighborhood. This is my attempt at replicating it. It's particularly good on whole-grain bread with lettuce, tomato, and sprouts, but sometimes, I eat it straight out of the bowl.

Mix everything in the food processor until it forms a paste. (Small chunks are okay.)

Yield: 3–4 servings

PHILLY PORTOBELLO CHEESE STEAK

1 French baguette
1½ tablespoons olive oil
6 garlic cloves, minced
8 portobello mushroom caps, chopped finely
4–8 slices vegan cheddar cheese
Salt and pepper, to taste

Philadelphia is famous for its meat-laden, greasy cheese steaks. They are a lunch cart staple in the City of Brotherly Love and elsewhere in the United States. Fortunately, many restaurants in the city, like Govinda's, Gianna's, and the Basic Four Vegetarian Snack Bar, serve superior vegan versions. But there's something special about homemade cheese steaks, especially on a crusty French baguette. They're a snap to make and use only pantry basics.

1. Slice baguette lengthwise and remove most of the soft middle to form concave pockets. (Save the middle for bread crumbs, bread pudding, or stuffing. You can freeze it in an airtight bag.) Slice baguette into 4 sections and set aside.
2. Heat oil in a large saucepan over medium-low heat. Add garlic and cook until it softens, about 5 minutes, taking care not to burn it. Add mushrooms and cook until they are very soft and tender.
3. Divide mushroom mixture among the 4 bread sections. Add 1-2 vegan cheese slices per section and serve.

Yield: 4 large cheese steaks

Variations

When sautéing the mushrooms and garlic, add any of the following:
an onion, minced, a very thinly sliced bell pepper (red or green),
parboiled broccoli rabe, or spinach.

SANDWICH MOUSSE

Since I live and work in the city, I'm surrounded by some stellar restaurants. Fighting the urge to eat lunch out every day can be difficult, to say the least. This sandwich spread helps me resist the temptation. I often make a batch on Sunday nights to ensure I have a sandwich filling for the workday lunches ahead.

I love the gentle salmon color that pink beans exude, but you can substitute any variety of canned beans. The sumac also adds color and a pleasant lemony undertone (you can find it at spice stores or Middle Eastern groceries).

Use this spread to fill sandwiches or wraps, adorned with sprouts and tomatoes. Or use it to make a grilled sandwich, along with sliced onion. You can also serve this mousse as a dip with crudités or crackers.

Mix everything in a food processor until smooth. Err on the side of over-processing.

Yield: 2 generous cups

- 1 15-ounce can pink beans, drained and rinsed
- 2½ tablespoons fresh squeezed lemon juice
- 3 healthy tablespoons tahini
- 2 tablespoons nutritional yeast
- 1 large garlic clove
- 1 carrot, sliced roughly
- ½ teaspoon salt
- 1 tablespoon dried or fresh parsley
- 1 teaspoon sumac (you may substitute 1 tablespoon lemon juice instead)

PLANNING A PICNIC

First, we need to change the way we think about picnics. To picnic properly, you don't need a park. You can picnic in the airport during a layover. Or on your office floor with a coworker. Or on your front stoop with your loved ones. The joy comes from eating homemade food in an unexpected locale. Picnic is just English for al fresco.

To pack a successful picnic lunch, you only need to remember two words: portable and non-perishable. Think PB & J, soup in a thermos, savory breads, cookies, apples, and oranges. Oh, and chocolate, too!

Bring a tablecloth to sit on. You can find inexpensive retro versions at your local thrift store. Don't forget the cloth napkins. They're classy and environmentally friendly.

½ cup watermelon chunks, seeds
  removed

½ cup pineapple chunks

½ cup strawberries, hulled and
  cut in half

I mango, cut into chunks (or
  about I cup frozen)

I organic orange, deveined and
  cut into sections

¼ cup cantaloupe chunks

¼ cup honeydew melon chunks

¼ cup red seedless grapes

I banana, sliced

Sabayon Sauce (see page 199)

FRUIT SALAD WITH SABAYON SAUCE

During the workweek, fruit salad carts can be found on every other corner in Philadelphia. When I worked in an office, I used to rely on them when I wanted an inexpensive-yet-healthy lunch. Luckily, fruit salad is easy to throw together at home. The addition of Sabayon Sauce elevates this healthful dish from lunch cart to lunch art. It also makes an elegant, light dessert.

1. Mix all fruits except banana and chill.
2. Arrange in dishes and top with banana and Sabayon Sauce. Or pour sauce into a small pitcher and allow guests to pour for themselves.

Yield: 4 servings

Variations

Feel free to tailor the fruit combinations depending on your taste and what's in season. Other excellent additions: raspberries, blueberries, cherries, kiwi, and papaya. You can also use peeled and sliced apples or pears, but be sure to add a squirt or two of lemon juice to prevent them from browning.

WHEAT-FREE SOFT PRETZELS

Philadelphia, my home city, is synonymous with soft pretzels slathered with mustard. You can buy them at street carts throughout the city. But to be honest, I'm not crazy about these giant hunks of white flour. So using spelt flour, I make my own wheat-free soft pretzels. I eat them plain, coated with lots of Earth Balance, or topped with cinnamon-sugar. They make wonderful lunch bag treats—but they taste best the day you make them.

1. In a large bowl, mix 2½ cups flour, yeast, salt, and water with agave or rice syrup. Knead until very smooth and pliable, about 5 minutes. (I use my KitchenAid mixer with the bread hook.) Add more flour in ¼ increments if dough appears too sticky. Cover tightly with plastic and let rest at room temperature for about 40 minutes.
2. Preheat oven to 475°F. Grease two cookie sheets or silpat mats.
3. Divide dough into:

       8 pieces if you are making medium pretzels
       16 pieces if you are making mini pretzels
       24 pieces if you are making pretzel sticks
4. Using a silpat mat for the rolling process takes the headache out of cleaning up.

To roll dough into large pretzels: Roll each dough ball into a 2-foot-long thread. It will be quite skinny—this is normal. Make a U shape, then twist the two ends once near the top. Fold twisted ends over to meet the bottom of the U.

To roll dough into mini pretzels: Same as above, except roll each dough ball into a 1-foot-long thread.

To roll dough into sticks: Roll into pieces approximately 6 inches long.

5. Dip in water/sugar/salt mixture. Add salt if desired, then let rest on cookie sheets for about 5 minutes.
6. Bake for 5 to 10 minutes, depending on the size, until golden. Check often to make sure they do not burn. Baking times will vary greatly.
7. Remove from oven and brush with all of the Earth Balance. Enjoy as is, or roll/sprinkle with the cinnamon-sugar topping.

Yield: 8 medium pretzels, 16 mini pretzels, or 24 pretzel sticks

2½–3 cups white spelt flour, sifted

2½ teaspoons instant yeast (or 1 packet instant dry yeast)

¼ teaspoon salt

1 teaspoon agave nectar or brown rice syrup, dissolved in 1 cup warm water (microwave water for about 1 minute on high)

A bowl filled with water, 1 teaspoon sugar, and a dash of salt

Toppings
¼ cup melted Earth Balance

Cinnamon-Sugar
8 tablespoons sugar
6 tablespoons cinnamon

HONEYDEW-POMEGRANATE JIGGLERS

4 cups honeydew melon chunks
¾ cup sugar
3 tablespoons agar flakes
1 cup pomegranate seeds (seeds from roughly one fruit)

After finishing your lunch, you want something fruity to cleanse your palate. But the sugar low that comes with a heavy slice of pie would definitely compromise your afternoon meetings. Wouldn't you rather savor sparkling ruby pomegranate seeds suspended in a celadon sea? These colorful jigglers give you all the nutrients and fiber of fruit and a wow factor, to boot. I suspect that kids will love them, especially if you make them in animal and flower molds. They remind me of the colorful slabs of homemade soap sold in stores like Lush. Fortunately, they taste much better!

Why not surprise your child by putting these jigglers in her lunch box? Then again, why not also surprise your spouse or partner with a few of these little gems?

1. In a blender, process the honeydew chunks into a smooth liquid.
2. Pour into a medium saucepan. Add the sugar and agar flakes. Stir well and let rest for 10 minutes to ensure that agar dissolves properly.
3. Bring mixture to a boil, stirring occasionally. Boil for 1 minute, then immediately remove from heat. Let sit for 1 more minute and skim off any foam.
4. Stir in the pomegranate seeds and pour into an oiled dish or into oiled molds.
5. Put in refrigerator to harden. (Agar jellies also harden at room temperature, but I think they taste better chilled.)

Yield: about 24 jigglers

Tip

To save your kitchen from looking like a murder scene and being stained with pomegranate juice, remove the seeds from the pith in a large bowl of water.

PAN BAGNAT

Pan Bagnat is a popular Provençal sandwich. It's essentially like eating a portable Niçoise Salad, and the flavors taste especially satisfying when paired with a nice firm bread to sop up the dressing. If you're taking this to work for lunch, pack the salad and bread separately, then assemble just before eating. (Making the salad the night before helps minimize early morning frenzy.)

1 loaf of round bread (called a boule), cut in half
Niçoise Salad (see page 121)

1. Cut the bread in half. Scoop out the whites, and save them for another use (e.g., bread crumbs or stuffing).
2. Fill the bread pockets with the salad, cut the halves in half, and serve.

Yield: 4 servings

ELEGANT LUNCH SANDWICH

This type of fancy-pants sandwich is often served to business people—at exorbitant costs—for lunch at chi-chi city eateries. Pack one for lunch—along with a real cloth napkin—whenever you need a little extra elegance. It's truly addictive.

2 slices black bread
2 tablespoons vegan cream cheese
½ avocado, sliced
¼ cup your favorite sprouts
1 tablespoon Pear-Pepper Chutney, or more to taste (see page 194)

1. Slather one slice of bread with the cream cheese. Arrange the avocado slices on top, then decorate with the sprouts.
2. Spread the other slice of bread with the chutney. Top the sandwich and enjoy immediately.

Yield: 1 sandwich

HOMEMADE WHOLE-GRAIN TORTILLAS

2 cups whole-grain flour
1 teaspoon salt
½ teaspoon chipotle chili powder
(optional; gives the tortillas a
spicy kick and an orange tint)
5 tablespoons vegan shortening,
softened and cut into tiny
chunks
¼–½ cup water

Whether you live in the city, the country, or anywhere in between, one thing is for sure: We Americans are addicted to those humongous, store-bought tortillas. They're very versatile and can be instantly transformed into burritos, wraps, tacos, and anything else we can think of. Lord knows I've bought my share of them. But you need to read the labels. Many tortillas are loaded with preservatives, hydrogenated oils, and other unmentionables.

Making your own tortillas is easy and smugly self-satisfying, especially if you have a silpat mat. It's also empowering to know that you can have fresh, cheap tortillas anytime you want them, using just a few pantry staples.

1. In a large bowl, mix together flour and salt (and chili, if using), and then using a pastry cutter or two knives, cut in the shortening. Once the mixture resembles cornmeal, add water, 1 tablespoon at a time, until the mixture holds together. Knead for about 5 minutes, until smooth.
2. Cover and chill for at least 2 hours so dough will be easy to handle.
3. Remove from refrigerator. Divide into 10 small or 5 large balls.
4. To roll, put a small ball in the center of your silpat. Roll as thinly as possible, adding more flour as needed. Set aside.
5. Heat a nonstick or cast-iron frying pan to high. Do not grease. Brown the tortillas on one side for about 15 seconds, then flip and repeat on the other side. Small bubbles will appear when they are done.

Yield: about 10 small or 5 large tortillas

LUNCH MUFFINS

With so much stimulation and so many people competing for jobs and attention, city life inevitably challenges your comfort zone and forces you to think outside the box. These grown-up muffins are a perfect example. Who on earth said that muffins should be relegated to breakfast alone?

These savory muffins are perfect to pack in a bagged lunch or to take along on a picnic. I like them heated, with the tiniest "schmear" of Earth Balance. But they're also good at room temperature, just as they are.

1. Heat oven to 400°F. Grease a muffin tin, or line with muffin papers.
2. Mix dry ingredients in a large bowl. Mix milk, oil, and pesto in a medium bowl. Stir wet ingredients into dry, being careful not to overmix.
3. Fold in tomatoes and olives. Batter will be very thick. If it is not manageable, add more milk, in 1-tablespoon increments.
4. Divide mixture between 6 muffin cups. Bake 20 to 25 minutes until a cake tester comes out clean. Let cool on rack for 5 minutes before removing from tins.

Yield: 6 muffins. Recipe is easily doubled

1 cup flour
1 heaping tablespoon soy flour
1 teaspoon baking powder
¾ teaspoon salt
½ cup plus 1–2 tablespoons rice milk
3 tablespoons olive oil
3 heaping tablespoons pesto
24 cherry tomatoes, quartered
⅓ cup oil-cured black olives, chopped

VEGAN BROWN BAG

Got sandwich block? Here are five for the road:

- Cashew butter and thinly sliced banana
- Cucumber and Vegenaise
- Vegan cheese and spicy mustard on brown bread
- Tomato and pesto on a baguette
- Almond butter and apple butter on whole-grain bread

CHICKPEA-CHILI BURGERS

1 15-ounce can chickpeas, rinsed and drained
2 tablespoons roasted red peppers
½ onion, chopped
2 cloves garlic, sliced
1 tablespoon olive oil
½–¾ teaspoon chili powder
¼ teaspoon paprika
½ teaspoon salt
2 slices stale, whole-grain bread, crumbled
Up to 4 tablespoons stock or water
Up to ¾ cup rolled oats

Many urban restaurants now offer some sort of veggie burger as a lunch option. They're fine in a pinch, but these slightly sweet, slightly spicy patties might cause you to rethink your definition of a vegan burger. They taste especially wonderful with a slice of vegan cheddar and all the usual burger fixin's. Enjoy them with a side of sweet potato fries.

1. Mix everything but the bread, stock, and oats in a food processor. To process, add enough water to make it smooth. You'll need to scrape down the sides of the bowl from time to time. Blend in crumbled bread and process until fairly smooth, adding stock as needed. Dough should be sticky but malleable.
2. Transfer to a large bowl and add enough oats so that you can pick up dough in your hands without it sticking. Refrigerate for at least 1 hour before forming into patties.
3. Fry in a bit of olive oil until each side is golden.

Yield: 6 burgers

PORTOBELLO BURGERS

2½ tablespoons extra-virgin olive oil
4 large portobello mushroom caps with gills removed
Splash balsamic vinegar
Splash soy sauce
Salt and pepper, to taste
Fixin's: vegan cheese, lettuce, tomato, onion, relish, ketchup, etc.

In the United States, city streets are lined with ubiquitous burger joints that appeal to battle-weary office workers. But this meaty portobello burger won't clog your arteries or empty your wallet; now that's what I call a happy meal!

1. Heat oil in a large frying pan over medium heat. Add mushrooms and drizzle facing sides with vinegar, soy sauce, salt, and pepper. Cook for about 3 to 5 minutes, then flip and repeat on other side, cooking until mushrooms are soft. Add a sprinkle of water or broth if 'shrooms start to dry out.
2. Serve on a bun with your fixin's of choice.

Yield: 4 burgers

Wine Pairing

Dolcetto from the Piemontese village of Dogliani tends to have a great balance of juiciness and earthiness and would pair beautifully with the meaty portobello.

TOMATO PIE

Tomato pie—thick, chewy pizza crust slathered with marinara sauce—is a favorite lunchtime standby of vegans and omnivores alike, and no wonder: It's inexpensive, tasty, and filling. Did you know you can make an entire tomato pie for about the same cost as purchasing just one slice? So why not make your own tomato pie, bring it to work, and have a pizza party with your colleagues?

1. Brush a medium cookie sheet with about 1 teaspoon of olive oil. Sprinkle with about 1 teaspoon cornmeal.
2. After dough has been made according to the directions on page 105 and has risen, punch it down, knead it gently, then roll it out slightly and stretch it onto the oiled cookie sheet. Cover and let it rise for about 30 minutes. Meanwhile preheat your oven to 400°F.
3. Using a ladle, spread the marinara sauce over the dough. Use a little or a lot, depending on your taste (I use about ½ inch of sauce). Bake for about 20 minutes, or until golden brown and sauce is warmed through.
4. Add nutritional yeast or vegan cheese, and desired toppings. Cut into slices and serve.

Yield: I pizza, serves about 8

1 teaspoon olive oil

1 teaspoon cornmeal

Focaccia dough (see page 105)

John's Marinara Sauce (see page 193)

3 tablespoons nutritional yeast or vegan parmesan

Salt, pepper, oregano, and hot pepper flakes, to taste

1 large organic potato, scrubbed
   and poked all over with a fork;
   then microwaved until soft
Salt and pepper

Toppings
Top with any of the following, or
   any combination:
Earth Balance and herbs
Olive oil and herbs
Any salad dressing plus steamed
   broccoli or cauliflower
Vegan sour cream
Guacamole (see page 111)
Leftover Chocolate-Chipotle Chili
   (see page 137)
Leftover Cauliflower-Chickpea
   Tagine (see page 77)
Welsh Rarebit sauce (see page 74)
Tapenade (see page 116)
Winter Pesto (see page 185)
Sun-Dried Tomato Pesto (see
   page 184)
Tamarind Barbecue Sauce (see
   page 195)
Béarnaise Sauce (see page 196)

BAKED POTATO BAR

I feel like I'm stating the obvious, but you don't have to pay an arm and a leg for an overpriced baked potato lunch at your local food court. Inexpensive, healthy, and versatile, baked potatoes are the ultimate brown bag lunch food.

If your office has a microwave (and if it doesn't, you might want to rethink your job), you can nuke the potato at lunchtime, then crown it with your topping of choice. Baked potatoes are also a great way to resurrect leftovers like Chocolate-Chipotle Chili or Cauliflower-Chickpea Tagine.

Carefully cut a cross into microwaved potato, then use your fingers to coax up the starch. Adorn with your favorite topping.

Yield: 1 serving

TUSCAN BRAISED BEANS

Whether you're a harrowed stay-at-home mom or Wall Street broker with zero cooking skills, you'll find yourself whipping up these tasty beans often. They take only about 5 minutes of hands-on time. Pack some in a container for lunch with an extra drizzle of good extra-virgin olive oil and a sprinkling of nutritional yeast. Enjoy a salad or a piece of fruit afterwards, and you'll have eaten much healthier than you would have at the food court.

2 tablespoons olive oil
2 tablespoons lemon juice
1 teaspoon white vinegar
2 14-ounce cans cannellini beans, rinsed and drained
2 bay leaves
7 cloves garlic, peeled and bruised (leave whole)
2 teaspoons dried powdered sage
Salt and pepper to taste
Nutritional yeast and extra-virgin olive oil

1. Preheat oven to 425°F.
2. Mix oil, lemon juice, and vinegar and pour into the bottom of a 9 x 9-inch baking dish. Add beans, bay leaves, and garlic. Toss gently, then add the sage and toss again.
3. Cover with foil and bake for 20 minutes, or until beans are soft and warmed through. Season to taste. Garnish with yeast and/or oil, as desired.

Yield: 6 servings

5 EASY WAYS TO LIGHTEN YOUR CARBON FOOTPRINT

1. Pack your lunch using primarily locally grown food.
2. Always carry a portable, reusable shopping bag in your purse or coat.
3. When dining out, bring your own chopsticks and your own plastic containers for leftovers.
4. Buy in bulk, when possible, to reduce packaging.
5. Walk as much as you can: to the market, to work, to dinner. Good for mama earth and your waistline!

GRILLED CHEESE AND BANANAS

2 slices thick French bread (about
  6 x 3 inches)
1 tablespoon Earth Balance
½ banana, very thinly sliced
2 slices vegan cheese (American
  or cheddar work best here)

Cheese and bananas are a common pairing in both Puerto Rican and Brazilian cuisine. During my pre-vegan days, I tried a grilled cheese and banana sandwich at a little restaurant in the Leblon section of Rio de Janeiro, and since then, I've been intrigued by this quirky combination. Both kids and adults will enjoy this delicious sandwich.

1. Spread one side of each slice of bread with Earth Balance. On dry side, place banana and cheese, then finish with the other slice of the bread, dry side in. Heat a small skillet to medium.
2. Place sandwich buttered sides out. Cook undisturbed until golden on the bottom, about 3 minutes. Flip and cook on the other side until golden. Slice on the diagonal and serve.

Yield: 1 serving

MINTY MEDITERRANEAN SALAD

½ teaspoon Dijon mustard
3 tablespoons vinegar
4 tablespoons lemon juice
3 tablespoons extra-virgin olive
  oil
3 tablespoons fresh parsley,
  chopped
4 tablespoons fresh mint, chopped
1 garlic clove, minced
½ onion, thinly sliced
2 tomatoes, diced
1 green or red pepper, seeded
  and diced
½ English or 1 Persian cucumber,
  sliced
½ carrot, grated
1 stalk celery, sliced thinly
Handful of olives, pitted
Crusty French bread

Practically every city block features a generic ethnic salad bar/grocery. Convenient? Yes. Variety? Yes. But since you pay by the pound, a hungry worker can go broke pretty quickly. It's just as easy to pack your own lunch salad. Store the dressing in a separate container and toss just before eating to avoid salad sogginess. This recipe is easily doubled or tripled.

1. Place mustard in a small bowl and whisk together with the vinegar and lemon juice. Slowly whisk in the oil. Stir in the herbs and the garlic. Set aside to allow the flavors to blend while you prepare the vegetables.
2. Place vegetables in a large bowl and toss gently with dressing. Serve with crusty French bread.

Yield: 2 servings

SOUP KITCHEN

*F*rom Tokyo to Paris, walk through any city at lunchtime, and you'll see diners in restaurants, slurping on soup. It's a fast, cheap, healthy, and easy meal for busy urbanites to consume. Soup is also economical, generally healthy, and easy to prepare. Served with bread and a salad, you can build an entire meal around a humble pot of soup.

Since many soups are inherently vegan (think lentil soup, think minestrone), it's a good dish to serve to vegan-phobic omnivores or skeptics.

PUMPKIN-DAAL SOUP

1 onion, chopped

2 tablespoons olive oil

1¼ cups pumpkin puree (pure puree—without sugar or other added ingredients)

2 cups plain soy or rice milk

½ cup split red lentils (masoor daal)

1 heaping teaspoon yellow curry paste

2 tablespoons sugar or agave nectar

½ teaspoon coriander

½ teaspoon turmeric

1 teaspoon vegan Worcestershire sauce (or soy sauce or Braggs)

½ teaspoon sea salt

Pinch nutmeg

Freshly ground pepper to taste

Cilantro or parsley for garnish

When Jack Frost first visits and leaves behind his signature nip in the air, it's time to make this warming, Indian-influenced soup. It's loaded with fiber and flavor, thanks to the curry paste and coriander. I like to serve it with crusty bread for dipping, and a large green salad.

1. In a large pot, sauté onion in oil over medium heat until brown. (Not just translucent. Brown! The edges should be dark.)
2. Add the pumpkin and remaining ingredients, except for the garnish.
3. Cook until the lentils are soft—about 25 minutes. Adjust seasonings and serve.

Yield: 6 servings

Variation

I like the lumpy texture of this soup, but feel free to puree all or part of it with an immersion blender if you are more inclined toward smoother soups.

TALK SOUP!

Soup: Basically liquid food, often containing solid pieces of food, usually eaten warm

Stew: An extremely thick, filling soup

Consommé: Clear soup

Broth/Stock: Clear liquid that is the flavor base of most soups

Potage: A thick and usually creamy soup

Stoop: This term, invented by Rachel Ray, is a soup that's thinner than a stew, but thicker than a soup.

HOT & SOUR COCONUT SOUP

February colds are the worst. I threw together this soup one day, mid-cold, when I was craving Thai flavors to speed up the healing process and clear my sinuses—but was too sick even to pick up takeout. The fusion of hot, sour and sweet, and the carby goodness of the rice noodles turned out to be just what the doctor ordered.

1. Sauté onion, garlic, celery, carrot, and ginger in oil on medium heat until soft. Add hot-and-sour paste and sauté a few minutes until combined. Add protein, agave, and mushrooms, sauté for a few more minutes, then toss in the coconut milk and water. Bring to a boil and add lime juice.
2. Add noodles. Stir well and turn heat down to low. Cook on low until noodles are soft, about 15 minutes. Careful not to overcook!
3. Garnish with fresh Thai basil, chopped scallions, or cilantro.

Yield: 6 servings

1 onion, chopped
2 cloves garlic, minced
1 stalk organic celery, sliced
1 carrot, cubed
1 1-inch piece of ginger, grated
1 tablespoon canola oil
½–1 heaping tablespoon hot-and-sour paste, to taste (tom yum)*
1 15-ounce can mock curry abalone or 1 cup seitan or firm tofu, cubed
2 tablespoons agave nectar (or vegan sugar)
6 dried shiitake mushrooms, chopped (fresh are fine, too)
1 14-ounce can coconut milk (lite is fine)
2 cans water (use the coconut milk can)
Juice of ½ lime
⅓ pound rice noodles, broken
Fresh Thai basil, scallions, or cilantro for garnish

* Be sure to read the ingredient list on the label. Not all tom yum paste is vegan.

BABCI'S POLISH MUSHROOM SOUP
(ZUPA ZE SWIEZYCH GRZYBÓW)

2 tablespoons canola oil
1 large onion, chopped
5 whole black peppercorns
4 whole balls of allspice
4 cups chopped, fresh wild
  mushrooms (to be authentic,
  use Polish mushrooms like
  borowiki; otherwise, shiitake,
  porcini, oyster mushrooms,
  cremini, and/or cepes make
  wonderful substitutes)
6 cups vegetable broth
3 tablespoons flour
½–1 cup vegan sour cream (add
  less for a thinner soup, more for
  a thicker, richer soup)
1 pound small red potatoes,
  scrubbed and cut into quarters
Parsley, for garnish
Salt and lots of black pepper

Growing up in a small boondockian town in the coal-mining region of Pennsylvania, all my friends had a nana. I wanted a nana. But I had a babci (pronounced: BOB-chee; Polish for "grandma"). Now, I'm proud that I did.

Babci had magical jars of herbs in her cupboard. Her garden was a spectrum of pastel rose petals, peppermint petunias, and tangled mint and thyme. On Saturday, I walked across town to scrub her floor. Babci always rewarded me with a crisp dollar bill and stories of the "old country," growing up on a farm on the Poland-Belarus border. She arrived in New York City by boat, all alone at fourteen, with $18 in her pocket and speaking not a word of English. I inherited her love of adventure, and a slew of recipes by osmosis. This is just one of them.

This recipe originally appeared in *Végétariens* magazine, in France.

1. Heat the oil over medium heat. Add the onions, peppercorns, and allspice. Sauté for about 5 minutes, then add the mushrooms. Sauté another 5 minutes, then pour enough broth in the pan to just cover the vegetables.
2. While the vegetables are cooking, whisk together the flour and sour cream in a medium bowl until there are absolutely no lumps. Then slowly add this mixture to the soup pot, a bit at a time, mixing continually until completely blended. Add the remainder of the broth and the potatoes.
3. Simmer the soup, partially covered, over medium-low heat until the mushrooms and potatoes are soft and cooked, about 1 hour. Add a bit more water or broth periodically if you need to.
4. When the soup is ready, puree about half of it in the blender and then add it to the pot. Adjust seasonings. Serve with a dollop of sour cream and a bottle of Pilsner or wheat beer.

Yield: 6 servings

Variations
Omit the potatoes and serve this soup over cooked wide noodles
or cooked brown or long-grain rice.
If you like a chunkier, more stewlike soup, omit the puree step. Conversely, if
you want the soup to be completely smooth, puree the whole batch.
For a lighter soup, use soy milk or rice milk instead
of the vegan sour cream.

ROASTED ROOT VEGETABLE SOUP

When autumn morphs from crisp to cold and I put away my summer clothes, colorful root vegetables call out to me from the farmer's market stalls. When you roast root veggies—an easy task—they mellow and exude a sophisticated, subtle smokiness. Depending on which roots you choose, this thick soup takes on a lovely, painterly hue, anywhere from ochre to burnt sienna to raw umber. Serve with crusty whole-grain bread and a side salad, or over cooked grains like spelt or brown rice. This soup freezes well.

1. Preheat oven to 400°F.
2. Oil a 9 x 13-inch pan and toss in all ingredients, mixing well with your fingers. Cover with foil and roast for about 35 to 40 minutes, or until vegetables are soft.
3. You can enjoy the vegetables as is; for a soup, remove bay leaf and carefully puree in a blender, in batches, with 2 cups of soy milk and 2 cups of vegetable broth.

Yield: 4 servings

3 cups mixed root vegetables, peeled and cut into 2-inch cubes (e.g., carrots, yams, turnips, parsnips, winter squash, potatoes)
1 onion, peeled and quartered
A few garlic cloves, peeled
4 tablespoons olive oil
1 tablespoon soy sauce
Handful dried coconut
½ teaspoon dried coriander
1 tablespoon basil
1 bay leaf
Salt and freshly ground pepper, to taste

GREEN GODDESS SOUP

3 tablespoons olive oil

1 large onion, chopped

5 cloves garlic, sliced

½ teaspoon salt

1 10-ounce package frozen spinach

1 12-ounce aseptic container of soft silken tofu

4 cups rice milk

½ avocado, sliced

¾ cup broccoli sprouts (or other favorite sprout)

4 heaping tablespoons nutritional yeast plus extra for sprinkling

2 vegetable bouillon cubes

¼ teaspoon nutmeg

Freshly ground black pepper, to taste

When I look out of the window of my city loft, I see bricks, steel, and concrete. While I love the industrial urban landscape, during the winter months, it can grow a bit gray. Sometimes, I just need a little infusion of greenness to pick me up. That's usually when I make this celadon-hued soup.

This is one of the easiest-to-make soups I know. Yet the rich and creamy finished product can fool your guests into thinking you spent hours slaving over a hot stove—and that you've given up your vegan lifestyle. Serve it with a strongly flavored whole-grain roll, toasted and slathered with Earth Balance or extra-virgin olive oil. A glass of Pinot Grigio will tease out the nutmeg's earthy sweetness.

1. Heat oil in a large Dutch oven over medium-low heat. Add the onion and, about 1 minute later, the garlic. Sprinkle with salt. Sauté until translucent—about 5 minutes.
2. Add the rest of the ingredients and bring to a boil. Turn heat down to medium and simmer for about 20 minutes, until everything is soft.
3. Carefully puree in a blender in 2-cup increments (please hold the lid down).
4. Sprinkle each bowl with about 1 tablespoon of nutritional yeast. Serve with plenty of toasted whole-grain bread for dunking.

Yield: 6 servings

ITALIAN WEDDING SOUP

This soup is a mainstay in largely Italian South Philadelphia. I'm still unclear as to the origins of its name, since apparently, it is not served at Italian weddings. Maybe it got its name from the perfect marriage of flavors used in the soup—bitter, sweet, and salty. It's the perfect use for escarole.

1. Mix bread crumbs and milk in a medium bowl. Let sit while you gather the remaining ingredients. Using your hands, mix in the remaining soy ball ingredients. Form into small meatballs (about the size of an acorn or smaller) and set aside.
2. In a large soup pot, heat oil over medium-low and sauté garlic until soft. Toss in the escarole and cook until the color deepens and the leaves wilt. Add the broth, porcini mushrooms, and nutritional yeast. Cook over medium-low, covered for about 30 minutes. Just before serving, gently spoon in the soy balls. Cook for 5 minutes. Season to taste with salt and pepper. Serve with sliced whole-grain bread.

Yield: 8 servings

Soy Balls

½ cup whole-grain bread crumbs
½ cup nondairy milk
1 pound ground meat alternative
2 teaspoons dried sage
1 teaspoon dried parsley
2 cloves garlic, crushed
1 tablespoon olive oil
3 tablespoons nutritional yeast
¾ teaspoon organic lemon rind or
   3 drops lemon oil
Salt and freshly ground pepper,
   to taste

Broth

3 tablespoons olive oil
5 cloves garlic, sliced
2 heads escarole, sliced
8 cups vegetable broth
1 handful dried porcini
   mushrooms
1 tablespoon nutritional yeast
Salt and freshly ground pepper,
   to taste

ENLIGHTENED VEGETABLE BARLEY SOUP

3 tablespoons olive oil
I large onion, chopped
I carrot, diced
2 stalks celery, sliced
2 cloves garlic, sliced
7 cups vegetable broth
2 tablespoons dried porcini
  mushrooms
½ cup pearl barley
½ pound assorted mushrooms,
  sliced (e.g., cremini, shiitake,
  oyster)
I tablespoon shoyu or soy sauce
2 tablespoons Amontillado sherry
2 tablespoons chopped parsley
Sea salt and freshly ground
  pepper, to taste

Winter soups are meant to warm, but some can sit like lead in your stomach—not exactly conducive to busy urban life. This soup does the trick—but it doesn't leave you feeling heavy and sleepy after you're finished eating. It's a great chill chaser.

1. Set a large pot over medium heat. Add oil, let it warm, and then sauté onion, carrot, and celery until almost translucent. Add garlic and sauté another minute, then add the stock.
2. Using your fingers, grind the porcini mushrooms into dust and sprinkle into the soup. Toss in barley, mushrooms, and shoyu and stir well.
3. Turn heat to low. Cover and simmer until carrots and barley are cooked—about 45 minutes. Just before serving, add sherry and parsley and adjust seasonings.

Yield: 8 servings

CHILLED ZUCCHINI SOUP WITH DILL

4 medium zucchini, sliced
2 medium onions, chopped
  roughly
6 cups vegetable broth
I bunch of dill, with any tough
  stems removed
Salt and pepper to taste

About twenty years ago, I was a cubist (definition: worker whose office is a cubicle) working at a firm in Philadelphia that managed the assets of extremely wealthy people; those with net worths of under $3 million were not accepted as clients (slackers!). Needless to say, I was like a fish out of water and eventually left to pursue my graduate degree in English. But I felt like I was rich when a colleague named Katie shared this easy recipe with me. Although I've tweaked it a bit over the years, this soup has consistently remained a go-to meal on humid August days, when the farmer's markets overflow with cheap, baseball-bat-size zucchini. The dill infuses the soup with an almost buttery silkiness. It's also good warm.

1. Dump everything except the dill into a large pot. Cover and bring to a boil. Boil for 10 to 15 minutes or until onions and zucchini are soft.
2. Remove from heat and allow to cool. Chill further in refrigerator. Add dill. Puree with an immersion blender or in a regular blender, and serve.

Yield: 6 servings

10-MINUTE CORN CONSOMMÉ

City people, generally speaking, are busy people. Even though I work at home, I don't always have time for a proper lunch or dinner. With this soup, there are no excuses for fast food. It's on the table in about 10 minutes. It's also extremely inexpensive.

1. Bring corn and broth to a boil. Cover and boil gently for 5 minutes or until warm.
2. Puree with an immersion blender or in a regular blender. Strain, if you are fussy about presentation. (I'm not, plus I love those corny bits.) Season and serve.

Yield: 6 servings

2½ cups frozen corn
6 cups vegetable broth
1 healthy pinch of one of the following: azafran, smoked Spanish paprika, or chili powder
Salt and pepper to taste

Variations

Toss an onion, some garlic, or a tomato into the mix.
You can also substitute peas for the corn, skip the pinch of spicy seasonings, and use good quality curry powder instead.

10 ADDITIONS TO LIVEN UP SOUPS

1. Pesto
2. A drizzle of truffle oil
3. A shot of vinegar (try different kinds, like balsamic, champagne, etc.)
4. Sesame oil—just a few drops
5. A few spoons of nutritional yeast
6. A shot of any creamy sauce (e.g., Béarnaise or Béchamel)
7. Finely chopped roasted red peppers
8. A dollop of Vegenaise
9. A dab of wasabi or horseradish
10. A few spoons of sherry or Marsala (especially wonderful in mushroom and creamy soups)

HEARTY ADZUKI BEAN SOUP

5½–6 cups vegetable broth
 (depending on how thick you
 want the soup)
1½ cups dried adzuki beans,
 rinsed and picked over
½ cup dried mushrooms (shiitake
 or other Asian variety)
½ onion, roughly chopped
2 cloves garlic
1 tablespoon soy sauce
1 tablespoon agave nectar
1 2-inch piece kombu (optional)*
¼ cup toasted, slivered almonds,
 for garnish
Sesame oil, for drizzling
Salt and pepper to taste

* Kombu infuses soup with a very
 subtle hint of the sea, but it also
 adds important nutrients.

Adzuki beans are petite red beans that are usually used in Asian dishes. They are subtly sweet and are amazingly filling. Here, I've paired them with dried mushrooms, toasted almonds, and a drizzle of sesame oil. (I prefer the flavor-packed black sesame oil.) One small bowl of this healthy, fiber-filled soup will keep even the busiest city slicker energized until the next meal.

1. Bring broth to a boil. Add all remaining ingredients, except almonds and sesame oil, and simmer, covered, for about 1 hour, or until beans are very soft.
2. Puree with an immersion blender or in a regular blender. Salt and pepper to taste.
3. Drizzle with sesame oil, garnish with some toasted, slivered almonds, and serve.

Yield: 6 servings

Wine pairing
The salty-sweetness of this soup pairs exceptionally
well with a dry Pinot Grigio.

NASI GORENG SOUP

4 cups vegetable broth
1 heaping tablespoon vegan Nasi
 Goreng paste
1 cup cauliflower florets
1 cup wide rice noodles, dry
Hot sauce, to taste
Soy sauce, to taste
Rice vinegar, to taste
2 tablespoons basil

Nasi Goreng is an Indonesian rice dish that I love to order out and occasionally make at home, thanks to a jar of Nasi Goreng paste that I bought at an Asian supermarket. One night, I saw the half-used jar of paste, staring me down from its perch on my refrigerator shelf, and I thought to myself, "If it tastes good with rice, it will taste even better with rice noodles." And I was right. This is how Nasi Goreng soup was born. Paired with Satay Seitan, it makes an excellent Southeast Asian-inspired meal.

1. In a large saucepan, add broth, paste, and cauliflower. Bring to a boil and boil for about 4 minutes, or until cauliflower is softish.
2. Add rice noodles. Boil 1 more minute. Turn off heat.
3. Add basil. Season with hot sauce, soy sauce, and rice vinegar, to taste. Serve when noodles are tender—another 2 to 3 minutes.

Yield: 4 servings

CAMEROON MAFÉ

Mafé is a West African peanut-based stew. Ingredients vary from country to country and kitchen to kitchen, but I'd guess that 99 percent of mafés are meat based. The flavors of my vegan version hail predominantly from Cameroon. For texture and chewiness, I used texturized vegetable protein (TVP) instead of chicken or beef. The sweetness of the carrots and ballerina lightness of the zucchini are yin to the creamy peanut butter yang.

Serve this piquant dish over brown rice with a healthy dollop of harissa (see page 188). A velvet shiraz will tease out the complex undertones.

1. In a food processor, combine tomatoes, garlic, ginger, and ½ cup broth until smooth. Set aside.
2. In a large soup pan, heat oil over medium-low and sauté onion until clear. Add carrots, and cook for 5 minutes until pre-softened. Toss in TVP, 3 cups broth, peanut butter, bay leaves, zucchini, and tomato mixture. Bring to a boil, then simmer partially covered, for 25 minutes or until veggies are soft. Add more broth in ½ cup increments if needed.

Yield: 6 servings

1 cup cherry tomatoes or 1 large tomato, diced
10 garlic cloves
2-inch piece ginger, peeled
½ cup plus 3 cups vegetable broth
3 tablespoons canola oil
2 onions, finely chopped
6 carrots, chopped in half, then into 1-inch pieces
2 cups textured vegetable protein (TVP) chunks or crumbles
1 cup peanut butter
3 bay leaves
3 zucchini, sliced
Harissa (condiment)

CLARA'S PASTA E FAGIOLI

Funny how whether you live in the city, the 'burbs, or the country, we generally all turn to the same foods for comfort. For me, nothing beats this filling, warming soup, especially with garlic bread for dunking. There are a skillion Pasta e Fagioli variations, but I like my mother-in-law Clara's interpretation the best.

1. In a large soup pot, sauté garlic in oil on medium-low until soft. Do not burn. Add tomatoes. Simmer on low for 10 minutes.
2. Add beans along with liquid from the can (or drain, and add 1 cup of water or broth). If you prefer a thinner soup, just add more broth. Simmer for 30 more minutes. Add herbs, salt, pepper, and crushed red pepper during the last 5 minutes.
3. Cook the pasta according to the package directions. Drain well and add to soup.

Yield: 6 servings

3 tablespoons olive oil
1 garlic clove, chopped
1 28-ounce can crushed tomatoes
2 16-ounce cans cannelini beans
1 teaspoon dried basil or ¼ cup fresh basil
1 teaspoon dried parsley or a few sprigs of fresh parsley
Salt and pepper to taste
¼ teaspoon crushed red pepper
1 pound ditalini or elbow macaroni

REGINA'S
RED BEET SOUP

3 tablespoons olive oil

1 onion, sliced

1 16-ounce can red beets, drained and julienned (or 2–3 small red beets, peeled, boiled until soft, and julienned); reserve 2 cups cooking liquid

1 cup broth

2 teaspoons white vinegar

Salt and pepper to taste

1 cup vegan sour cream

I firmly believe that the best soup recipes come from family matriarchs. My Aunt Regina (we called her "cioci," which is Polish for "aunt") was and continues to be an incredible inspiration to me. From her, I gained a penchant for travel and a love of city life—and of red beet soup. This recipe is hers, veganized by adding nondairy sour cream. I grew up eating this lovely, Pepto-Bismol pink potage.

1. In a large soup pot, sauté onion in oil until soft. Add red beets, broth, 1 cup of red beet water, vinegar, and seasonings. Simmer on low for about 20 minutes.
2. With a ladle, transfer about 1 cup of the soup liquid to a large bowl. Whisk in the sour cream well. Then add back to the soup pot. If you'd like, you can puree the soup with an immersion blender, but I prefer the earthy slivers of onion and beet.

Yield: 6 servings

SMOKY
SPLIT PEA SOUP

2 tablespoons olive oil

2 large carrots, diced

2 organic celery stalks, diced

1 medium onion, diced

3 garlic cloves, peeled and sliced

6 ounces tempeh bacon, chopped

1 bay leaf

1 tablespoon soy sauce

1 teaspoon dried thyme

1½ cups dried split peas

1 rutabaga, peeled and diced

8 cups vegetable stock

2 tablespoons white wine

Pea soup is a nutritious meal in itself, especially when served with fiber-filled Six-Flour Dunkin' Bread (see page 69). Somehow, it always tastes magically comforting. It's like a hug in a bowl—something city dwellers and country dwellers alike want to come home to. My version gets its smoky essence, and an extra shot of protein, from tempeh bacon. It's one of those soups that tastes even better the next day.

1. In a large soup pot, heat oil over medium. Sauté carrot, celery, onion, and garlic until soft, about 10 minutes. Add tempeh, and cook another minute or two.
2. Add bay leaf, soy sauce, thyme, peas, rutabaga, and broth. Bring to a boil and then reduce heat to low. Simmer covered for at least 1 hour, or up to 2 hours. About 15 minutes before serving, stir in the white wine and remove lid.
3. You can eat this soup as is, which is essentially a split pea chowder, or you can puree or partially puree it with an immersion blender. (I do the latter.)

Yield: 6–8 servings

QUINOA SOUP

Most North Americans eat quinoa in casserole or side dish form. But go to Lima, and you'll find this light, flavorful soup on almost every menu. Lima has its share of damp and foggy winter days, and this soup is like a little taste of warming sunshine, warming you up on a damp winter day. Unfortunately, it's usually made with chicken broth, which is why I decided to veganize it.

1. In a large soup pan, heat oil over medium heat. Sauté onions and garlic until soft, about 3 to 5 minutes. Add achiote and broth. Bring to a boil and then add the quinoa. Boil gently for about 10 minutes.
2. Lower heat to a hearty simmer. Add potatoes and cook, covered, until tender, about 10 more minutes. Then add the nutritional yeast and milk. Cook until warmed through, about another 10 minutes.
3. If soup should dry out at any point, add more vegetable broth by the ½ cup.
4. Add parsley, and season with salt and pepper to taste.

Yield: 6 servings

1 tablespoon olive oil
1 small red onion, minced
4 garlic cloves, minced
2 tablespoons achiote, dissolved in 6½ cups vegetable broth
2 cups quinoa, rinsed
3 organic potatoes, peeled and cubed
½ cup nutritional yeast
1 cup rice or soy milk
3 tablespoons fresh chopped parsley
Salt and pepper to taste

ISLAND GUMBO

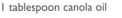

This sunny, spicy soup, inspired by the Caribbean, is just what the doctor ordered to take you through to springtime or any time you need a tropical-inspired pick-me-up.

1. In a large soup pan, heat oil over medium heat. Sauté onion and garlic until soft, about 5 minutes, then add flour and cook until it starts to brown.
2. Add remaining ingredients, except for grain. Bring to a boil. Add grain, cover, and cook for an additional 20 to 40 minutes (depending on which grain you choose), or until vegetables and grain are cooked. Add salt.

Yield: 8 servings

1 tablespoon canola oil
2 onions, chopped
5 cloves garlic, minced
2 tablespoons flour
2 stalks celery, chopped
1 habañero pepper, seeded and minced (wear gloves!)
1½ teaspoons paprika
2 red or orange peppers, seeded and chopped
4 cups vegetable stock
1 28-ounce can crushed tomatoes
8 ounces fresh or frozen okra, chopped
1 14-ounce can pigeon peas
1 cup corn
1 cup peas
3 tablespoons fresh parsley, chopped
1 tablespoon fresh thyme
½ cup barley, millet, or rice
1 teaspoon salt

LF $

2 tablespoons extra-virgin olive
  oil
1 large bunch of Swiss chard or
  beet greens, coarsely chopped
  (remove large stalks)
1 onion, minced
4 garlic cloves, minced
4 tablespoons tomato paste
8 cups vegetable broth
½–1 tablespoon harissa (see page
  188), or about ½–1 teaspoon
  chili flakes
Juice 1 fresh organic lemon
Zest 2 fresh organic lemons
1 teaspoon cumin
8 ounces angel hair or cappellini,
  broken
1 15-ounce can chickpeas, rinsed
  and drained
Salt and ground black pepper to
  taste

TUNISIAN SOUP

Snow-covered sidewalks. Fanglike icicles hanging from overpasses. Faces buried behind layers of hats, scarves, and shawls. In winter's dead center, city life screams monochrome.

That's when I need to make this soup. It makes me realize, rather hopefully, that somewhere in Tunis a North African vegetarian is happily slurping this typical potage under perpetually sunny skies. Eaten with some crusty bread, this hearty soup is a filling wintertime meal.

1. In a large soup pan, heat oil over medium heat. Sauté greens, onion, and garlic until soft, about 10 minutes. Add tomato paste and cook another few minutes until combined.
2. Add remaining ingredients, except for pasta and chickpeas, and bring to a boil. Simmer, covered, for about 40 minutes. Add noodles and chickpeas and cook for another 10 minutes. Season with salt and pepper.

Yield: 6 servings

FEIJOADA

Salvador de Bahia is the black heart of Brazil. Originally a center of slave trade, it resurrected itself and became the cultural and musical epicenter of Brazil, borrowing influences from African, indigenous, and European traditions. Music seems to flow through Salvadorians' blood; walk down any street, and the pounding beat of the samba drum is never far away.

Slaves originally made Feijoada from pork scraps and black beans. Now considered Brazil's national dish, it's customarily eaten on Sunday night (as I learned in Salvador, where some version was headlined on practically every restaurant's menu). Feijoada is hearty, healthy, and filling: classic comfort food. And a certain amount of improvisation is encouraged! It's usually garnished with orange slices and manioc flour, also known as farofa.

My vegan version uses tempeh bacon to infuse the beans with the dish's signature smoke. Serve over beans with a Copacabana Caipirinha (see page 202).

4 cups dried black beans
8–10 cups water or broth
2 bay leaves
2 tablespoons olive oil
1 large onion, chopped
4 cloves garlic, chopped
¼ teaspoon hot pepper flakes
2 8-ounce packages of tempeh bacon, crumbled (or 1 8-ounce pack tempeh bacon and 1 8-ounce pack of sweet soy sausage, crumbled)
4 cups cooked rice
Organic orange slices, for garnish

1. Soak the beans overnight, or for at least 8 hours, in a large bowl with enough water to cover the beans. Drain and place in a large soup pot. Add enough water or stock to cover beans and slowly bring to a boil over medium heat.
2. Add the bay leaves to the beans. Simmer uncovered for about 2 hours or until soft, adding more water or broth as needed.
3. Heat oil in medium sauté pan over medium heat. Add the onion, garlic, and pepper flakes and cook until soft. Add this and the tempeh bacon to the beans.
4. Simmer for another hour (or two, if you have the time!), adding water as needed. Partially puree with an immersion blender (or remove a cup or two of beans and puree them in the blender).
5. Serve over rice with orange slices—and manioc flour if you can find it!

Yield: 8 servings

POTATO-LEEK SOUP

3 tablespoons olive oil

2 large leeks, washed well and sliced

3 garlic cloves, sliced

1 pound potatoes, peeled and cubed

8 cups vegetable stock

2 tablespoons fresh parsley, chopped

Salt and freshly ground pepper, to taste

This basic, farm-inspired soup makes icy city winters a bit more bearable, especially when served with a few thick slices of crusty bread.

1. In a large soup pot, heat oil over medium-low heat. Add leeks and garlic, and cook until soft, about 5 minutes. Add potatoes and stock and bring to a boil.

2. Turn heat to low and simmer, covered, for about 30 to 50 minutes, or until potatoes are soft, stirring occasionally. Add parsley and seasonings.

3. Puree or partially puree, using a blender or immersion blender.

Yield: 8 servings

Variation

For a richer soup, substitute soy or rice milk for the stock.

CUT THE FAT

Try these tips to slim down your cooking:

- When making soups, instead of sautéing onions and garlic in oil, simply let them cook in the broth.
- When baking, substitute applesauce for up to half of the called-for amount of oil or Earth Balance.
- Measure! Rachel Ray may tell you to "eyeball it," but your waist says, "Pull out the measuring spoons!"
- When sautéing onions, instead of adding more oil, sprinkle onions with salt. This draws out the water and prevents them from burning.
- Instead of adding more oil to pasta or other dishes, try a bit of vegetable broth.

SIX-FLOUR DUNKIN' BREAD

I love artisanal bread and fancy city bakeries. But I'm too frugal (some may say "cheap") to fork out $4 for a loaf on a regular basis. I'm no artisan, but I developed this dense, fiber-filled loaf especially for dunking into hearty soups like Smoky Split Pea (see page 64), Roasted Root Vegetable Soup (see page 57), or Pumpkin Daal (see page 54). This bread is dark, rich, and sops up the soup nicely, while still holding its own shape long enough for you to take a bite. It's easy to make, but you need to be close at hand to wait for the dough to rise several times. In other words, it's the perfect "snowed-in" recipe and tastes great the next day for breakfast, toasted and slathered with jam.

1. Heat the milk and water to lukewarm—not too hot, about wrist temperature. (I microwave mine in a Pyrex beaker for about 1½ minutes. Remember, microwave times vary.) Dissolve the sugar and yeast in this heated liquid and let it stand for about 5 minutes or until foamy.

2. Pour liquid into a large bowl and, using the kneading hook on your mixer (I use my KitchenAid), add 1 cup each of whole wheat and spelt flour, about ½ cup at a time. Add vital wheat gluten and knead until well mixed. Cover with foil and put in a warm place. Allow it to rise until it's doubled in bulk—30 to 60 minutes (rising time can vary depending on the season, region, and weather).

3. Using the kneading hook, work in oil, molasses, and salt. Then add the oats and remaining flours, ½ cup at a time, finishing off with 1 to 2 cups of spelt flour. Continue kneading about 5 to 10 minutes. Dough is ready when it is smooth, elastic, and easy to handle.

4. Place dough in an oiled bowl. Turn it to make sure oil covers dough ball evenly. Cover with foil and let rise until doubled, about 1 hour.

5. After the second rising, punch down the dough and preheat the oven to 375°F. Oil two loaf pans.

6. Knead the dough lightly by hand. Divide in two, and form into loaves. Place into loaf pans, and sprinkle with your seeds of choice, if desired. Cover with foil, and allow to rise until dough is about ⅔ to ¾ the height of the pan.

7. Bake for about 30 to 45 minutes, or until the loaves sound hollow when tapped. Allow to cool at least 15 minutes before slicing.

Yield: 2 loaves

1 cup soy or rice milk
½ cup water
1 teaspoon sugar
2 tablespoons yeast
1 cup plus ¼ cup whole-wheat flour
1 cup plus 1–2 cups spelt flour
1½ teaspoon vital wheat gluten
4 tablespoons olive oil
4 tablespoons molasses
1½ teaspoons sea salt
1 cup instant oats
¼ cup soy flour
¼ cup teff flour
½ cup chickpea flour
2 tablespoons sesame, nigella, poppy, or sunflower seeds to sprinkle on top (optional)

Tip

I say, if you're going to go to the trouble of baking homemade bread, making 2 loaves at once turns out to be a time- and money-saver. Freeze one, and eat the other immediately.

DIY STOCK

Cities are only as great as their citizens. The same concept is true of soups: They are only as good as their ingredients, the flavor foundation of soups. Crappy stock = crappy soup.

Since I'm a busy lady, I lean heavily on store-bought stocks. But I do like to make my own. Not only does homemade stock taste fantastic, it's also super-economical, especially when you consider the price of store-bought versions.

This is not so much a recipe as it is inspiration. Every homemade stock tastes different depending on the cook and the ingredients you have on hand. Use this as a starting point to create your own stocks. The best advice I can give you is to taste, taste, taste! Keep doctoring your stock until you say "mmmm" after a spoonful. If your stock tastes good, chances are your soup will, too.

- Whenever you're chopping vegetables, save the tasty but unpretty bits and store them in a large plastic container in the freezer. This includes mushroom stems, onion ends, organic onion skins, organic potato peels, carrot tips, etc. (Don't save celery ends, though; they tend to dominate a stock.)
- Also save and freeze any flavorful liquid used to cook potatoes, onions, or dried mushrooms.
- To this end, when your dinner guests don't finish their wine, pour the contents into a ziploc freezer bag or your stock liquid container. You can use this to flavor your stock. (I got this tip from watching a Nigella Lawson show. I love that she's a blue blood *and* thrifty.) Don't use too much wine—I find up to ¼ cup in a pot of stock is plenty.
- When you have amassed about 2 cups of vegetables, it's time to make stock. Fill a large pan with about 8 cups of water. Add all of your frozen veggie ends and any liquid flavorings you have amassed. Bring to a boil, and then simmer for several hours, adding more water as needed. Strain and add any fresh herbs you like.
- Freeze this stock or use it immediately.

Yield: 8 cups

MELTING POT

Today, most major cities are microcosms of the world, made up of diverse peoples who bring with them exotic foods from faraway lands. Many ethnic recipes are intrinsically vegan, due to religious or economic reasons. So urban vegans have ready access to endless inspiration—via ethnic neighborhoods, restaurants, and grocery stores.

MODULAR PAKISTANI KIMA

[LF] [$]

1 large onion, chopped
3 cloves garlic, minced
3 tablespoons olive oil

Pick one:
2–3 cups chopped kale
2–3 cups chopped spinach
2–3 cups chopped mustard greens

Pick one:
1 12-ounce box soy "meat" grounds
1 15-ounce can beans of your choice
1 cup texturized vegetable protein

Pick one:
1 cup peas
1 cup chopped carrots
1 28-ounce can crushed tomatoes
1 cup water or vegetable stock
2 potatoes, diced
3 to 5 tablespoons curry powder (I go for the full monty)
1 dash each of cinnamon, ginger, and turmeric
1½ teaspoons sea salt

Urban vegans are busy vegans. But that doesn't mean you have to pull out the take-out menus. This easy one-pot curry is a snap to throw together using a series of mix-and-match ingredients that you already have on hand—even after the most hectic of days. Serve it over steaming hot basmati rice.

1. In a large pot over medium-low heat, sauté the onion and garlic in oil until soft. Add your green of choice (for instance, kale) and sauté about 5 minutes.
2. Add remaining ingredients. (If using peas, toss them in during the last 10 minutes of simmer time.) Bring to a boil and then lower heat and simmer, covered, 40 to 50 minutes, until all vegetables are soft. Curry should not be too soupy. If it's too watery, remove lid and cook another 5 minutes.

Yield: 6–8 servings

YOUR FRIENDLY NEIGHBORHOOD ETHNIC MARKET

It's full of foods you've never tasted, words you can't pronounce, and alphabets you can't read. So how do you navigate an ethnic market?

Come prepared. Research the items you want to buy online and prepare a list.

Ask for help. Explain what you are making, and the owners will be more than happy to assist you.

Take note of what others are buying. If there's a flock of customers buzzing around the tapioca-coconut desserts, for example, chances are it must be good (don't forget to ask about the ingredients).

Stock up on the familiar. Items in ethnic markets, such as soy sauce and exotic rices, tend to be much cheaper than in your trendy neighborhood gourmet shop.

Check out the freezer. If you're into mock meats, Asian markets offer an astonishing variety.

MOROCCAN MILLET TIMBALES

"Timbale" means "drum" in Italian. The independent film *Big Night* popularized this mythical rice dish. My compact version was inspired and necessitated by my compact city kitchen.

When you unmold these little millet packages, they resemble colorful little disks. These nifty timbales are a nutritious side dish and a tasty accompaniment to any Middle Eastern entrée. I love them drizzled with Tahini Sauce (see page 186). They're also versatile—simply play around with the herbs and spices, or just use whatever you have on hand.

1. Spray two muffin tins or twelve ramekins with cooking spray and set aside.
2. In a large saucepan, bring broth to a boil. Add millet, saffron, and carrot. Cover, reduce heat to low, and simmer until all the water is absorbed, 22 to 24 minutes.
3. Remove from heat and stir in remaining ingredients gently with a rubber spatula, mixing until everything is combined. Press the mixture into the greased muffin tins or ramekins, a few tablespoons at a time, and press it down gently and level out with the back of the spatula.
4. Refrigerate until set, at least 2 hours. To remove, trace the edge of the muffin tin or ramekin with a butter knife and then very gently lift out the timbale; they can be fragile. Enjoy at room temperature or heated.

Yield: 12 timbales

Cooking spray

2½ cups vegetable broth

1 cup millet

1 tablespoon saffron

1 carrot, grated

1 garlic clove, crushed

10 black olives, pitted and minced

2 tablespoons lemon juice

1 tomato, diced

1 tablespoon agave nectar

1½ teaspoons cumin

½ teaspoon cinnamon

½ teaspoon turmeric

1 tablespoon coriander

2 tablespoons cilantro, chopped

3 tablespoons extra-virgin olive oil

¼ teaspoon sea salt (or to taste)

Freshly ground pepper

Variations

Provençal Timbales: Omit cumin, cinnamon, turmeric, and cilantro. Instead, when stirring millet mixture, add 2 tablespoons fresh chopped parsley, 2 tablespoons herbes de Provençe, and 1 tablespoon capers, rinsed and chopped.

Italian Timbales: Omit cumin, cinnamon, turmeric, and cilantro. Instead, when stirring millet mixture, add 2 tablespoons fresh chopped parsley, 4 tablespoons fresh chopped basil, and 1 teaspoon oregano.

WELSH RAREBIT

2 tablespoons Earth Balance

2 tablespoons whole-grain flour

1 cup beer

6 ounces vegan cheese, grated (I recommend Mature Cheddar Cheezly)

1 healthy pinch dried mustard

2 healthy pinches cayenne pepper

2 tablespoons nama shoyu or soy sauce

½ large ripe tomato, chopped fine

Freshly ground pepper

4 slices whole-grain bread, toasted and slathered liberally with Earth Balance

There's a hip corner restaurant in Philadelphia, called Jones, that only serves "retro," nonvegan comfort foods, like meat loaf and Jello. It inspired me to update—and veganize—this classic retro treat, which is essentially a deconstructed grilled cheese sandwich.

1. In a large saucepan over medium heat, melt the Earth Balance. Sprinkle the flour over it and let it brown—about 2 minutes.
2. Whisk in the beer, a tiny bit at a time so the sauce doesn't get lumpy. Toss in the cheese, mustard, cayenne pepper, and shoyu or soy sauce. Whisk continuously until blended well—about 10 minutes.
3. Add the tomato and cook about 5 more minutes. Sauce should be thick and creamy. Adjust seasonings.
4. Spread sauce over toasted bread, slathered with Earth Balance.

Yield: 4 servings

Variations

Instead of bread, serve sauce over a toasted English muffin, bagel, or even cooked legumes or a cooked whole grain like wheat berries.

CURRY CASHEW CASSEROLE

I'm not usually big on casseroles. But the fact is, busy working stiffs like me need a good casserole recipe to pull out of a hat in times of exhaustion, desperation, or procrastination. This creamy, Thai-influenced entree is one of my go-to simple suppers. It only requires about 15 minutes of hands-on time, yet it tastes like you traveled all the way to Bangkok (or at least your favorite Thai restaurant) for takeout. Serve it over any whole grain. Although rice is the most obvious choice, I'm partial to a bed of spelt, since its inherent sweetness offsets the heat and sourness of the curry.

1. Preheat oven to 400°F.
2. In a large bowl, whisk together the cashew butter, rice milk, and basil. Add the curry paste, ½ teaspoon at a time, until the sauce is as hot as you like. (I add the full 2 teaspoons.) Be sure to whisk well so no clumps remain.
3. Toss all the other ingredients in a large casserole. Use a spatula to roughly break up the tomatoes, then pour on the cashew sauce. Stir well until all ingredients are combined and well coated.
4. Cover with foil and bake for 40 minutes. Remove foil and bake another 15 to 20 minutes, or until sauce has thickened.

Yield: 6 servings

½ cup plus 1 tablespoon cashew butter

½ cup rice milk (or soy milk)

2 tablespoons fresh basil, chopped very fine

1–2 teaspoons red curry paste

1 head broccoli, chopped into 1-inch pieces, or one 1-pound bag frozen broccoli

1 15-ounce can whole tomatoes, including juice

1 16-ounce can chickpeas, drained and rinsed

1 large onion, chopped

¼ teaspoon salt

Optional additions

8 ounces mushrooms, thinly sliced

1 red or yellow pepper, thinly sliced

1 yellow squash, sliced

Variations

Substitute peanut or almond butter for the cashew butter.
(But it really tastes best using cashew butter!)

FOIL-ROASTED BEETS WITH WASABI VINAIGRETTE

4 red beets
6 tablespoons extra-virgin olive oil
2 tablespoons balsamic vinegar
1 tablespoon parsley, chopped fine
2 teaspoons rice vinegar
2 teaspoons wasabi paste
2 garlic cloves, crushed
Salt, to taste

Being a nice Polish girl, red beets have always held a special, nostalgic place in my heart. And even though I realize wasabi is uniquely Japanese, each time I taste it, it still reminds me of the horseradish-infused Polish dishes I ate during my childhood in the boondockian Pennsylvania coal regions. This Warsaw-meets-Tokyo juxtaposition inspired my simple autumnal salad. The inherent sweetness and earthy innocence of the red beets is dazzled by the urbane spiciness of this wasabi vinaigrette—just as a coal miner's granddaughter like me was dazzled by the spice and tang of city life.

1. The easiest way to cook beets is to roast them in foil. Wash them, cut off the green tops, and wrap them individually in aluminum foil. Place them on a cookie sheet and roast for about 45 minutes at 400°F. (When they're done, you can easily pierce them with a fork.)
2. While the beets are cooling, mix the remaining ingredients well.
3. When cool, peel the beets and toss them with the Wasabi Vinaigrette. Serve warm, cold, or at room temperature.

Yield: 4 servings

Variation

Use horseradish instead of wasabi.

CAULIFLOWER-CHICKPEA TAGINE

Most cities have at least one wonderful, veg-friendly Moroccan restaurant. Philadelphia has several. But let's face it: Sometimes, you just want to savor an earthy tagine without having to deal with belly dancers shaking their assets in your face—especially on weeknights (some men might disagree). Now that I think of it, when I was in Morocco, I didn't see any belly dancers. I did see ladies—and men—very modestly dressed, covered from head to toe in loose, non-formfitting attire. And I sampled my fair share of tagines.

I like to serve this over the more traditional whole-wheat couscous. But it's just as good served over other whole grains like spelt, farro, and barley. It's also substantial enough just as it is.

1. In a large pot, heat oil over medium heat, and sauté onions until translucent. Add garlic and sauté another minute. Add a bit of salt to slow down the cooking, if needed.
2. Add remaining ingredients, except almonds. Bring to a boil, then lower to simmer. Cook covered for about an hour, or until all vegetables are soft. Top with almonds before serving.

Yield: 6 servings

1 tablespoon olive oil

1 large onion, thinly sliced

3 garlic cloves, slices

1 large head cauliflower, broken into florets

3 carrots, sliced thinly

1 15-ounce can chickpeas, drained (or 2 cups fresh-cooked chickpeas)

1 15-ounce can crushed tomatoes

1 cup vegetable broth

¼ cup raisins

1 cinnamon stick

1 teaspoon turmeric

1½ teaspoons cumin

½ teaspoon harissa (see page 188; use less, or just a dash of cayenne, if you're not a fan of heat)

¼ cup toasted, slivered almonds

Salt, to taste

GRANADA PAELLA

2 tablespoons olive oil

3 cloves garlic, minced

1 cup red pepper, chopped

1–2 links of vegan chorizo, crumbled (I prefer Trader Joe's brand; I use 1 large link)

2 cups Arborio rice

½ cup peas (frozen is fine)

2 tomatoes, cubed

1 teaspoon saffron

4–5 cups vegetable stock

Sea salt, to taste

Organic lemon wedges, for garnish and finishing

Granada, Spain, is one of my favorite cities in the world—especially at night. Wandering through the silent, curving streets after midnight feels just slightly dangerous, as if you are peeking in someone else's window. Except in this case, the window is an entire city with a culture all its own. The silence is inevitably shattered, at some point, by an angry flamenco guitar and the loud, off-key singing of some bar patron who's had too much sangria.

When you're making this paella, I strongly suggest you play some flamenco music. Maybe the Gipsy Kings or Ojos de Brujos. The Spanish are not shy about singing out loud. Nor should you be. Sing. Even if you don't know the words. Even if you can't carry a tune. Even if you don't speak Romani. Then reward yourself with this paella.

1. In a large pot (or paella pan, if you have one), heat the oil over medium-low heat. Sauté the garlic until clear. Be careful not to burn it!
2. Raise heat to medium and add peppers. Sauté for 1 to 2 more minutes, then add the chorizo. Sauté for 10 more minutes then add the rice. Stir until it's coated with the now-reddish oil, and cook for a minute more.
3. Add peas, tomatoes, saffron, and stock. Bring to a boil, then lower to simmer and cover pan. Cook for 15 to 20 minutes or until most of the water is absorbed. If paella starts to dry out, add more broth in ¼ cup increments. It should be just slightly wet—slightly wetter than risotto.
4. Adjust seasonings. Garnish with a lemon wedge. Squeeze lemon juice onto paella and serve.

Yield: 8 servings

Variations

Substitute 1 cup white beans and ½ teaspoon red pepper flakes
for the chorizo. You can also substitute 1 cup chopped seitan.
Add 1 teaspoon fennel seeds while you add the stock.

Wine Pairing

Garnacha from Spain or a Grenache-Syrah blend from Rousillion,
the French side of Catalonia.

SPICY INDIAN EGGPLANT

Let's face it. Unless you have your very own Indian grandma at your disposal, the best Indian food you will find is out at Indian restaurants. Bharta is a vegan-friendly dish I used to often order out. But lately, I find it too oil-laden for even a hedonist like me to enjoy. I created this lighter version so I could have my bharta and eat it, too. (Although it's not exactly fat-free, it's light enough to be virtuous in my eyes.) It's easy to make, even if you've never had success with Indian-centered meals.

1. Preheat oven to 400°F. Prick eggplants all over with fork and place on a greased cookie sheet. Roast until soft and saggy, about 45 minutes. Let cool, then skin and mash. You can peel away the skin, or include it. Your choice. (I include the skin.)

2. In a large pan, heat oil over medium heat. Add onion, garlic, and ginger and sauté until soft, about 5 minutes. (If they start to brown too quickly, lower heat and sprinkle on some salt to draw out the water and slow down the cooking.)

3. Turn heat to medium-low and add the spices. Cook about 5 minutes, then add the tomatoes.

4. Cook 5 more minutes, then add the eggplant. Cover and simmer over low heat for about 45 minutes. Serve over basmati rice or another whole grain.

Yield: 6 servings

4 small eggplants, destemmed

2 tablespoons canola or peanut oil

1 large onion, chopped

5–6 cloves garlic, minced

2-inch piece ginger, peeled and minced

1 tablespoon dried coriander

1 teaspoon fennel seeds

1 teaspoon cumin

¾ teaspoon nigella or black mustard seeds

½ teaspoon garam masala

½ teaspoon cayenne pepper (or less, to taste)

Salt, to taste

1 15-ounce can crushed tomatoes

PORTOBELLO BURRITOS

1 teaspoon plus 1 teaspoon olive oil

¼ teaspoon red pepper flakes

1 red pepper, thinly sliced

1 large onion, thinly sliced

2 cloves garlic, minced

3 portobello mushroom caps, sliced

1 16-ounce can black beans, drained and rinsed, or refried beans

2 cups cooked rice (a great use for leftover rice)

2 tablespoons ground cilantro

2 teaspoons cumin

1 teaspoon coriander

½ teaspoon chili powder

1 16-ounce jar salsa

10 tortillas (store-bought, or make your own—see page 46)

Vegan cheese (optional)

Salt, to taste

Cilantro for garnish

Chopped lettuce, tomatoes, garlic, onion, and/or avocado for garnish

For years, this has been one of my go-to meals. I've made double batches to serve at dinner parties, and I've also made it just for myself. It tastes so authentic that, for a moment, you might think you're in Mexico City. I suggest listening to Julieta Venegas or Lila Downs while you chow down on these muy bueno burritos.

1. Heat oven to 400°F. Grease a large baking pan.
2. In a large skillet, heat 1 teaspoon oil and red pepper flakes over medium heat. Sauté peppers, onion, and garlic for 5 minutes on medium. Add a pinch of salt to draw out the moisture. Add the portobello mushrooms, and cook until soft, about 20 minutes.
3. Meanwhile, mix beans, rice, spices and one teaspoon olive oil. Add sautéed vegetables to this mixture and stir well.
4. Place a few tablespoons of salsa in the bottom of the baking pan. Stuff tortillas with a few tablespoons of the rice mixture and a few thin slices of vegan cheese, if desired. Keep stuffing toward you. Roll "east and west" ends closed, and then roll the burrito closed from south to north. Place burritos in pan, and cover with salsa. Bake for 20 minutes. Serve. Adorn with garnish and vegan sour cream, if desired.

Yield: 6–8 servings

Variations

Replace rice with any kind of cooked grain (e.g., couscous, spelt, millet, barley).

RED CABBAGE WITH CARAWAY SEEDS

I grew up in the coal regions of Pennsylvania eating mounds of cheap, flavorful green cabbage. When I moved to the city, the exotic spectrum of colorful veggies in farmer's markets and even grocery stores astounded me. As an urban dweller, I started making the dishes I grew up with, using an entirely different painter's palette. Try purple, red, or green cabbage to make this hearty side. It pairs wonderfully with any German or Eastern European food, but it's lovely on its own, with rye bread. It's great with soy kielbasa, too.

1 tablespoon olive or canola oil
1 large onion, sliced thinly
1 large head red cabbage, julienned
1 teaspoon caraway seed
Lots of freshly ground pepper
Salt to taste

1. In a large stockpot, sauté the onion in the oil over medium heat until clear.
2. Turn the heat to medium-low, and add the cabbage and caraway seed. Cook until very soft, stirring occasionally—about 10 to 15 minutes. Season to taste.

Yield: 6 servings as a side

TRAVELING VEGAN— TIPS FOR EATING OUT AND PACKING

- Pack snacks that are easy to tote and easy to get through security, like power bars, whole pieces of fruit, nuts, and PB&Js on whole-grain bread.
- Ask airlines about "Asian vegetarian" (often foreign airline code for vegan) in-flight meals (but don't expect them to be tasty).
- While at the airport, read labels—you may be surprised at your finds.
- Research vegan restaurants at your final destination on www.HappyCow.net.

GOBHI ALOO

3 tablespoons neutral oil

½ teaspoon black mustard seeds

1 medium onion, chopped finely

1–2 teaspoons salt

2-inch piece ginger, peeled and chopped finely

2 teaspoons garam masala

1 teaspoon ground coriander

1 teaspoon cumin

¾ teaspoon turmeric

¼ teaspoon cayenne pepper

4 medium potatoes, cut into ½-inch pieces

1½ cups canned crushed tomatoes

2 heads cauliflower, cut into small florets

3 tablespoons water

I've consumed more than my share of Aloo Gobhi in Indian eateries from New York to New Delhi. This entree is easy for busy restaurant chefs to veganize, since they can make it quickly using oil instead of ghee. My pet peeve about this dish has been consistent: too many potatoes (aloo) and not enough cauliflower (gobhi). In my home-cooked version, I've switched things around a bit to include a greedy amount of cauliflower, with just a modest dose of potatoes. Serve over basmati rice. This tastes even better the next day!

1. In a large stockpot, heat oil over medium heat. Toss in the mustard seeds to pop, and cover. Once you hear that the mustard seeds have popped, carefully open the lid and toss in the onion, salt, and ginger. Add the remaining spices, one at a time, stirring well after each addition. Cook for an additional minute or so, then add potatoes. Stir well then lower heat and cook for another 2 to 3 minutes. Mixture in the pan will seem very dry at this point.
2. Add tomatoes, cauliflower, and water. Mix very well. Cover and simmer on medium-low for 30 to 40 minutes, or until vegetables are tender.

Yield: 6 large portions

BEAN AND BULGUR TACOS

When we think of tacos, we tend to think of crunchy, nacho-like taco shells, filled with a generic beefy chili. But go to Mexico City, or any Mexican city or town, and you'll find that most Mexicans prefer their tacos soft, with chunky fillings.

You'll get more than your fair share of fiber from these tacos, especially if you serve them with the Homemade, Whole-Grain Tortillas (see page 46). Top them with a dollop of vegan sour cream or guacamole, your favorite salsa or a healthy drizzle of the Passion Fruit–Cilantro Sauce, and plenty of shredded lettuce to temper the heat.

1. In a large saucepan, heat broth, onion, pepper, bulgur, hot pepper, and spices. Bring to a boil, and then cover, simmered for 15 minutes. Stir in the beans and cilantro, then cook another 10 to 20 minutes, or until all liquid is absorbed and mixture is dry enough to spread on tacos.
2. To serve, put a small amount of the filling in the center of a taco shell. Top with your garnishes of choice and some Passion Fruit–Cilantro Sauce, and then fold in half and enjoy. Not in the mood for tacos? The filling is also delicious served over brown rice.

Yield: 8 servings

1 cup vegetable broth

1 small onion, finely chopped

½ red pepper, very finely diced

½ cup bulgur

½–1 small hot pepper, deseeded and very finely minced (add for heat, according to your preference)

½–2 teaspoons chipotle pepper powder (add for heat, according to your preference)

1 teaspoon cumin

¾ teaspoon salt

1 15–16-ounce can black beans, drained and rinsed

1–2 tablespoons fresh cilantro, chopped

Passion Fruit–Cilantro Sauce (see page 194), shredded lettuce, sliced avocado, guacamole, and/ or vegan sour cream, for topping

Soft tacos or tortillas

CHICKPEA PAPRIKASH

$

4 tablespoons olive oil

2 tablespoons best-quality paprika

3 medium onions, peeled and chopped

½ teaspoon salt or more, to taste

2 15-ounce cans chickpeas, drained, rinsed, and lightly mashed

1½ cups vegetable broth

1 large tomato, chopped

3 Cubanelle or Hungarian wax peppers, seeded and chopped

4 cloves garlic, peeled and minced

Freshly ground pepper, to taste

½ cup soy yogurt or sour cream

3 tablespoons flour

I used to think paprika was just another banal kitchen spice until I visited Budapest. There, I learned to recognize how complex this earthy condiment is. The best paprika is grown in Szeged. There are two basic varieties: sweet and hot. I've used them both in this recipe with good success.

Serve over noodles, rice, bulgur, or more authentically, over Spaetzle (see page 85).

1. In a large stockpot, heat oil and paprika over medium-low heat. Let the paprika color the oil red and allow to cook for a minute or so. Add the onions and salt and cook until onions are soft, about 5 minutes.

2. Add everything but the yogurt/sour cream and flour. Bring to a boil, then cover and lower to a simmer. Cook for about 30 minutes or until peppers are soft.

3. In a small bowl, whisk together the sour cream and flour. Add about ½ cup of the rich paprika sauce you've just made to this mixture and whisk it all together. Make sure no lumps remain; it needs to be perfectly smooth. Then slowly add this slurry back to the pot. Heat on low for ten more minutes before serving.

Yield: 8 servings

EDIBLE SOUVENIRS

While on vacation, why not bring home exotic vegan foods as vacation souvenirs? Your family will appreciate them much more than another tacky shot glass. Here are just a few ideas:

Peru: Quinoa, granola

Caribbean: Guava cheese, rock cakes

Argentina: Olive spreads

France: Liqueurs like Cointreau

UK: Marmalades and jams

SPAETZLE

I had never heard of Spaetzle until I visited Munich, where I ate it topped with mushrooms. It was love at first bite. Now I make this eggless version all the time.

Serve tossed with oil or Earth Balance, salt, pepper, and a bit of nutritional yeast or topped with Chickpea Paprikash (see page 84) or Marsala Mushroom filling (see page 148). Since it's on the bland side and is easy to digest, a dish of spaetzle is also wonderful when you're feeling under the weather.

For best results, you'll need a spaetzle press or potato ricer. (I use the latter.) You could also force the batter through a colander. Before I had a ricer, I used to just drop the batter by teaspoons into the water. The spaetzle weren't as pretty, but they tasted just as good.

1 cup flour
⅔ cup soy or rice milk
2 tablespoons extra-virgin olive oil
½ teaspoon baking powder
½ teaspoon salt

1. Bring a large saucepan of salted water to a boil.
2. In a large bowl, whisk together all the ingredients. Batter will be very thick. Put about a tablespoon of batter into your press or ricer and squeeze dough into boiling water. When spaetzle rise to the top (almost immediately), transfer them, using a slotted spoon, to a colander. (If you're using a spoon, drop by teaspoons into the boiling water.)
3. Repeat this until you've used up all the batter. Immediately toss spaetzle with oil or Earth Balance and serve.

Yield: 6–8 servings

HAVANA BEANS AND RICE

1 pound dried black beans, rinsed and soaked overnight

4 cups vegetable broth, plus more if needed

6 cloves garlic, peeled and minced

1 red bell pepper, diced

2 onions, peeled and chopped

8 ounces tempeh bacon, diced

½ teaspoon liquid smoke

1 tablespoon paprika

1½ tablespoons cumin

1 bay leaf

½ teaspoon achiote powder

¼–½ teaspoon red pepper flakes

1 tablespoon rum

2–3 cups cooked white or brown long-grain rice (cook rice in vegetable stock instead of water)

Red or white wine vinegar or sherry vinegar

Salt and pepper

I must admit I had some trepidation about including this recipe. For one thing, it's almost cliché to include a recipe for beans and rice in a vegan cookbook. Another reason is that beany-ricey dishes seem to add to the myth that this is all that vegans eat.

But this earthy Cuban version truly transcends the stereotypes and makes you want to mambo. Serve it with Pan-Fried Plantains. (See recipe below.)

1. In a large pot, cook the beans in broth until soft.
2. Add garlic, pepper, onions, tempeh bacon, liquid smoke, paprika, cumin, bay leaf, achiote, red pepper flakes, and rum. Simmer, covered, on low for about 1 hour, adding more water or broth as needed.
3. Drain beans, and gently mix with rice. Just before serving, drizzle with a bit of vinegar. Add salt and pepper to taste.

Yield: 6 servings

PAN-FRIED PLANTAINS

3 ripe medium plantains

2 tablespoons Earth Balance

1–2 tablespoons brown sugar (optional)

Dash cinnamon (optional)

Plantains are a mainstay of Caribbean cuisine. Even though they aren't indigenous to cities with colder climates, you can still find them in markets everywhere. Not only are they plentiful; they're also inexpensive, filling, and healthful.

I like my plantains on the sweet side, in which case they need to be rather soft before frying (the plantain skin should be almost black). If you prefer a starchier, more potato-like texture, use plantains that are on the yellower side, but keep in mind, you will probably need to cook them longer.

1. Peel the plantains and slice them on the diagonal, about ⅛ to ¼ inch thick.
2. In a large saucepan, melt the Earth Balance. Add the plantain slices and fry until crispy. The plantains' own sugar will caramelize as it's heated. Once the first side is as brown as you like it, flip and repeat on the other side.
3. If using, sprinkle sugar and cinnamon over plantains, and mix to ensure they're evenly coated. Serve warm.

Yield: 6 servings

EGGPLANT PARMA

$

When I was a kid, my mom used to bread and fry eggplant rounds for dinner and tell us they tasted like pork chops. Eggplants do have a meaty, filling texture, and you can find endless varieties in city farmer's markets: purple, white, Sicilian, Asian.

In this famous dish, most recipes have you fry the eggplant before baking. I save a few calories, not to mention time and cleanup, by instead brushing them with oil and then baking them.

1. Heat oven to 400°F. Spray two large cookie sheets with cooking spray, or brush with oil.
2. Slice the eggplants very thinly (about ⅛ inch or less). Place them in a colander and sprinkle generously with salt. Allow to sit for 30 minutes. (This step is not usually needed if you are using very small eggplant.) Rinse well and drain.
3. Pour the bread crumbs into a shallow dish. Brush the eggplant slices with olive oil then dip them in the bread crumbs. You may have to use your fingers to push the crumbs onto the slices. Place on cookie sheets, being careful not to overlap. Bake for 20 to 30 minutes, or until eggplants are soft.
4. Lower oven to 350°F. Pour some sauce into the bottom of a 9 x 13-inch baking dish. Place a layer of eggplant on top of the sauce and then sprinkle liberally with nutritional yeast, and season to taste with salt, pepper, and dried basil. Repeat until you have used up all the eggplant—about three layers. Finish with a layer of sauce, and sprinkle with a final topping of nutritional yeast and vegan mozzarella, if using.
5. Bake for 30 minutes. Allow to cool for 10 minutes before serving.

Yield: 6 servings

3 medium eggplants
1½ cups bread crumbs *
½–1 cup extra-virgin olive oil
John's Marinara Sauce (see
  page 193)
½–1 cup nutritional yeast, plus
  extra for sprinkling
Salt and pepper to taste
3 tablespoons dried basil
1 package of vegan mozzarella,
  shredded (optional)

* Make your own bread crumbs
  by whizzing about 6 slices
  of stale bread in the food
  processor. Add any herbs you
  like.

Variation
Substitute zucchini for the eggplant.

Wine pairing
Valpolicella, a versatile red from the Italian province of Verona,
marries well with the marinara and eggplant.

FETTUCINE ALFREDO

1 pound fettuccine, linguine, or other flat pasta

1 tablespoon kudzu root (you may substitute cornstarch or arrowroot)

1⅓ cups soy milk

6 tablespoons Earth Balance

2 tablespoons nutritional yeast

1–1½ teaspoons salt (This may seem like a lot, but this helps give the sauce a more authentic Alfredo flavor. Start with less if you're skeptical.)

Additional nutritional yeast or vegan Parmesan for sprinkling

Freshly ground pepper

My husband used to work in Perugia, Italy, the city that's famous for Perugina chocolate. He's more opinionated, critical, and honest about Italian food than anyone I know. So when he said that this dish was "like a good North-ern Italian sauce, but without the cholesterol and fat," I took it as the best compliment ever. It's not exactly fat-free—but then again, what comfort food in its right mind is?

1. Start cooking pasta according to package directions.
2. Dissolve kudzu in soy milk. Melt Earth Balance over medium-low heat and sprinkle on nutritional yeast. Whisk together to make a roux, then slowly whisk in the milk and add salt. Turn heat to low, and cook until thick, whisking occasionally, about 15 minutes.
3. Toss over drained pasta and sprinkle generously with more nutritional yeast or vegan Parmesan. Add pepper to taste.

Yield: 4 large or 6 small servings

Variations

After adding milk, add any of the following to the sauce:
crushed garlic, 3 tablespoons chopped fresh herbs, 3 tablespoons chopped sun-dried tomatoes.

FARFALLE WITH FENNEL

I love the urbane, ever-so-faint licorice flavor of fennel. It's just a humble root vegetable that you can find in any market, but somehow, it exudes sophistication. In this recipe, I've paired fennel with some of its best culinary friends. The sweetness of the raisins and sun-dried tomatoes contrast beautifully with the creamy texture and flavor of the pine nuts.

1. Start cooking pasta according to package directions.
2. Meanwhile, in a large pan, sauté garlic and red pepper in olive oil over medium-low heat. Cook slowly, being careful not to brown garlic, until soft. Add fennel and cook 10 minutes longer, until soft.
3. After you drain pasta, mix with fennel mixture. Just before serving, add raisins, sun-dried tomatoes, and pine nuts. Drizzle with additional oil, if desired, and sprinkle with nutritional yeast or vegan Parmesan and sea salt.

Yield: 6 servings

1 pound farfalle
8 large garlic cloves, evenly sliced
Pinch red pepper flakes (optional)
½ cup extra-virgin olive oil
2 large fennel bulbs, roughly chopped
¼ cup raisins, plumped in water then drained
¼ cup sun-dried tomatoes, chopped
¼ cup pine nuts, toasted
Best quality extra-virgin olive oil, for drizzling
Nutritional yeast or vegan Parmesan, for sprinkling
Sea salt
Fennel fronds, for garnish

SPICY UDON NOODLES

Udon noodles are wheat-based Japanese noodles that you can find in any Asian grocery (substitute spaghetti if you can't find them). Here, I pair them with a spicy satay-esque sauce. This dish is easy to throw together and, after a busy day at the office, will save you from reaching for the take-out menus.

1. In a medium bowl, whisk all the sauce ingredients together until smooth.
2. Fill a large pot with water. Add onion, edamame, ginger, and garlic and bring to boil. Add noodles and cook according to package directions.
3. Drain, toss with sauce, top with herbs, and enjoy with chopsticks.

Yield: 6 servings

Sauce
1 tablespoon vegan sate paste, or Microwave Satay Sauce (see page 187)
2 heaping tablespoons creamy peanut butter
3 tablespoons soy sauce
3 tablespoons water
Splash of dark sesame oil
Splash ume vinegar
Pinch chili pepper

Base
1 large onion, thinly sliced
1 cup frozen, shelled edamame
2-inch piece ginger, sliced
2 cloves garlic, sliced
1 pound udon noodles
Fresh coriander or parsley for garnish

SPAGHETTI CON SALSA FRESCA

1 pound spaghetti

4 tablespoons olive oil

8 large garlic cloves, evenly sliced (Yes, 8. Use less if you're not a fan.)

Pinch red pepper flakes (optional)

6 large, ripe tomatoes, roughly chopped

⅛ to ¼ cup dry white wine, to taste

18 basil leaves

Sea salt and pepper

Best quality extra-virgin olive oil, for drizzling

Nutritional yeast or vegan Parmesan, for sprinkling

Most of us equate pasta sauce with traditional Italian sauce, aka "gravy." This deconstructed tomato sauce relies on summer's ripest farmer's market produce. Because it's barely cooked and relies on summer's freshest ingredients, you get a lot of flavor for very little effort—a true blessing during a steamy city heat wave.

1. Start cooking pasta according to package directions.
2. Meanwhile, sauté garlic (and red pepper, if you're using it) in olive oil over medium-low heat until soft. Be careful not to brown. Your nose should tell you when it's done.
3. Toss in tomatoes. Break down slightly with spatula and cook down over medium heat until soft and orange. Turn heat to high, add wine, and let the alcohol cook off for about a minute.
4. Turn heat to low while pasta cooks.
5. After you drain pasta, mix with sauce and using kitchen scissors, snip basil leaves over pasta. Season with salt and pepper to taste. Finish with a drizzle of extra-virgin olive oil and a sprinkle of nutritional yeast or vegan Parmesan.
6. Serve with a green side salad and a loaf of crusty Italian bread.

Yield: 4 to 6 servings

Wine Pairings

French or Italian Mediterranean rose, Soave Classico, or Montepulciano d'Abruzzo.

SPAGHETTI ALLE MELANZANE
(SPAGHETTI WITH EGGPLANT)

When eggplant is abundant, my first instinct is to make vegan eggplant parmesan. My second instinct is to make this easy pasta dish. There's something to be said for occasionally ignoring your instinct.

1. Dust eggplant generously with salt and let sit in a colander about 20 minutes (the larger the eggplant, the longer it should sit). Rinse away bile. Set aside.
2. Sauté onion and red pepper in 4 tablespoons olive oil over medium heat until clear and then add garlic. Be careful not to burn. Add eggplant and basil and sauté until eggplant is very soft and cooked through, about 25 minutes (it will look brown and mushy and taste mellow and pasty). Add olive oil as needed in 1-tablespoon increments. Covering the pot with a lid will help the eggplant cook with less oil. Add canned tomatoes and cook partially covered for about 30 minutes, or thick.
3. Start cooking pasta al dente according to package directions. Add pasta to the eggplant and toss over lowest heat.
4. Serve with vegan Parmesan.

Yield: 4 to 6 servings

8 small eggplants, cut into ½-inch cubes
Salt
1 onion
Up to ½ teaspoon red pepper flakes, to taste
4 tablespoons olive oil, plus more as needed
10 large garlic cloves, sliced
3 tablespoons fresh basil, chopped, or 1 tablespoon dried
1 28-ounce can crushed tomatoes
1 pound spaghetti
Vegan Parmesan

Wine Pairing
Barbera d'Asti

ORECCHIETTE CON BROCCOLI

6 tablespoons best-quality olive oil, plus up to 2 additional tablespoons *

10 garlic cloves, sliced

½ teaspoon red pepper flakes

1 teaspoon light miso paste

2 heads broccoli, chopped

1 pound orecchiette

Vegan Parmesan or nutritional yeast, for sprinkling

Salt, to taste

* Lower the fat: To lighten the recipe, add about ¼ cup vegetable broth to the pan instead of the extra oil

I make this dish often, for dinners in or whenever I'm hosting a party. I've substituted miso paste for the traditional anchovies; it gives you the same salty taste of the sea. Orecchiette means "little ears," and they are the perfect little containers for this sauce.

1. Heat 6 tablespoons oil over medium-low heat. Sauté garlic and red pepper flakes until garlic is very soft, about 10 minutes. Do not burn or brown garlic; it should be clear and infuse the oil with its aroma. Turn heat down or remove pan from the burner as needed. Add miso paste and mix into the oil mixture, using a flat whisk.

2. Meanwhile, start boiling a large pot of water, which will serve to cook both the broccoli and the pasta (one less dish to wash!). When boiling, toss in florets and cook until soft but not mushy, about 7 minutes. (This depends on your taste. Cook longer if you like mush—or less if you prefer crunch.) Remove with slotted spoon and add to the garlic mixture, adding more oil as needed. Then cook pasta in the same water according to package directions.

3. Toss with pasta. Sprinkle with vegan Parmesan or nutritional yeast, if desired, and drizzle with more extra-virgin olive oil.

Yield: 4 to 6 servings

Variation

Orecchiette with Cauliflower (Orecchiette con Calviore):
Substitute cauliflower for the broccoli and add a healthy pinch—
or two or three—of cayenne pepper.

Wine Pairing

Frascati

SPAGHETTI CARBONARA

Carbonara sauce is traditionally made with bacon or pancetta, eggs, and sometimes cream. But it's not bacon per se that truly flavors this dish—it's really just the smoke and the fat. In my version, tempeh bacon infuses an eggless, but nevertheless decadent, sauce with an earthy smokiness—without a hint of saturated fat, cholesterol, or cruelty. This is a perfect urban dinner party entrée: Even omnivorous guests will like it. Serve it with a spinach side salad and the same dry white wine that you use to deglaze the pan.

1. Dissolve kudzu and salt in ⅓ cup soy milk and set aside.
2. In large saucepan, heat oil over medium heat. Sauté tempeh bacon for about 5 minutes, or until heated through (you should be able to smell the smoky aroma). Turn up the heat to medium-high and pour in the wine to deglaze the pan. Cook for about 5 minutes, and transfer tempeh to another dish.
3. Melt Earth Balance in the same saucepan over medium-low heat and sprinkle in nutritional yeast. Whisk together to make a roux, then slowly whisk in 1 cup soy milk. Turn heat to low, and cook until thick, whisking occasionally, about 15 minutes. Add the tempeh, turn heat down very low, and simmer covered for about 10 to 15 minutes, stirring occasionally. Add salt and pepper to taste. Meanwhile, start cooking pasta according to package directions.
4. Toss sauce over drained pasta and sprinkle generously with more nutritional yeast or vegan Parmesan, and top with parsley.

Yield: 4 belly-busting or 6 average servings

1 tablespoon kudzu root (or substitute cornstarch or arrowroot)
1 teaspoon salt
⅓ cup plus 1 cup soy milk
1 tablespoon extra-virgin olive oil
6 ounces tempeh bacon, chopped fine (I use LightLife Fakin' Bacon.)
¼ cup dry white wine (like Pinot Grigio or Frascati)
6 tablespoons Earth Balance sticks
3 heaping tablespoons nutritional yeast
Additional nutritional yeast or vegan Parmesan for sprinkling
Freshly ground pepper and salt, to taste
1 pound spaghetti, fettucine, or linguine
2 tablespoons fresh parsley, chopped

Wine Pairing
Frascati

FRESH PASTA

2 cups flour

¾ teaspoon salt

2½ tablespoons extra-virgin olive oil

Up to ¾ cup water

Fortunately for me, some of the best Italian restaurants are located in Phila-delphia, and they usually have fresh pasta on the menu. Unfortunately, the pasta is almost always made with egg. But you don't need egg to make pasta dough from scratch. Ask any Italian nonna. All you need is flour, olive oil, salt, water—and a rolling pin or pasta machine.

Cut this pasta into tagliatelli or lasagna sheets. Or use it to make the Porcini Ravioli on page 147.

1. Using the bread hook on a stand mixer or handheld mixer, beat together flour, salt, and olive oil. Add water, about 1 tablespoon at a time, until the dough forms a ball. Continue kneading until very smooth. Dough should not be sticky.
2. Cover, set aside, and let rest for a half hour. Then use a rolling pin to roll into thin sheets—as thin as possible, about ¹⁄₁₆ inch thick. Cut into fettuccine, tagliatelli, or lasagna sheets. Or make other varieties using a pasta machine. Follow the manufacturer's directions.
3. Fresh pasta cooks very quickly. Cooking time varies depending on the thickness and cut of the dough. Cook in a large amount of well-salted water until dough floats and is al dente. Err on the side of caution and taste it even before you think it's done. Mushy pasta is one of the culinary seven deadly sins.

Yield: enough pasta for 4–6

Variations

Work any chopped fresh herb you like into the dough.
(Basil is especially nice.)

HOUSE PARTY

*H*osting parties and get-togethers is de rigueur for urban dwellers. But it can be intimidating knowing your vegan food will be scrutinized. These recipes are designed to impress your guests—even omnivorous ones.

20 TIPS FOR A STRESS-FREE DINNER PARTY

TWO WEEKS AHEAD

1. **Make lists.** Create a guest list. Jot down what you plan to serve. Create attainable "to-do lists" as the big day gets closer.
2. **Keep it simple.** Now's not the time to attempt recipes worthy of Michelin stars. Choose proven standbys.
3. **Plan a balanced menu.** You don't want your guests waddling away overstuffed. If your main course is heavy, plan on sorbet or fruit for dessert. If your main dish is light, go all out with a decadent dessert.
4. **Don't forget the spirits.** Do some research to ensure you have the proper wine pairing to complement your meal.
5. **Remember—you don't have to do it all.** Quality store-bought items are delicious lifesavers. In a pinch, I buy vegan fruit pies at Whole Foods and serve them a la mode, with a scoop of vanilla soy milk. No one has ever complained.
6. **Remind yourself that it's supposed to be fun.** Perfection seeking is so, well, unrealistic. Manage your own, too-high expectations accordingly. Plan on fun, not frenzy.

ONE WEEK AHEAD

7. **Shop for less perishable items,** like wine, crackers, and nuts. You'll be so glad you did.
8. **Plan what you'll wear and try it on.** Nobody needs a fashion crisis on the night of the party.
9. **Make like a DJ.** Choose tunes to set the mood. Arrange the CDs in your player beforehand.

A FEW DAYS AHEAD

10. **Make whatever you can in advance.** Dip. Cheesecake. Party nuts. If you can prepare it ahead, don't hesitate.

ONE DAY AHEAD

11. **Buy the perishables**—fresh veggies, flowers, etc.
12. **Set the table.** Lay out serving dishes and music.
13. **Chop to it.** Prep any items that need chopping or mincing, like onions, garlic, or carrots.

THE NIGHT OF

14. **Don't forget the candles.** And dim the lights. Ambiance is half the battle—and is conducive to relaxation.
15. **Delegate.** Tell your family what needs to be done. Ask them to help—nicely. Then thank them—profusely.
16. **Accept help from guests.** They're offering to clean up? Who in their right mind would say no?
17. **Remember to enjoy.** Take a deep breath—and a sip of wine. Savor the food. Listen to your friends' stories. Tap your toes to the music.
18. **Send 'em home with doggy bags.** You don't want to be bogged down with a ton of leftovers. And your guests will appreciate having yummy food to reheat the next day.
19. **Have a large glass of water before you retire.** Hydration now is especially important if you've had a few drinks or salty foods.
20. **Leave it till tomorrow.** Too pooped to clean up? Tomorrow is another day.

HEDONIST'S STUFFED MUSHROOMS

Everyone loves stuffed mushrooms. Mine get their name from liberal dousings of extra-virgin olive and truffle oils. Make these bite-size appetizers when you want to impress omnivores—or vegans, for that matter. Feel free to improvise—use walnuts, pine nuts, different herbs, or whatever else you have on hand.

1. Separate the mushroom caps from the stems. Chop the stems and set aside. Put caps on an oiled tray. Sprinkle them lightly with salt, and brush them with olive oil.
2. In a large frying pan, heat 3 tablespoons of oil. Sauté the onion and garlic until translucent. Sprinkle with salt, then add the mushrooms, seitan, and herbs. Sauté until mushrooms are cooked, about 7 minutes, adding more oil as/if needed.
3. Put sautéed mixture in food processor, along with nuts. Process until grainy and spreadable, adding more olive oil, if needed.
4. Using a teaspoon, stuff the mushroom caps with the mixture, molding a slightly rounded dome with the spoon. Drizzle with more olive oil and bake at 375°F for about 10 minutes. Finish with a drizzle of truffle oil.

Yield: 20 mushrooms

20 medium to large button or baby bella mushrooms

Up to 6 tablespoons olive oil and more for drizzling

½ onion, chopped

2 cloves garlic, chopped

¼ cup seitan, chopped (optional, but it adds a nice texture)

1 teaspoon thyme

½ teaspoon oregano

Pinch nutmeg

Salt and freshly ground pepper, to taste

4 tablespoons chopped pecans, toasted

Truffle oil, for finishing (optional, but incredible!)

Variations

Use any kind of toasted nut or seed—
or any combination—that you have on hand.

LF

CONFETTI QUINOA

2 tablespoons olive oil

1 onion, chopped

2 stalks celery, preferably organic, chopped

4 carrots, diced

4 cloves garlic, minced

1 cup quinoa

2 cups water or vegetable stock

2 bay leaves

2 tablespoons organic lemon zest

2 tablespoons fresh lemon juice

1 cup peas (frozen is fine)

Salt and pepper to taste

The Incas called quinoa the "mother of all grains," and it's no wonder. This little wonder is packed with protein, fiber, iron, and calcium. This easy side salad is a mosaic of color, flavor—and nutrition. Luckily, you don't have to travel all the way to Lima to try it.

1. Heat oil over medium-low in large saucepan. Sauté onion, celery, carrots, and garlic until translucent, about 7 minutes.
2. Add quinoa and water and the remaining ingredients, except for peas, to the veggie mixture. Reduce heat to low, and simmer about 10 minutes. Add the peas and simmer another 10 minutes, or until all water is absorbed (check periodically). Fluff with a fork, adjust seasonings, and remove bay leaves. Serve warm, room temperature, or cold.

Yield: 4 to 6 servings

Variation

Use orange zest and juice instead of lemon.

COUSCOUS MOSAIC

My oldest sister, Babs, has four grown children. And my nieces and nephews now have families of their own. That means a large extended family of— you guessed it!—omnivores. I came up with this recipe when I was invited to a gathering at Babs' house "across the bridge" from the city, in suburban New Jersey. I wanted to make something nutritious that most people there would enjoy. Turns out this urban recipe was a huge suburban hit.

The best part of this recipe is how embarrassingly easy it is to prepare. Ask the kids to help out.

1. Mix oil, vinegar, garlic, salt, and pepper in a small bowl to make the dressing.
2. Gently mix remaining ingredients in a large bowl and toss with dressing.

Yield: 6 servings

6 tablespoons olive oil
2 tablespoons red wine vinegar
2 garlic cloves, minced
Salt and pepper to taste
1 cup cooked whole-wheat couscous, fluffed with a fork
1 large carrot, grated
Zest 1 organic lemon
Juice ½ lemon
1 small onion, minced
½ cup peas (frozen is fine)
¼ cup raisins
¼ cup slivered almonds, toasted
5–7 basil leaves, minced
8 dried apricots, chopped into chocolate-chip-size pieces
1 can pinto beans, rinsed and drained

SHERRY-INFUSED PÂTÉ

1 cup chopped pecans
4 tablespoons plus 2 tablespoons extra-virgin olive oil
4 cloves garlic, sliced
1 pound cremini mushrooms, sliced
½ cup Amontillado sherry
Salt and freshly ground pepper, to taste

During a trip to Spain and Portugal, I sampled my fair share of sherries. This pâté is my homage to this amazingly complex libation. A blast of Amontillado sherry sweetens and deepens the flavor of this dip—infusing it with that mysterious "je ne sais quoi." Or should I say "No sé lo que"?

1. Heat a dry skillet to medium high. Toast the pecans, tossing constantly, until golden and fragrant. Remove from heat and remove pecans from pan so they don't continue to cook. Drop them into the food processor and whir them into a fine flour.

2. In a large pan, heat 4 tablespoons of the olive oil over medium-low heat. Sauté the garlic until it begins to soften. Be careful not to brown! Add the mushrooms, stirring and sautéing until they darken and are very soft. Once this happens, raise heat to high and toss in the sherry. Deglaze the pan. Once the alcohol evaporates, continue cooking on medium heat until the pan is almost devoid of liquid. At this point, carefully transfer the mushroom mixture to the food processor with the sherry. Process until smooth, adding the additional 2 tablespoons of olive oil (more or less) as needed.

3. Add salt and pepper to taste. Serve with French bread, crackers, vegetables, or crisp bread.

Yield: 1 large bowl—about 2 cups

Variation
Use Madeira or Marsala instead of sherry.

Wine pairing
Amontillado or Manzanilla sherry, Madeira, or Marsala
(pair with the type of alcohol you use)

BRUSCHETTA, SEVERAL WAYS

This tomato bruschetta is my idea of perfection on a plate—simple ingredients, easy to prepare and easy to enjoy. Bruschetta is a huge hit at parties. Make one version—or several—and arrange them on a large plate so your guests can nibble away.

1. For the bruschetta base, heat oven to 350°F. Place bread slices on cookie sheet and drizzle with olive oil. Place in heated oven and toast until just golden, about 10 minutes (check earlier!).
2. Let cool.
3. Mix all ingredients for topping in a large bowl. Top toasted bread rounds.

Yield: enough topping for 6–8 pieces of bruschetta

Bruschetta Base

1 loaf French or Italian bread, sliced into ½-inch-thick rounds
Extra-virgin olive oil

Tomato Bruschetta Topping

6 Roma tomatoes, chopped
6 cloves garlic, minced
6 tablespoons extra-virgin olive oil
18 fresh basil leaves, minced
1 tablespoon parsley, minced
¼ teaspoon dried oregano
Salt and pepper to taste (add salt just before serving. Salt draws water from the tomatoes.)

Mushroom Bruschetta Topping

Sherry-Infused Pâté (see page 100)

Bean Bruschetta Topping

Sandwich Mousse (see page 41). Top with freshlychopped tomatoes and basil.

Additional Bruschetta Toppings

Vegan tapenade
Roasted red pepper hummus topped with roasted red peppers
Tofu-basil ricotta and oil-packed sun-dried tomatoes
Minced garlic, olive oil, and a drizzle of truffle oil

MINI-RICE CROQUETTES WITH WASABI-MISO DIPPING SAUCE

½ avocado

4 tablespoons nutritional yeast, plus 3 tablespoons extra for rolling

½ teaspoon basil

½ teaspoon parsley

½ teaspoon oregano

Healthy pinch nutmeg

Salt and pepper, to taste

1 cup cooked white or brown rice, cooled

1–2 tablespoons broth or water

Wasabi-Miso Dipping Sauce (see page 188)

Every urbanite seems to have a carton of leftover take-out rice hogging up room in the fridge. That's what inspired this recipe. The nutmeg and oregano add an element of brightness and surprise—contrasting nicely with the sweetness and heat of the dipping sauce. Serve these room temperature—with chopsticks!

1. Preheat oven to 350°F.
2. Using a fork, mash avocado in a large bowl. Sprinkle in yeast and herbs, and then add rice. Using a potato masher, mash this mixture until it is malleable, adding water as needed to help it stick together. Form into tiny balls (about ¾ to 1 inch in diameter).
3. Roll each ball in nutritional yeast and then place on a greased cookie sheet. Bake for about 25 minutes, turning balls every 5 minutes or so to ensure even browning. You could also fry these lightly in olive oil. Serve with dipping sauce.

Yield: 12–16 croquettes

SAVORY FRENCH TERRINE

Making a terrine seems like the sole birthright of willowy French women who wear intricately knotted scarves. But as you'll see, making a terrine is easier than pronouncing "Champs Elyssées." This cheeselike terrine makes a wonderful appetizer, spread on crackers (try the Peppery Party Crackers on page 110) or crispbreads. You can also make an adorable sweet version for dessert (see page 164).

1. Wrap tofu in clean tea towels or paper towels. Place on a dish, cover with another dish, and then press between two large books, such as dictionaries. Let sit for 30 minutes. Replace towels and let sit for another 30 minutes. With paper towels still swaddling tofu, gently squeeze out as much water as possible. Please don't skimp on these steps—they are crucial to the success of the recipe.

2. Meanwhile, spray a mini loaf pan (or other suitable rectangular mold) with cooking spray. Then line with plastic wrap, making sure there is some overhang. Smooth out any wrinkles and spray with cooking oil. Set aside.

3. After the tofu has been sufficiently pressed, use your hands to break it into cottage cheese–size crumbles. Add the nutritional yeast, olive oil, and seasonings, if using, and mix in with your fingers.

4. Using your knuckles, mash this mixture until it is absolutely smooth and creamy. Using a spatula, spoon a layer into the prepared pan and tamp it down well to ensure that it's firm and even. It should be about ½ inch thick. Follow with a layer of your filling. This layer should be about ⅛ inch thick, give or take. Follow with a layer of tofu. Continue in this manner, lasagna-style, ending with a tofu layer. You can use just one filling or several different ones—it's up to you.

5. Cover terrine with plastic-wrap overhang. Refrigerate for at least 4 hours or preferably overnight. Slice with a very sharp knife.

Yield: 12 servings as an appetizer

1 pound extra-firm tofu
2 tablespoons nutritional yeast
1 tablespoon extra-virgin olive oil
Freshly ground black pepper

Fillings
½ cup to 1 cup one or more of
  the following:
  tapenade
  roasted red peppers
  sautéed mushrooms
  thinly sliced tomatoes or
  zucchini
  hummus (try the Smoked
    Paprika Hummus on page 38)
  vegan paté (try the Sherry-
    Infused Pâté on page 100)

Optional
Add 1 tablespoon fresh or dried
  herbs. Some good options
  include basil, oregano, fresh
  parsley, or herbes de Provençe.
  If you use rosemary, use only a
  small amount to avoid having it
  overpower the dish.

SEITAN

1 cup vital wheat gluten

1⅓ cups best-quality broth, for mixing

6 cups best-quality broth, for simmering

1 tablespoon canola or other neutral oil

Every urban vegan needs a kick-ass seitan recipe. Mine is so simple you will squeal.

Making seitan often intimidates novice vegan chefs, but really, there's nothing to fear—except over-simmering. If you let your seitan linger too long in the broth, the results can be rubbery. Another thing that will ruin seitan is tasteless broth. Either use homemade or the best quality broth you can find. I swear by Better Than Bouillon Vegetable.

I especially like to shape my seitan into nuggets and serve with the Microwave Satay Sauce (see page 187), followed by a huge bowl of Nasi Goreng Soup. But you can make this seitan into any shape you like or need—cutlets, chunks, nuggets—the sky's the limit. If you create steaks, coating them in flour before sautéing or baking them helps give the seitan a nice crust.

1. Mix wheat gluten and 1⅓ cup broth. Knead for 5 minutes. (Using your mixer's kneading blade is absolutely acceptable. I use my KitchenAid mixer.) Let rest for 5 minutes.
2. Cut seitan in nuggets or desired shape. Pieces will swell when you cook them, so cut them slightly smaller than your desired size.
3. Bring broth to a boil in a large saucepan. Gently drop in seitan. Turn down heat to low, and simmer for 1 hour.
4. Drain well. Heat a wok or nonstick skillet to medium high. Add oil, and then sauté nuggets until browned, stirring constantly. Serve on skewers with Microwave Satay Sauce for dipping,
5. If you're not using the seitan immediately, you can cover it with broth and store it in the refrigerator for up to 1 week. You can also store it in a plastic container, covered with broth, in the freezer for up to 6 months.

Yield: 6 servings

FOCACCIA

Focaccia is easy to make, especially when you mix the dough in the food processor like I do. Since most people don't know this coveted secret of the initiated, focaccia is the perfect bread to serve at your parties—or to bring along to someone else's party. Pretend that you slaved for hours over a hot oven, kneading until your arms ached, while your guests marvel at your amazing baking abilities.

Focaccia is the perfect bread to serve along with dips like Sherry-Infused Pâté (see page 100) and Smoked Paprika Hummus (see page 38). You can also slice it longways and use the thin slices for panini or any sandwich. Then again, you can just eat it as it is, which is my favorite way. There are a million topping variations, so dress it up—or leave it naked—as you see fit.

1. Brush a medium cookie sheet with about 1 teaspoon of olive oil. Sprinkle with about 1 teaspoon cornmeal.
2. Remove the blade of your food processor. Sprinkle the yeast in your food processor cup. Pour the warm water over it, and add the sugar. Stir well with a fork and let stand for about 5 or so minutes. It should start to bubble, foam, and/or appear to "move" slightly. This is the water at work, waking up the dormant yeast.
3. Add about 1 cup of flour and the salt. Attach the blade and process briefly to mix. Slowly add the remaining flour, about ½ cup at a time, processing between additions. Stop adding flour when the dough starts to form a dough ball and sticks to the sides of the processor. At this point, let it rotate about 25 times in the food processor.
4. When you remove the dough, it should be very smooth and stretchy. Oil it, place it in a large bowl, and cover with foil or, better yet, a tea towel that's been soaked in hot water and wrung out. Place in a draft-free area of your kitchen and let it rise until it doubles, about 1 hour.
5. Punch down the dough and knead it for a few minutes. Roll it out slightly and stretch it onto the oiled cookie sheet. Again, cover and let it rise for about 30 minutes. Meanwhile preheat your oven to 400°F.
6. Just before baking, use a chopstick or your fingers to make rows of small craters in the dough. At this point, sprinkle with sea salt and, if desired, add your toppings of choice. Brush with 1 tablespoon of oil. Bake for about 17 to 20 minutes, or until golden brown.

Yield: 1 focaccia

1 teaspoon plus 1 tablespoon olive oil

1 teaspoon cornmeal

2¼ teaspoons dry yeast

1 cup lukewarm water (not too hot, not cold or cool)

½ teaspoon sugar

3–3¾ cups flour

1 teaspoon sea salt

Optional toppings:

1 tablespoon fresh or dried rosemary

½ cup olives (green or black), sliced, or oil-packed sun-dried tomatoes

½ cup green or red grapes

1 onion, sautéed in 1 teaspoon olive oil and 1 tablespoon basil, mixed with a spritz of best-quality balsamic vinegar

1 cup mushrooms, sautéed in garlic and 1 teaspoon olive oil; pan deglazed with 1 teaspoon flour and Marsala wine

2 tablespoons nutritional yeast mixed with 1 teaspoon thyme

16 small organic potatoes, cut
  into sixths (peel or don't: up to
  you, as long as they're organic)
2–3 tablespoons extra-virgin olive
  oil
40 cloves of garlic, unpeeled but
  separated (about 3 small heads)
½ teaspoon each of chopped
  rosemary, thyme, and sage
2 bay leaves
Sea salt and freshly ground pepper
  to taste

POTATOES WITH 40 CLOVES OF GARLIC

If you're a garlic lover, you probably did back flips when you read the title of this recipe. Less enthusiastic about garlic? Fear not. Roasting the garlic calms its bite, subduing it into a mellow, creamy spread for the potatoes. The unctuous roasted garlic cloves taste equally great spread on the potatoes—squeeze out a little dab before each bite—or on a baguette. This is a great ice breaker dish to serve at parties, and since you don't even have to peel the cloves, it's host/hostess-friendly, to boot. Serve hot or room temperature.

Don't get too hung up about counting the garlic cloves. There's a classic French dish called "Chicken with 40 Cloves of Garlic," and I was determined to create a kinder recipe that had as much garlic bravado.

1. Preheat the oven to 370°F.
2. Toss all ingredients into a large casserole pan and bake, covered, for about 45 minutes to 1 hour, until the potatoes and garlic are soft.
3. To eat, squish some garlic onto each potato chunk and enjoy.

Yield: 8 servings

HERBED BEURRE

When you're hosting a party, make it easy on yourself and buy spanking-fresh artisan breads and rolls from the corner bakery. Serve them with this flavorful spread. Use your favorite herbs, seasonal herbs, or a combination. Just make sure they're fresh. You can put this recipe together in less than 5 minutes. It offers a lot of taste for very little effort.

Using a handheld beater, whip Earth Balance until fluffy. Add lemon juice and then gently stir in herbs.

Yield: ½ cup

1 stick (½ cup) Earth Balance, softened
Splash lemon juice
2 tablespoons fresh herbs (e.g., rosemary, basil, tarragon, chives, dill), minced as finely as you can manage

SPINACH WITH PINE NUTS AND RAISINS

Just because you're having a party doesn't mean you can't serve wholesome food. This healthful, Sicilian-inspired side tastes exotic enough for a dinner party yet healthful enough so you won't feel too guilty about indulging in dessert.

1. In a medium saucepan over medium-low heat, heat the oil and cook the garlic until soft, about 2 to 3 minutes.
2. Add raisins and zest and cook another minute or so.
3. Toss in the pine nuts, turn up the heat, and add the wine. Stir, then add the spinach. Stir gently or toss with tongs until spinach is wilted. Season with salt and pepper, to taste, and serve.

Yield: 4 servings

2 tablespoons olive oil
5 cloves garlic, minced
2 tablespoons raisins, plumped in water
½ teaspoon organic lemon zest
2 tablespoons pine nuts, toasted
1 tablespoon white wine
5–6 cups spinach, trimmed and chopped
Salt and pepper, to taste

Variations

Substitute sultanas or dried cranberries for the raisins.
Substitute arugula for the spinach.

SWEET POTATO SALAD

2 pounds sweet potatoes
1 6-ounce packet tempeh bacon, steamed for 10 minutes, then crumbled
4–6 scallions, sliced
1 red pepper, seeded and diced
¼ cup fresh parsley, chopped
¼ cup fresh basil, chopped
3 tablespoons champagne or white vinegar
6 tablespoons extra-virgin olive oil
Salt and freshly ground pepper

When you're having a party buffet or a picnic, everyone expects you to make a potato salad. Being a city girl who prides herself on being different, this is exactly why I make a sweet potato salad instead. So go ahead, pimp your potato salad with abandon!

1. Peel sweet potatoes and cut into 2-inch pieces. Boil in a medium sauce-pan, until soft, about 10 minutes. Place in a bowl of cool water.
2. In a large bowl, gently toss sweet potatoes with remaining ingredients. Allow to sit for a few hours before serving so the flavors can meld. Serve at room temperature.

Yield: 6 servings

ARTY-FARTY PARTY NUTS

1¾ cups your favorite unsalted mixed nuts (try almonds, pecans, macadamia, Brazil nuts, peanuts, pistachios, hazelnuts, walnuts, pine nuts, and peanuts)
2 tablespoons raw sunflower seeds
2 tablespoons cacao nibs
1 tablespoon Earth Balance
1 tablespoon agave nectar
1 tablespoon dried rosemary
⅛–¼ teaspoon cayenne pepper, to taste
¼ teaspoon cinnamon
Sea salt to taste (I use about ½ teaspoon)

Rosemary and cacao? I know what you're thinking—what a kooky combination. But city life swells with unexpected juxtapositions. These nuts are endearingly offbeat, a little spicy, a little showy, and undeniably sweet—just like your artiest, fartiest friends.

The bitterness of the cacao complements the fragrant rosemary and sweet agave nectar, and then you're left with a subtle hint of heat via the cinnamon and cayenne. Try some kooky combinations of your own—both in and out of the kitchen—and see where you land. The more you encounter, the more elastic your definition of "normal" becomes.

1. Preheat oven to 375°F. Spread nuts, sunflower seeds, and cacao nibs on a cookie sheet. Toast for about 10 minutes or until golden brown. Your nose is more accurate than your kitchen timer, and if you pay attention, it will tell you when the nuts are done.
2. Meanwhile, melt together the Earth Balance and agave nectar. Pour into a medium bowl
3. Remove nuts from oven. Pour into bowl with Earth Balance and agave nectar. Toss with rosemary, cayenne pepper, cinnamon, and salt. Serve warm.

Yield: a scant 2 cups

BAGNA CAUDA

"Bagna Cauda" (pronounced bayn-ya code-a) means "hot bath" in Italian. It's an appropriate moniker since this simple dip is served warm and bathes fresh bread and veggies with an earthy, garlicky goodness. Although it's peasant food at its finest, it somehow evokes an urbane style and sophistication—probably thanks to the extravagant amount of fat! Please use the best quality olive oil you can find; you need to build this dip on a firm foundation of flavor.

1. Grind porcini mushrooms into a fine powder in a coffee or spice grinder or a food processor.
2. Heat the oil and Earth Balance in a small saucepan. Over medium-low heat, sauté the garlic, being very careful not to brown. Once translucent, sprinkle in the porcini powder and whisk in the miso, broth or water, and tamari. Stir very well. If mixture seems too thick, add more water, about 1 teaspoon at a time.
3. Serve warm, with bread and fresh vegetables for dipping.

Yield: about 1 cup

1 tablespoon dried porcini mushrooms
6 tablespoons best-quality extra-virgin olive oil
4 tablespoons Earth Balance
3 garlic cloves, finely minced
1 teaspoon miso paste
1 tablespoon vegetable broth or water
Dash of tamari
Fresh bread and vegetables (e.g., thinly sliced carrots, sliced zucchini, celery, endive, scallions, and radicchio) for dipping

PEPPERY PARTY CRACKERS

1 cup whole-wheat flour

4 tablespoons nutritional yeast

1 tablespoon freshly ground pepper (no substitute for fresh)

¾ teaspoon sea salt plus extra for sprinkling

½ teaspoon dry mustard

2 tablespoons olive oil

4–6 tablespoons soy yogurt or rice milk

Sure, you can drop $4 for a box of fancy crackers at a ritzy gourmet shop. Or you can throw together a batch of these crispy little numbers for under $1.

Making your own crackers may sound intimidating, but in reality, thanks to your food processor, it's a snap and a surefire way to impress the hell out of your guests. These crackers are perfect for dipping into the Smoked Paprika Hummus (see page 38) or Sandwich Mousse (see page 41), or for supporting chunks of your favorite vegan cheese. A few homemade crackers also make a nice topping for soups.

To form the crackers, I use a pastry cutter because it's quick and simple. But you can make them in any shape you want. You can even get all Martha Stewart on me, and use small cookie cutters to create shapes that fit your party's theme. (For example, use a wedding bell cutter for a bridal party.)

You really need to roll the crackers as thinly as possible—at least ⅛ inch thick, but ideally even thinner. Using a silpat really helps, and keeps cleanup to a minimum. Once rolled, you simply transfer them to your baking sheets with a spatula.

1. Preheat oven to 375°F. Grease two medium cookie or baking sheets.
2. In the food processor, whiz all dry ingredients together to mix. With the processor running, add the oil, and then the yogurt or milk, about ½ tablespoon at a time. (The less you use, the drier and better your crackers will taste.) The dough is done when it sticks together and you can handle it.
3. Divide dough in half and roll as thinly as possible. Poke rolled-out dough evenly all over with the tines of a fork. Sprinkle dough with extra sea salt, and gently press in.
4. Cut crackers into desired shapes. Transfer to baking sheet and bake for 7 to 9 minutes, or until just starting to turn golden.
5. Transfer to wire cooling racks. Crackers will harden as they cool.

Yield: about 60 small crackers

GUACAMOLE

In the seaside city of Playa del Carmen, Mexico, there's a touristy little restaurant called Palapa Hemingway. The food's good, the margaritas are lethal, and they still make guacamole fresh at your table. I got the confidence to make my own guac by watching the chefs nonchalantly work their magic on local avocados. Seeing someone else do it in real time really demystified the process.

There are as many guacamole recipes as there are cooks, so use this one as a springboard, and then add or subtract ingredients to make it your own. Serve it with nachos, use it to dress your burritos, or slather it on sandwiches.

1. Using a fork, mash avocadoes in a medium bowl.
2. Add lime juice, onion, pepper, cilantro, salt, and pepper. Drizzle with oil and serve immediately.

Yield: a healthy cup

2 ripe avocadoes

Juice 1 lime

2 tablespoons very finely minced onion

¼–½ jalapeño pepper, very finely minced

2 tablespoons chopped fresh cilantro

½ teaspoon salt, or to taste

Freshly ground pepper to taste

Drizzle of extra-virgin olive oil

Variations

Add any of the following: ½ tomato, diced; 2 tablespoons minced red or green pepper, 2 tablespoons fresh corn.

3½ tablespoons olive oil

3 cloves garlic, minced

1 small onion, finely minced

3–4 cups whole-grain flour

1½ teaspoons salt

¾ cup oil-cured black olives,
   pitted and chopped

3 tablespoons dried rosemary

2 teaspoons yeast

1–1½ cups warm water (not too
   hot, but not lukewarm)

ROSEMARY-OLIVE BREAD

When they eat a slice of this bread, your guests will assume, at least for a moment, that you bought this loaf fresh from the farmer's market in the center of Aix-en-Provence. Thanks to the assertive aromas in the olives and rosemary, you get a lot of flavor for very little work.

1. In a small saucepan, sauté the garlic and onion in 1 tablespoon of the oil over medium heat until soft, about 5 minutes. Let cool.

2. In a large bowl, mix 3 cups flour, salt, olives, garlic, onion, and rosemary. Stir in yeast, and then add the water. Add more flour as needed, in ½ cup increments. Knead until smooth, using the bread hook on your mixer. Cover with aluminum foil and let rise in a warm place until doubled in size, about 1 hour.

3. Punch down dough and then knead on a silpat or floured board for about 5 minutes. Form into a boule—a round loaf—and place on a greased cookie sheet. Let rise for a half hour.

4. Preheat the oven to 400°F. Brush loaf with remaining olive oil and bake for 25 to 30 minutes, or until loaf sounds hollow when tapped. Cool completely on a rack before slicing.

Yield: 1 loaf

YEAST KNOW-HOW

Don't go broke buying those expensive, single-use packets of yeast. Buying yeast in bulk costs almost ten times less than single packs. Even if you only bake a few times a year, consider splitting a pound packet of yeast with a friend or neighbor. And don't pay too much mind to the expiration date. I've used yeast for as long as a year after the expiration date with great results.

CHOCOLATE-COVERED GINGER

Chocolate and ginger are an unlikely pair, but together, make wonderful dinner guests—kind of like James Carville and Mary Matalin. This combination proves that culinary opposites can also play quite nicely together: The chocolate's deep, sweet intensity lends a certain gravitas to the ginger's lightness while balancing its heat.

⅓–½ cup dark chocolate chips or buttons
¾ cup unsulphured, crystallized ginger pieces

This treat is best enjoyed in small doses. One or two pieces, savored slowly and deliberately, are enough. I suggest making chocolate-covered ginger as a mignardise—a tiny palate-cleansing nibble to serve after a heavy meal. Please don't skimp on ingredients. Buy unsulphured, crystallized ginger and best-quality dark chocolate.

1. Cover a cookie sheet with wax paper. Nuke chocolate in the microwave on medium power until melted, about 2 minutes, stirring halfway through.
2. Dip crystallized ginger pieces in the chocolate and lay on the wax paper to cool. You can certainly dip the entire piece, but I prefer to leave a hint of the yellow ginger seductively exposed.
3. Leave to cool at room temperature, or, if you're in a hurry, place in the freezer for about 15 minutes.

Yield: about ¾ cup

Variations

Use tamarind paste in place of ginger. Roll paste into ½-inch balls and dip in chocolate. Add a dash of chili pepper, if you dare.

WRAP-ARTISTRY

When you're having a cocktail party or informal gathering of friends, serving a tray packed with colorful wraps is a no-brainer. You can make them a few hours ahead of time, leaving you time to mingle with your guests, instead of fussing in the kitchen at the last minute (and inevitably spilling something on your best party frock). There are flavor combinations for every taste, limited only by your imagination. Wraps are also a great way to use up leftovers, and they make fun lunchbox treats.

Here's a wrap algorithm I frequently use for informal parties. Please don't consider this a recipe to follow exactly; it's just a blueprint to help you get in touch with your inner wrap artist. Interpolate, extrapolate—and mix and match—depending on your own taste and available ingredients.

1. Lay tortilla in front of you on your working surface. Arrange or spread your filling on the wrap, leaving about a 1-inch border all the way around. Arrange vegetables for crunch and freshness on top and drizzle with about 1 teaspoon to 1 tablespoon of your dressing. Add extras, if desired.
2. Fold the right and left sides of the wrap inward slightly. Press gently to create a seam. Now tightly roll the top half toward you, tucking in any straggling fillings as needed. Slice in half on the diagonal and secure with a toothpick.
3. Arrange on a tray, open side up. The more crowded the tray and the greater varieties of wraps (red, green, brown, etc.) you use, the more attractive the tray will look.

Yield: as few as 1 or as many as you need

The wraps

24 large tortillas—get a variety (spinach, whole wheat, chili, tomato) to make the tray as colorful as possible; or make your own—see page 46

Fillings

Sandwich Mousse (see page 41)

Sherry-Infused Pâté (see page 100)

Seitan Sandwich Spread (see page 40)

Tapenade (see page 116)

Sun-Dried Tomato Pesto (see page 184)

Sliced avocadoes, drizzled with lemon or lime juice (to prevent browning)

Vegan cheese

Hummus

Baked, broiled, or pan-fried tofu

Crumbled tempeh that has been baked, broiled, or pan-fried

Chili (be judicious about how much you use, so the wraps don't get soggy)

Vegetables

Mung bean sprouts

Baby spinach

Mesclun

Arugula (very nice with the Sandwich Mousse)

Shredded carrots

Thinly sliced tomatoes

Thinly sliced onions

Thinly sliced bell peppers

Dressings

Any of the sauces from the Saucy Vegans chapter, or your own favorite homemade or store-bought sauces

A drizzle of your favorite salad dressing

Mustard

Vegenaise

Aioli

Extras

Fresh herbs

Toasted nuts

Leftover whole-grain salads (such as Curried Wheat Berry Salad, see page 119), about 1 tablespoon per wrap

PASTITSIO

Everyone loves this rich, creamy Greek pasta. One taste of its exotic hints of cinnamon, nutmeg, and allspice, and you'll swear you just landed in Athens. It's perfect for sit-down meals and buffets alike, but if you're expecting a crowd, it's easily doubled. It's a bit labor-intensive, so making the sauces ahead of time makes it more manageable. Trust me, this recipe is worth the effort.

Architecturally speaking, pastitsio has great "posture"; it's lasagna-like, except that it's made with ziti. If you eat it straight out of the oven, it will taste great, but it will fall apart. Better to make it the night before, then reheat it to help it stand as tall as possible.

1. Preheat oven to 375°F. Grease a medium lasagna pan or a large casserole dish. Round, oval, square, rectangular—any shape will work.
2. Heat oil in large sauté pan over medium heat. Add onion and garlic and cook until clear, about 10 minutes. Add the tomatoes, herbs and spices, and wine. Stir in the crumbles. (If you're using the kind that comes in a plastic tube, be sure to break it up into tiny pieces using your spatula.) Stir in salt and cook for about 20 minutes. Remove from heat.
3. In a large bowl, stir the cooked pasta with ½ of the Béchamel Sauce.
4. Place ⅓ of the pasta in the dish. Cover with ⅓ of the tomato sauce. Repeat this twice more. Cover with remaining Béchamel, then adorn with either the nutritional yeast or the bread crumbs. Bake for 30 to 45 minutes or until firm.

Yield: 8 to 10 servings

1 tablespoon olive oil
1 onion, minced
3 garlic cloves, minced
1 26-ounce can chopped tomatoes
1 tablespoon oregano
1 tablespoon dried parsley
1 teaspoon thyme
½ teaspoon cinnamon
¼ teaspoon nutmeg
⅛ teaspoon allspice
1 bay leaf
Dash ground cloves
2 tablespoons dry red wine (optional)
1 14-ounce packet of ground beef–style crumbles (or 1¾ cup reconstituted Textured Vegetable Protein [TVP] crumbles)
½ teaspoon salt or more, to taste
¼ cup nutritional yeast or bread crumbs for topping
1 pound ziti, cooked al dente (err on the side of firmness), drained and cooled
Béchamel Sauce (see page 196)

MUSIC SOOTHES THE SAVAGE GUEST

Your music should complement your guests and your food, but it's all too easy to get into a musical rut. When choosing tunes, put your own personal preferences aside and keep your guests' tastes in mind. Mix up soft and hard, slow and fast, ethnic and homegrown.

Instead of playing Top 40 pop music, consider jazz or ethnic music. Or try pop music in another language (try Laura Pausini, Carla Bruni, or Julieta Venegas); it will add an element of urbane sophistication to your party.

HERBY POLENTA

Polenta is a mainstay in northern Italian cities like Milan and Torino. Since it requires very little prep time and tastes good hot or cold, I think it's the perfect party dish. You can mingle with your guests instead of slaving over a hot stove. If you can, save yourself some stress and make the sauce a day ahead. Use fresh herbs. They really make a difference here.

2 cups vegetable broth

½ cup soy or rice milk

1 cup fine cornmeal

3 tablespoons–½ cup nutritional yeast, to taste, plus more for sprinkling

3 tablespoons fresh basil, or 1 teaspoon dried

1½ tablespoons fresh oregano, or ½ teaspoon dried

1 teaspoon fresh rosemary, chopped, or ½ teaspoon dried

Salt and pepper, to taste

1 recipe of your favorite sauce (try John's Marinara, see page 193, Winter Pesto, see page 185, Red Pepper, see page 197, or Walnut, see page 192. A doctored-up store-bought jar of tomato sauce also works.)

1. In a large saucepan, mix the broth and milk. Bring to a gentle boil and in a continuous stream, whisk in the cornmeal, whisking constantly to avoid lumps. Reduce heat to low and cook another 5 to 10 minutes, or until very thick. (If mixture is too thick to stir, add more milk or broth, 1 tablespoon at a time.)
2. Stir in the nutritional yeast and herbs, and adjust seasonings. Top with your sauce of choice and additional nutritional yeast, if desired.

Yield: 8 servings

TAPENADE

This olive-and-caper dip is a shining star in restaurants, gourmet shops, and farmer's markets in cities across Provence. Each city has its own subtly different interpretation of this French classic. Most tapenades get their shot of sodium from anchovies, but mine relies on a teaspoon of miso paste.

Tapenade is lovely on crackers or French bread, but it's also wonderful slathered on sandwiches in place of mayo or Vegenaise spread, as a bruschetta or crostini topper, or tossed with pasta, pine nuts, nutritional yeast, and a bit of fresh basil, with a little extra olive oil for thinning.

1 cup Niçoise olives, or any black olives, pitted (preferably oil-cured)

2 tablespoons capers, rinsed

4 tablespoons extra-virgin olive oil

2½ tablespoons freshly squeezed lemon juice

2 large garlic cloves, peeled

1 teaspoon miso paste

½ teaspoon dried thyme

¼ teaspoon Dijon mustard

Freshly ground black pepper

1 teaspoon cognac (optional, but highly recommended!)

Mix everything in the food processor until smooth.

Yield: 1 cup

Variations

Substitute green olives. Add a few oil-cured, sun-dried tomatoes.

Urban Garden

Sure, it's been called the concrete jungle, but if you look around your city, you'll find much lushness and greenery by way of parks, farmer's markets, urban gardens, and community gardens. As a result, a spectrum of produce is available year-round, from the exotic to locally grown, to inspire and add color to your cooking.

RAW SLAW

½ head Savoy cabbage, finely shredded

½ head red cabbage, finely shredded

1 carrot, peeled and finely shredded

4 garlic cloves, minced

½ red bell pepper, julienned

1 cup bean sprouts (I used mung beans)

7 tablespoons extra-virgin olive oil

3 tablespoons shoyu or soy sauce

2 tablespoons apple cider vinegar

1 tablespoon agave nectar

2 teaspoons nigella seeds

Need some crunch with your lunch? Subtly sweet and sour, this raw cole-slaw is a kaleidoscope of vitamins and fiber, and it's a snap to prepare with fresh market veggies. Ideally, you should let this salad sit for an hour before serving to allow the flavors to integrate, but it's fine if you just can't wait.

1. In a large bowl, toss the vegetables.
2. Mix the olive oil, shoyu, vinegar, agave nectar, and nigella seeds, and pour over the veggies. Toss well and serve.

Yield: 6 servings

NIBLET SALAD

1 tomato, chopped

1 can corn, drained

2 tablespoons toasted, slivered almonds

4 tablespoons raisins

Optional additions: olives, sliced green grapes

This deceivingly simple salad is a kitschy throwback to the 1950s. It relies on a combination of canned goods and staples. (Fresh is always better, but doesn't every city pantry have a can of corn waiting to be used up or donated to the food drive?) It's perfect to bring along to a summer picnic in the park—just double or triple the recipe. So put on your apron and pull out your can opener.

Toss all ingredients together in a large bowl. Dress with Basil-Flax Dressing (see page 124) to taste.

Yield: 4–6 servings

CURRIED WHEAT BERRY-SPELT SALAD

I live right near Chinatown in Philadelphia, and I walk to my favorite Malaysian restaurant at least once a week to indulge. But you can't eat out every night, right?

Curry paste gives many Southeast Asian dishes that special tang. It's a phantasmagorical blend of sweet, hot, and sour ingredients, which may or may not include galangal, chilies, ginger, turmeric, lemongrass, and kaffir lime. You can find it in most Asian markets.

The slightly chewy whole-grain base of this salad obediently absorbs the curry-paste dressing. I think it tastes better if you let it sit overnight. Adjust the amount of curry to your own taste. Personally, I like a heaping teaspoon!

1. Let raisins soak in water for about 10 minutes until plump. Bring water to a boil. Add the wheat berries and spelt. Cover and simmer for 90 to 120 minutes or until all the water is absorbed
2. Meanwhile, make the dressing. Mix together the olive oil, tahini, lemon juice, agave nectar, salt, curry paste, and spices. Add cooked grains, onion, pepper, carrot, and drained raisins. Toss gently. Adjust seasonings as needed.
3. Serve chilled or room temperature.

Yield: 6–8 servings

¼ cup raisins, soaked
3 cups water
½ cup wheat berries
½ cup spelt
3 tablespoons extra-virgin olive oil
1 tablespoon tahini
2 tablespoons lemon juice
4 tablespoons agave nectar
¾ teaspoon salt
½–1 teaspoon yellow or red curry paste (start with less)
½ teaspoon cumin
¼ teaspoon turmeric
½ small onion, minced, or several green onions, sliced
½ cup green pepper, minced
½ cup carrot, shredded

Variation

Substitute farro for all or part of the wheat berries or spelt.

SPINACH-FENNEL SALAD

1 large bunch organic spinach (about 4 cups)

1 fennel bulb, sliced very thin

3 tablespoons chopped pecans, toasted

2 tablespoons dried cranberries

Salt, freshly ground pepper to taste

Creamy Avocado Dressing (see page 124)

Spinach and fennel are two vegetable powerhouses that are even more formidable when used in tandem: Fennel's heady licorice aroma teases out the spinach's grassy innocence. The creamy avocado dressing, pecans, and cranberries provide sophistication, texture, sweetness, and a little needed decadence. Sometimes, after a particularly trying workday, we'll just eat a huge bowl of this salad for dinner, with whole-grain bread to mop up any extra dressing.

Please try to buy organic spinach, if possible. Non-organic is often rife with pesticides.

Gently toss all ingredients. Dress with Creamy Avocado Dressing.

Yield: 4 (or 2 as a main course) servings

HOW TO START A COMMUNITY GARDEN

Put those vacant lots to good use!

1. **Get organized.** Meet with like-minded people who are motivated to make the garden happen.
2. **Agree on garden goals.** Vegetable patch or floral retreat? Make sure you're all on the same page.
3. **Assess the site.** Is the soil safe for planting? Is it sunny? Do you have access to water?
4. **Make a list.** Check it twice. Figure out what resources you need to make the garden happen, including manpower, tools, etc.
5. **Design the garden.** (This is the fun part.) See if local university students can contribute design ideas gratis.
6. **Plan it.** Develop a task list, assignments, and a time line. Hold regular meetings to keep volunteers accountable.

JICAMA SALAD

Jicama is something like a cross between a potato and an apple. Like tofu—and any true urbanite—it happily absorbs the influences of any ingredients you add. I like to pair it with sweet agave nectar, corn and red pepper, and just a hint of heat. This salad is extremely refreshing on a hot summer day. It's the perfect accompaniment to the Portobello Burritos (see page 80).

In a large bowl, mix all ingredients. Let flavors meld at least 6 hours before serving.

Yield: 6 servings

1 medium jicama, peeled and diced

1 red bell pepper, diced

1 mango, peeled and diced

½ cup corn kernels (frozen is fine)

1 garlic clove, minced

4 tablespoons lime juice

3 tablespoons agave nectar

1 healthy pinch of chili powder or red pepper flakes

¼ teaspoon salt or more, to taste

Variations

Add one avocado, chopped. If you're a fan of heat,
add one small chili, chopped very fine.

NIÇOISE SALAD

City summers can get intensely humid and steamy, since the high buildings and concrete trap in the heat. During the hot weather, I often don't feel like eating a huge meal—or cooking one, for that matter. For this reason, dinner salads are lifesavers during the warmer months. Niçoise Salad is a favorite, because the flavors and preparation are simple yet immensely satisfying. Eating this healthful dinner makes you feel like you took a trip to Nice. For now, anyway, organic lettuce is much cheaper than an airplane ticket.

In a very large bowl, toss all the vegetables. Stir in the Dijon Vinaigrette and decorate the plate with about 4 or 5 olives. Serve with good French bread to mop up any extra dressing.

Yield: 4 servings

1 head organic red or green leaf lettuce, torn into bite-size pieces

4 small organic potatoes, baked or microwaved until soft, then chopped into large chunks

2 cups green beans, cooked until tender crisp (canned and drained also works here)

½ cup red bell peppers, thinly sliced, or roasted red peppers, chopped roughly

16 cherry tomatoes, halved

Dijon Vinaigrette (see page 125)

½ cup Niçoise olives, for topping

A baguette, for dipping

Variations

Add mesclun or frisee to the lettuce. Add cubed cucumbers,
grated carrots, or thinly sliced zucchini.

FAT-FREE PAPAYA SALAD

Juice 1 lime

3 to 4 tablespoons agave nectar (to taste)

3 cloves garlic, crushed

2 tablespoons rice vinegar

1 tablespoon water

1 teaspoon soy sauce

Salt to taste

¼ to 1 Thai hot chili, minced very finely (to taste, start with ¼ pepper. I use the whole thing!)

2 scallions, minced

1 firm green papaya, peeled, de-seeded, rinsed very well (to remove any bitterness), and grated

1 organic red pepper, cut in quarters, and then sliced as thinly as possible

1 cup mesclun salad greens, lettuce, or spring mix

1 tomato, preferably Jersey, cut into 8 wedges

2 tablespoons crushed peanuts, for topping*

Thai basil, for garnish

* Disclaimer: This salad is only fat-free if you forgo the garnish. But the peanut topping is traditional. And a tiny bit of healthy fat won't kill you.

Immigrants to cities often alleviate their homesickness by emulating tradi-tional dishes that they would enjoy in their homeland. Sometimes, they have to make do with local ingredients—like Jersey tomatoes and mesclun. This Thai-inspired salad pairs nicely with the Spicy Udon Noodles (see page 89) or Curry Cashew Casserole (see page 75). It's especially refreshing on a hot summer night. Sometimes, we just have it for dinner. Did I mention that it's fat free?

If green papaya sounds intimidating, first watch the movie *The Scent of Green Papaya*. Then just think of green papaya as a giant cucumber. Working with it is pretty much the same.

1. Combine lime juice, agave nectar, garlic, vinegar, water, soy sauce, salt, chili, and scallions. Let sit for at least 15 minutes to allow flavors to blend.
2. Mix papaya, peppers, and dressing.
3. Divide mesclun between 4 plates. Place a high mound of papaya mixture in the center. Decorate with tomato wedges. Top with peanuts and snip-pets of Thai basil.

Yield: 4 servings as a side, or 2 for dinner

Variations

Instead of grating the papaya, you can also create a "carpaccio," by thinly slicing the papaya with a mandoline or spiral slicer. You can also add cucumber, carrots, radish, and mango.

CONTAINER GARDENING FOR URBAN DWELLERS

Not every urban dweller has the room for a garden. But some edibles, like peppers, eggplant, tomatoes, and herbs, can thrive in containers. In fact, many varieties were for-mulated especially for small spaces. Use large pots with excellent drainage and choose a high-quality, peat-based soil mix. Plants in containers need frequent watering, so check your plants daily.

POTATO-BEET SALAD

Beets and potatoes go together like Broadway and theater, like Greenwich Village and celebrities, like the East Village and vegans. My beet of choice for this side is the humble red beet: They lend some of their deep crimson color to the potatoes, making for a gloriously scarlet-pink dish. But you can use any color or variety of beet you have on hand. The nuttiness of the walnut oil complements the earthy flavors in these autumnal veggies.

1. In separate pans, boil potatoes and beets in plenty of water until soft, about 30 minutes. Drain. Peel when cool enough to handle. Slice thinly.
2. In a large bowl, combine vinegar, oils, and spices. Add vegetables and toss gently. Let sit for about 3 hours to allow the flavors to combine. Top with scallion. Season with salt and pepper, to taste. Serve at room temperature.

Yield: 4 servings

4 medium potatoes
4 beets
5 tablespoons white or champagne vinegar
2 tablespoons extra-virgin olive oil
2 tablespoons walnut oil
1 tablespoon ground coriander
½ teaspoon cumin
1 scallion, minced
Salt and freshly ground pepper, to taste

MISO-SESAME DRESSING

Okay, busy urbanites. There's no longer any excuse for not eating your greens. This dressing is pathetically easy to make, and it takes most salads from drab to fab.

Pour all ingredients in a mason jar. Shake well. Store leftover in refrigerator for up to 10 days.

Yield: 1 cup

2 teaspoons light miso
4 tablespoons olive oil
4 ounces rice wine vinegar
2 teaspoons sesame oil
1 teaspoon agave nectar
Pepper

BASIL-FLAX SALAD DRESSING

8 tablespoons flaxseed oil
4 garlic cloves, crushed
2 teaspoons chopped fresh basil
   (or 2 teaspoons and 1 large
   pinch of dry)
1 teaspoon dried oregano
4 tablespoons Braggs or soy sauce
Salt and pepper to taste
Pinch of pepper flakes (optional)

Want some omega-3s with your dinner? This basil-infused dressing gives you a little extra nutritional TLC—a must for urbanites, who are dodging free radicals left and right.

Put everything in a mason jar and shake vigorously until well blended. Tastes better if you let it sit overnight. Store leftovers in glass jar in refrigerator for a few days.

Yield: ½ cup

Variation

Add some red pepper flakes for a spicy dressing.

CREAMY AVOCADO SALAD DRESSING

Flesh of 1 avocado
2 tablespoons apple cider vinegar
1 tablespoon shoyu or soy sauce
1 teaspoon agave nectar
½ teaspoon dark sesame oil
¼ teaspoon salt
Drizzle lime juice
Freshly ground pepper to taste

Pico de Gallo, my favorite Mexican restaurant in Philadelphia, makes an incredible, gargantuan taco salad, served with copious slices of fresh avocado—so many that you get a little taste of creamy avocado in every bite. This dressing serves the same purpose.

Extra-creamy and full of lignans—anti-cancer phytochemicals—it really clings to a salad—and to your ribs. You can also use this on sandwiches as a substitute for mayonnaise or as a dip (Try it with endive!). This recipe is easily doubled or tripled.

Mix everything well using a blender or an immersion blender.

Yield: 1 cup

TRIPLE SESAME SALAD DRESSING

Tahini is sesame seed paste, and it's often used in Middle Eastern cuisine. I adore its slightly smoky creaminess, and I could eat it right out of the jar. Try different varieties and brands because, like wine, I think they impart subtleties of flavor that can affect your recipes. Browse in a Middle Eastern market and ask the merchants for their advice.

In this dressing, I tripled up on my love of sesame by adding to the tahini sesame seeds for a tiny bit of texture and dark sesame oil for a deeper layer of flavor. It's definitely a fusion dressing, since it also leans heavily on Asian flavors. It's wonderful over salad or steamed vegetables and rice.

Mix everything well using a blender or an immersion blender. Be careful about salting your salad when using this dressing. It is probably salty enough as is.

Yield: I cup

3 tablespoons white miso paste
I ½ tablespoons tahini
I tablespoon walnut oil
I tablespoon sesame seeds
I teaspoon sesame oil
4 tablespoons water
4 tablespoons rice vinegar
2 tablespoons ume plum vinegar
Dash cayenne pepper

DIJON VINAIGRETTE

Eat a meal in any French city, and this is the classic dressing that will infuse your salads with tangy flavor. (Where on earth did the U.S. version of "French" dressing come from, anyway?) Add any fresh herbs you have on hand, or omit the herbs altogether and enjoy this dressing's timeless and versatile sophistication. Please use the best Dijon mustard and extra-virgin olive oil you can find; they really make a difference (I sometimes eat good mustard straight out of the jar with a spoon). Try it on the Niçoise Salad (see page 121).

2 teaspoons Dijon mustard
4 tablespoons white vinegar
6–8 tablespoons extra-virgin olive oil
I garlic clove, crushed
½ teaspoon each dried thyme and parsley
Salt and pepper, to taste

1. In a large bowl, whisk together the mustard and vinegar. When it's completely emulsified, slowly whisk in extra-virgin olive oil to taste, and watch the color transform to a painterly ochre.
2. Add the whole crushed garlic clove, herbs, and salt and pepper to taste, and let the dressing rest for about 10 minutes. Store any leftovers in a glass jar in the refrigerator for a few days.

Yield: about ½ cup

MARSALA VINAIGRETTE

1 cup Marsala
2 tablespoons red wine vinegar
1 tablespoon lemon juice
2 shallots, chopped as finely as
  you can manage
1 garlic clove, minced
¾ cup extra-virgin olive oil
Salt and pepper to taste

An urban liquor cabinet is a well-stocked liquor cabinet. This is a great way to put a dent in your Marsala stash. It's slightly sweet and slightly nutty. Try it in a salad tossed with bitter frisee, sweet, ripe pears, and toasted walnuts.

1. In a small saucepan, bring Marsala to a boil. Boil gently until it's reduced by half.
2. Cool, then whisk with remaining ingredients. Adjust seasonings.

Yield: about 1 cup

HOMEMADE VEGAN BATH PRODUCTS

Instead of forking out big bucks to a spa, raid your pantry and make your own animal-free beauty treatments.

EASY PEPPERMINT FACIAL SCRUB
1 tablespoon rolled oats
1 teaspoon dried peppermint
½ teaspoon coarse salt

Mix ingredients and add enough water to form a paste. Wet your face, then take a heaping teaspoon of the scrub and rub it into your skin, gently exfoliating using circular motions. Rinse well, then finish with a dab of witch hazel if your skin is oily.

  Cover and store unused portion in the refrigerator for up to 4 days. Makes enough for 3 to 4 applications.

HOMEMADE BATH SCRUB
½ cup coconut, olive, or almond oil (if using coconut oil, make sure it comes to room
    temperature; if it's hard, microwave it on low power for a few seconds)
1 cup sugar or coarse salt
A few drops of your favorite essential oil(s)

Using a large spoon, mix ingredients in an airtight container. To use, scrub onto wet skin in shower and rinse.

E-Z RAW MASKS
1 avocado, for dry skin
½ cup mashed strawberries and 1 tablespoon agave nectar for oily skin

Wash your face. Rub chosen mask on skin and let dry for 30 minutes. Rinse well and tone, if desired.

BEANS AND GREENS

Not only is this Italian staple nutritious and inexpensive but it's also easy to prepare, giving you a lot of flavor for very little effort. Most people would consider Beans and Greens a side dish, which is why it appears in this chapter. But I must confess, we often eat this as an entrée, especially in the winter, with crusty Italian bread and a tomato side salad.

1. Fill a large pot with 2 inches of water and bring to a boil. Parboil the broccoli rabe, covered, for about 8 minutes.
2. Meanwhile, sauté the garlic and hot pepper flakes (if you're using these) over medium-low heat in olive oil until translucent. Be careful not to brown the garlic.
3. Drain the broccoli rabe. Toss it in with the olive oil and warm through over medium heat. Add wine, if desired, and let the alcohol cook off over medium-high heat. Remove from heat and add beans. Season with salt and pepper and garnish with flaxseeds. Sprinkle with vegan Parmesan or nutritional yeast, if desired.

Yield: 4 to 6 servings

1 large bunch broccoli rabe, chopped into 2-inch pieces
8 garlic cloves, minced (yes, you read right)
1 healthy pinch red pepper flakes (optional)
6 tablespoons olive oil
¼ cup dry white wine (optional)
1 16-ounce can beans, drained (pinto, chickpeas or navy beans—choose a color that contrasts nicely with the deep green broccoli rabe)
Salt and pepper, to taste
1 tablespoon ground flaxseeds
Vegan Parmesan or nutritional yeast for sprinkling (optional)

Variations

Use collard greens, mustard greens, bok choy, or kale instead of broccoli rabe. You can also use Swiss chard instead, but you will need two large bunches, since it shrinks greatly when cooked.

HARICOTS VERTS ET TOMATES

2 pounds green beans, trimmed
and cut into 1-inch pieces
2 tablespoons plus 1 tablespoon
extra-virgin olive oil
1 large onion, chopped
2 cloves garlic, minced
2 large tomatoes, chopped
2 tablespoons basil, chopped
1 teaspoon thyme
1 bay leaf
1 teaspoon sugar or agave nectar
Salt and pepper

It's just a fancy name for "green beans and tomatoes," but everything sounds more urbane in French, right? Make this Provençal-inspired side in the heat of summer, when beans and tomatoes are at their peak, and the prices hit rock bottom.

1. Cook green beans in boiling water for about 10 minutes or until tender-crisp.
2. Heat 2 tablespoons oil in a large saucepan and sauté onion and garlic over medium-low until soft, about 5 minutes. Add chopped tomatoes, herbs, sweetener, and salt and pepper. Cook for about 5 more minutes. Add the beans, cover, and cook until the tomatoes break down—about 15 minutes. Add a few tablespoons of water if needed.
3. Just before serving, stir in the remaining olive oil, and adjust seasonings.

Yield: 6 to 8 servings as a side

EASY ROASTED ASPARAGUS

3 tablespoons extra-virgin olive
oil
1 pound asparagus, trimmed—the
thinner the stalks, the better
2 tablespoons nutritional yeast
Freshly ground black pepper

Roasting asparagus in best-quality extra-virgin olive oil infuses it with a rich, dinner-party-worthy sophistication. But this recipe is so easy that you'll want to make it every night. The nutritional yeast adds a salty, cheeselike element, so it's a perfect side to serve to skeptical omnivores. Best of all, this dish takes only about 5 minutes to prepare.

1. Preheat the oven to 400°F.
2. Drizzle the bottom of a 9 x 9-inch pan or baking dish with olive oil. Arrange the asparagus and then drizzle the remaining olive oil over top. Sprinkle the nutritional yeast over top (feel free to add more if you're a "nooch" fan) and season with black pepper.
3. Cover with foil and bake for 15 to 20 minutes, until asparagus is cooked through and semi-soft.

Yield: 4 servings as a side

SNAP PEAS IN GARLIC AND OLIVE OIL

For me, shelling peas is an exercise more meditative than yoga. Sometimes the simplest foods are the best, and in my opinion, freshly shelled peas taste best in what I consider to be the perfect vegetable formula—garlic and best-quality extra-virgin olive oil.

1. Sauté garlic in olive oil over medium heat about 1 minute or until oil is infused with garlic flavor. Be careful not to burn.
2. Toss in peas and cook for about 4 to 5 minutes.
3. Remove from heat. Stir in lemon juice, and season according to your preferences.

Yield: 4 servings

3 cloves garlic, minced
1 ½ tablespoons best-quality
  extra-virgin olive oil
2 cups freshly shelled snap peas
1 tablespoon lemon juice
Salt, pepper to taste
Herbs (e.g., basil, oregano, thyme),
  optional

OVEN-ROASTED POTATOES WITH BASIL-FENNEL CREAM

I like to cheer for the underdog. In this case, the underdog is a ridiculously simple side dish. These olive-oil-roasted fingerling potatoes can effortlessly outshine many a main course—especially when paired with a sweet-basil and fennel-infused sauce.

Heat oven to 400°F. Line a roasting pan with foil (for easy cleanup). Drizzle the bottom of the pan with about 2 tablespoons of the olive oil. Toss in remaining ingredients except Basil-Fennel Cream Sauce, and mix well with your hands, ensuring that all potatoes shine with olive oil. Top with additional oil as needed. Bake for 25 to 30 minutes, or until soft. Serve with Basil-Fennel Cream.

Yield: 6 servings as a side

About ¼ cup extra-virgin olive oil
2 pounds fingerling potatoes,
  scrubbed
6 cloves garlic, sliced in half
2 tablespoons dried rosemary
½ teaspoon dried thyme
½ teaspoon sea salt
Freshly ground pepper
Basil-Fennel Cream Sauce (see
  page 185)

SNOW IN
THE SUMMER

1 tablespoon canola or peanut oil
2 garlic cloves, minced
1-inch piece ginger, grated
1 carrot, julienned
1 medium zucchini, julienned
½ pound snow peas, "topped and
   tailed"
Sesame oil and soy sauce for
   drizzling

In Philadelphia, August usually means oppressive heat waves, exacerbated by the high temperatures and humidity. Fortunately, fresh snow peas are abundant during this time, and they really lighten the spirit. Stir-frying them with a few seasonal ingredients makes a quick, refreshing summer side dish.

1. Heat oil in a wok over medium-high heat. Stir-fry garlic and ginger for about 1 minute, until fragrant. Add the carrot. Fry for about 1 to 2 minutes, moving constantly, until tender crisp. Add zucchini. Again, fry for about 1 to 2 minutes, moving constantly, until tender crisp. Finally, add peas and fry until warmed through but still crispy, about another minute or so.
2. Finish with a drizzle of sesame oil and soy sauce.

Yield: 4 servings as a side

BALSAMIC-ROASTED VEGETABLES

I know what you're thinking: "Balsamic vinegar is so 1990s." But every city girl knows that trends in food and fashion come and go, but classics like best-quality balsamic vinegar are as timeless as the little black dress.

The inherent sweetness of the peppers, onions, garlic, and yams ping-pong against the acrid, sweet-sourness of the vinegar, causing a pleasant tension on your palate. The eggplant dissolves and acts as a thickener of sorts. Although this is traditionally served as a side dish, you can toss in some chickpeas, seitan, or tofu, serve it over a whole grain, and call it Dinner. You can also add other vegetables, depending on your tastes and your pantry.

1. Preheat the oven to 425°F.
2. Place the vegetables in a large roasting pan. Add the oil, 2 tablespoons of the vinegar, ¼ cup of vegetable broth, plus the seasonings and salt. Mix all ingredients well (I like to use my hands.). Cover pan and place in the oven.
3. Check every 15 minutes or so to make sure there is enough liquid. Add more broth as needed. Roast for 30 to 45 minutes, or until vegetables are soft. Toss with additional vinegar and serve.

Yield: 6–8 servings as a side

4 peppers (any color will do), roughly chopped into 1½-inch pieces

3 small, organic potatoes, roughly chopped into 1½-inch pieces

2 yams or sweet potatoes, roughly chopped into 1½-inch pieces

1 small eggplant, roughly chopped into 1½-inch pieces

1 large onion, chopped into eighths

6–8 cloves garlic, peeled

1½ tablespoons extra-virgin olive oil

2 tablespoons plus 4 tablespoons good quality balsamic vinegar

¼–½ cup vegetable broth

1 tablespoon fresh or 1 teaspoon dried basil

1 bay leaf

Healthy pinch azafran (Spanish sweet paprika) or regular paprika

½ teaspoon sea salt

Variations

Add any of the following to the base vegetables, cut into 1½-inch chunks: carrots, turnips, zucchini, portobello or cremini mushrooms, or parsnips.

ACORN SQUASH WITH PECAN-CHERRY STUFFING

$

2 medium acorn squash, halved
   and deseeded

1 cup soy or rice milk

2 teaspoons sage

1 teaspoon oregano

8–10 slices of stale whole-grain
   bread, cubed (Not stale yet? Let
   it sit out overnight.)

2 tablespoons olive oil, plus about
   1 tablespoon for rubbing the
   squash halves

4 stalks celery, minced

2 onions, minced

½ cup shredded carrots

¼–½ cup dried cherries or fresh
   or dried cranberries

2 tablespoons toasted pecans,
   roughly ground

Salt and freshly ground pepper

4 tablespoons maple syrup or
   agave nectar

There's something so urbanely sophisticated about stuffed acorn squash. Maybe it's the squash's attractive scalloped edges, which remind me of the arabesque on the Alhambra in Granada, Spain. Adding a hint of dried cherries, an unexpected taste during autumn, makes this side even more highbrow. A filling (pun intended) everyday side dish, Acorn Squash with Pecan-Cherry Stuffing would be particularly appropriate at a Thanksgiving meal.

1. Preheat the oven to 400°F.
2. Rub the insides of the cut squash with olive oil. On a silpat or greased cookie sheet, bake the squash, cut-side down, for about 25 minutes, or until soft. Remove from oven, and allow to cool enough to handle.
3. Meanwhile, in a large bowl, mix milk and the herbs. Soak the bread cubes in this mixture and let sit for about 15 minutes. The bread should absorb all the liquid.
4. In a large saucepan, over medium-low heat, slowly sauté the celery, onion, and carrots in the olive oil, until soft, about 15 minutes.
5. Add the sautéed veggies to the bread, along with the cherries and pecans. Season with salt and pepper to taste.
6. Once the squash is cool, cut a slice from the "nipple" edges of the stems (ouch!) to make a base so they will not topple when they stand. Drizzle one tablespoon of maple syrup or agave nectar in each squash half, then fill the squash with the stuffing, forming a slight dome with a tablespoon. Drizzle with additional olive oil, if desired.
7. Bake for about 15 to 25 minutes, or until warmed through. Be careful not to burn.

Yield: 4 servings

Variations

Not in the mood for stuffing? You can fill this squash with just about anything. Start with these ideas: Cooked brown rice, walnut oil, cranberries, apples, and bread crumbs • Cooked millet, olive oil, black olives, capers, and tomatoes, with a healthy helping of basil. Millet is especially easy to mold and shape • Thai-style veggies, roasted in coconut milk and curry powder • Cooked whole-wheat couscous, olive oil, toasted almonds, chopped apricots, moistened raisins, and harissa • Potatoes, turnips, and parsnips, mashed with grated ginger, olive oil, and tons of garlic. A veritable carb-fest! • Leftover paella (see page 78) • Barley, tomatoes, green beans, olive oil, and onion, seasoned with herbes de Provençe, and nutritional yeast • Chopped pears and apples, cranberries, and pomegranate seeds, mixed with cooked spelt, za'tar, sumac, olive oil, lemon juice, and salt • Sherry-Infused Pâté (see page 100) • Beans and Greens (see page 127)

BRUSSELS SPROUTS AU GRATIN

Brussels is a fabulous city, and its signature veggie is equally amazing. Since these mini cabbages have such a strong flavor, it's best to dress them simply and let their distinctive taste shine through. The cheesy flavor imparted by the nutritional yeast helps mellow out their assertiveness.

1. Steam the brussels sprouts until tender-crisp.
2. Toss with Earth Balance and nutritional yeast. Place under the broiler for 5 minutes, or until the nutritional yeast starts to brown. Season with salt and pepper.

Yield: 4 servings

1 pound brussels sprouts, trimmed and cut in half
2 tablespoons Earth Balance, melted
2–3 tablespoons nutritional yeast
Salt and freshly ground pepper

CHICKPEAS WITH TOMATOES AND SPINACH

Whether it concerns design, architecture, fashion, or food, simplicity is an enduring ingredient for success. And not only are these Turkish-inspired beans easy to throw together but they're also a nutritional powerhouse. They usurp all of their creamy flavor from just a few ingredients: tomatoes, spinach, and a handful of kitchen spices.

1. Heat oil in a large saucepan. Cook garlic and onion until soft, then add chickpeas and stir to coat. Stir in the fresh and canned tomatoes. Cover. Cook for 5 minutes on medium heat.
2. Remove the lid, raise the heat, and cook until the tomatoes are soft. Stir in agave nectar and spices.
3. Turn heat to low. Add spinach in batches and cook until it wilts. Simmer for a few minutes, adjust seasonings, and serve as a side or over rice or another grain as a meal.

Yield: 4–6 servings

4 tablespoons olive oil
4 garlic cloves, sliced
1 small onion, chopped
2 14-ounce cans chickpeas, drained and rinsed
1 large tomato, diced
1 15-ounce can crushed tomatoes
1 teaspoon agave nectar
1½ teaspoons cumin
1 teaspoon ground coriander
Dash cinnamon
Salt and pepper to taste
1 pound spinach, washed and chopped

TRICOLOR QUINOA

2 cups vegetable broth
1 cup curly kale, chopped into
  small pieces
1 large carrot, finely diced
2–3 garlic cloves, minced
1 cup uncooked quinoa, rinsed
Freshly ground black pepper

Quinoa is quintessentially Peruvian. I saw it on many restaurant menus in Lima. But ironically, this tricolor quinoa reminds me of a Mexican or Italian flag. The bits of kale and carrot add texture and flavor—not to mention color!—to this über-grain.

1. Pour veggie broth into a medium saucepan. Add kale, carrot, and garlic, and bring to a boil, covered. When boiling, add the quinoa. Stir gently then turn heat to low.
2. Simmer, covered, about 25 minutes or until all the liquid is absorbed and veggies are soft. Add pepper to taste.

Yield: 6 servings as a side

Variation

Substitute finely chopped broccoli for kale.

PORCINI QUINOA WITH CAULIFLOWER AND TOASTED PECANS

2 cups vegetable broth
1 cup uncooked quinoa, rinsed
1–2 large garlic cloves, crushed
2 cups cauliflower, chopped into
  small pieces (frozen is fine)
¼ cup crushed, dried porcini
  mushrooms
1 tablespoon soy sauce
1 teaspoon herbes de Provençe
1 tablespoon walnut, flax, or
  extra-virgin olive oil
¼ cup toasted pecans
Freshly ground black pepper

One of the joys of city life is eating out. I dine out at least twice a week. Quinoa is such a versatile grain—yet I rarely see it served in mainstream U.S. restaurants, not even health-conscious ones. So I make it at home often. Porcini mushrooms, walnut oil, and toasted pecans bathe this super-grain in a mellow earthiness. Although it sounds like an autumn dish, it's light enough to enjoy during any season.

1. Pour veggie broth into a medium saucepan. Add quinoa, garlic, cauliflower, porcini mushrooms, soy sauce, and herbes de Provençe. Stir gently and bring to a boil, covered. Immediately lower the heat and simmer, covered, for about 15 minutes, or until all the liquid is absorbed and the cauliflower is soft.
2. Stir in oil and toasted nuts. Season with freshly ground pepper.

Yield: 6 servings as a side

HAUTE CUISINE
(NOT OAT CUISINE)

*I*t's time to dignify vegan food and escape cutesy names like "faux chicken" and "fakin' bacon." These elegant recipes call foods by their rightful names and are designed to take vegan cuisine to the next level. Make them when you want to impress someone—whether it's a die-hard omnivore or that cute vegan you have a crush on—or when you feel like your culinary skills need a bit of a challenge.

2 large sweet potatoes
2 tablespoons Earth Balance
½ teaspoon salt
¾–1 cup flour
Basil-Cream Sauce (see page 191)

SWEET POTATO GNOCCHI WITH BASIL CREAM SAUCE

Believe it or not, the best gnocchi I ever tasted were not in Rome or Florence. They came from a charming little restaurant in South America, in the small city of Colonia, Uruguay (many Italian immigrants happened to settle in Uruguay and Argentina). I still remember the cloudlike fluffiness of those handmade dumplings as if it were yesterday.

This surprise forced me to think outside the gnocchi box. How, I wondered, would gnocchi taste using a different carb as a base? To find out, I created these airy, autumnal gnocchi using sweet potatoes.

Don't be intimidated by making your own gnocchi. It's easy and fun. If you played with Play-Doh as a kid, then you won't have any problems.

1. Microwave sweet potatoes until soft, about 6 minutes. Using a potato ricer, squeeze filling from the sweet potatoes into a large bowl. Mash with Earth Balance and salt and then add about ½ cup of flour. Work through with your hands, adding additional flour 1 tablespoon at a time, until the dough is no longer sticky. Add as little flour as possible (this will depend largely on the humidity in your city). Roll a handful of dough out at a time into a ½-inch-wide rope. Using a knife, cut rope into ¼-inch nuggets.

2. Hold a nugget in the palm of your hand, and roll against the tines of a fork to create grooves. These indentations not only beautify the gnocchi but they also help "hold" the sauce.

3. Store finished gnocchi on a cookie sheet lined with wax paper, refrigerated, until ready to cook. Or freeze on a cookie sheet, and then transfer to an airtight, ziplock bag (will keep in freezer for about 1 month).

4. To cook the gnocchi, gently toss in a large pot of boiling, well-salted water. When they're done, gnocchi will float to the top. Remove immediately with a strainer. Drain well and toss with sauce.

Yield: 6 servings

Wine Pairing
Soave, Custoza, Beaujolais, or Bardolino

CHOCOLATE-CHIPOTLE CHILI

A good chili should showcase seamless layers of complexity. Perfecting this recipe took years of trial and error—and several trips to Mexico. But after about twenty iterations, I finally arrived at this version. Its smoky sweetness—and healthy dose of chocolate—diplomatically offsets the heat. Don't be intimidated by the long list of ingredients—this recipe is very easy. And the longer this chili cooks, the better it tastes, so make it when you have time to putter around the house. Serve it with white or yellow corn chips and a spinach salad with avocado.

1. Heat olive oil over medium heat in a large stockpot. Add onions and garlic and cook until glossy, a few minutes. Add celery, carrots, and pepper, and cook until soft, about 10 minutes. Add chipotle pepper and cumin. Stir to coat. Add tomato paste and stir to make a paste. Let heat through for a few minutes.
2. Add remaining ingredients, except chocolate, and bring to a boil. When boiling, add chocolate and stir well to mix. Lower heat to medium-low, and simmer covered, 25 minutes, checking consistency periodically, adding more water or stock as needed.
3. When carrots are soft, adjust seasonings and remove from heat.

Yield: 6–8 servings

3 tablespoons olive oil
1 large onion, chopped
4 cloves garlic, sliced
1 stalk celery, diced
1 carrot, diced
1 cup red and/or green pepper, chopped
1–2 teaspoons chipotle chili powder (start with 1½ teaspoons; I use the full 2)
2 teaspoons cumin
1 6-ounce can tomato paste
2 15-ounce cans beans of your choice, drained (I like pinto and cannelloni)
½ cup textured vegetable protein
1 28-ounce can tomato puree
1 cup corn (frozen is fine)
2 tablespoons parsley, chopped
2 tablespoons cilantro, chopped
1½ tablespoons agave nectar
½ teaspoon salt
½ teaspoon tamarind concentrate
¼ teaspoon cayenne pepper (optional—only if you like spicy chili)
Water or veggie broth to add, if needed
½ cup dark chocolate buttons or chips, minimum 60 cocoa

LEMON POPPY SEED TEMPEH

1 pound tempeh
Juice of 4 organic lemons
Zest of 4 organic lemons
6 tablespoons extra-virgin olive oil
4 tablespoons poppy seeds
2 tablespoons brown rice syrup, agave nectar, or maple syrup (in order of preference)
2 tablespoons cornstarch
3 scallions, chopped finely
Healthy pinch sea salt

It seems like every breakfast joint across the United States offers some version of lemon–poppy seed muffins and scones. But why should this glorious combination be confined to the breakfast table alone?

This simple recipe is packed with flavor. I like to serve it over the Confetti Quinoa (see page 98). The longer the tempeh sits in the marinade, the better, so if you do the prep work the night before, all you'll need to do the next day is to bake the tempeh.

1. Cut the tempeh into 4 triangles. In a medium saucepan, bring a half pot of water to a boil and add the tempeh. Turn heat to low and simmer for 10 minutes. This will chase away the tempeh's inherent bitterness.
2. In a baking pan, mix remaining ingredients. Use a whisk to ensure that the cornstarch and sweetener are completely dissolved. Coat the tempeh with the marinade and let sit for at least an hour, or ideally overnight. Be sure to "baste" the tempeh with more marinade from time to time.
3. Preheat oven to 400°F. Re-baste the tempeh once more and bake for 15 to 20 minutes, re-basting once about every 5 minutes. About halfway through, the sauce will begin to thicken and stick to the pan. At this point, just add a few tablespoons of water to thin it out and continue baking and basting.
4. Serve over your grain of choice with pan drippings.

Yield: 2 substantial or 4 light servings

Variations

Substitute orange zest and juice for lemon zest and juice.
Substitute sesame seeds for poppy seeds.

SALTIMBOCCA

Many vegans sing the praises of mock meat, but I could live quite contentedly without it. However, I enjoy the challenge of veganizing family's and friends' old favorite meat dishes. Everyone is pleased with the results of this Saltimbocca. Although I prefer to make things from scratch, every once in a while, store-bought products like vegan cheeses can be timesavers.

1. Preheat oven to 375°F.
2. Pound seitan cutlets until flat. Rub with scored garlic clove and coat with flour.
3. In a large saucepan over medium heat, melt together the Earth Balance and oil. Sauté the 3 garlic cloves until soft, then the cutlets, a few at a time, until browned on each side. Put one slice of "ham" on cutlets and place in a 9 x 13-inch baking dish.
4. Turn the pan with remaining oil/Earth Balance to high. Pour in wine and deglaze pan. Add sage. Lower heat and cook until thick.
5. Pour sauce over cutlets. Top with vegan cheese. Bake until brown, about 15 minutes.

Yield: 6 servings

8 thinly sliced pieces seitan
(¼-inch thick is ideal; see recipe on page 104)
1 whole garlic clove, scored to release flavor for rubbing, plus 3 garlic cloves, minced
¼ cup flour in a deep dish
¼ cup Earth Balance
¼ cup olive oil
8 slices vegan soy slices, "ham" style
1 cup dry white wine
(I recommend Pinot Grigio)
1 tablespoon fresh sage, chopped
8 vegan cheese slices, mozzarella flavor

FOOD CO-OPS 101

Food cooperatives, or co-ops, sell groceries—often locally grown—and other items at fair prices to their members. They are usually member-owned and run, and are committed to their community. To find a co-op near you, visit coopdirectory.org.

MILLET-CRUSTED MUSHROOM-LEEK PIE

2 cups leftover cooked millet or brown rice

2 heaping tablespoons plus ½ cup nutritional yeast

2 tablespoons extra-virgin olive oil

2 leeks, sliced thinly (Wash them well. They can be annoyingly sandy.)

1 pound cremini mushrooms, sliced

¼ teaspoon salt, or more to taste

Lots of freshly ground black pepper

1 tablespoon parsley

Healthy pinch nutmeg

2 tablespoons chickpea flour (aka gram flour)

Even if you don't live in the UK, these days, most large cities have at least a handful of authentic British and Irish pubs. But what do you do when faced with an after-hours pub-grub craving? Make this hearty pie, of course. Drawing on millet's inherent malleability, I use it as the base for my pie crust —much healthier than what you'll find in a pub. But you'll still want to wash this down with a pint of bitter.

1. Preheat oven to 375°F.
2. Spray a pie pan with cooking oil. Using your hands, mix the millet with the 2 heaping tablespoons of nutritional yeast. Press the millet mixture into the pie pan to form a crust. Set aside.
3. In a large domed pan, heat the olive oil over medium. Add the leeks and cook a few minutes until bright green. Add the mushrooms, salt, and pepper and cook down until both the mushrooms and leeks are very soft, about 25 minutes. Add the parsley and a healthy pinch of nutmeg and mix well. Remove from heat.
4. Carefully transfer the cooked vegetables into the food processor (be careful not to burn yourself). Pulse a few times, and then add the chickpea flour, ½ cup of nutritional yeast, salt, and pepper. Mix until it forms a fairly firm mousse. If it seems too wet, add a bit more chickpea flour and nutritional yeast, in alternating tablespoonfuls.
5. Transfer the mousse into the prepared pie shell. Use your spatula to flatten the top. Bake for 20 to 25 minutes, until firm. Let cool at least 10 minutes before serving. Use a very sharp knife to cut. This is also good served room temperature.

Yield: 4 servings

RISOTTO MILANESE

Risotto is perfect winter fare—warm, comforting, and filling—but many people are intimidated by it. Truth is, it's very easy and almost meditative to make. All you really need to do is measure and stir. Risotto Milanese is a good "primer" risotto. Traditionally made with veal marrow, mine gets its kinder, gentler earthiness from a handful of dried porcini mushrooms.

1. Prepare your stock. Toss in the celery, carrot, mushrooms, and parsley stalks and heat to a simmer. Have a ladle ready.
2. Sauté the onion in 4 tablespoons of the Earth Balance. Add salt as needed, to slow down the cooking time.
3. When the onions are soft, toss in the risotto and stir to coat. Cook for 1 minute on medium heat. Turn the heat up to medium-high and pour in the wine. Let it cook until the wine evaporates.
4. Turn heat to medium-low. Add broth, one ladle at a time. Allow rice to absorb broth and then repeat until rice is al dente, about 20 minutes.
5. Add the saffron, yeast, parsley, and remaining 1 tablespoon of Earth Balance. Stir well, then close the lid and turn off the heat. After about a minute, mix again, add salt and pepper to taste, and serve with extra nutritional yeast or vegan Parmesan.

Yield: 6 servings

6 cups veggie stock
1 celery stalk chopped in thirds
1 carrot, chopped in thirds
Handful dried porcini mushrooms
Handful parsley stalks
1 large onion, chopped
4 tablespoons plus 1 tablespoon Earth Balance
2 cups Arborio rice
½ cup dry Italian white wine (e.g., Pinot Grigio; If you don't drink, you can use extra broth.)
½ teaspoon Spanish saffron
4 tablespoons nutritional yeast plus extra for sprinkling
4 tablespoons parsley, chopped
Salt, pepper to taste

Wine Pairing

Valpolicella from Verona, or an unoaked Dolcetto from Alba

POIVRONS FARCIS

$

6 sturdy red bell peppers

3 tablespoons extra-virgin olive oil

⅛ teaspoon salt

2 stalks celery, chopped

1 onion, chopped

1 tablespoon fennel seeds

¼ cup chopped parsley

1 tablespoon herbes de Provençe

16 ounces veggie sausage (breakfast style is particularly good here) or 2 14-ounce cans light-colored beans or chickpeas

2 cups cooked barley

Salt and pepper to taste

These are not your grandma's stuffed peppers—unless, of course, she is vegan and lives in Avignon. Stuffed vegetables are a staple in the south of France. I sampled various vegetables "farcis" in restaurants throughout Nice, Marseille, and Aix en Provence and adored veg-friendly Provencal food so much that I brought home a few cookbooks.

This recipe is a bit time-consuming, but it's worth the effort, especially if you plan on serving these little beauties at a dinner party. Make the grain ahead of time to cut down the prep time. Serve with the Haricots Verts et Tomates on page 128.

1. Preheat oven to 450°F. Grease a high-sided baking dish.
2. Cut the tops off the peppers and discard any seeds. Set tops aside. Place the pepper "shells" in a roasting dish, drizzle with about a teaspoon of olive oil, and bake for 15 minutes, while you prepare the filling. (You need to "pre-soften" them.) When done, set aside.
3. Dice the red portion of the tops. Heat 1 tablespoon olive oil in a large skillet. Sauté the pepper tops, celery, onion, and fennel seeds over medium heat until soft, about 15 minutes. Covering the pan helps, especially toward the end. Add salt. Drizzle in a bit more oil if mixture gets too dry.
4. Mix in parsley and herbes de Provençe. Crumble sausage with your hands and mix this or the beans in, along with the barley. Mix very well, then, using a tablespoon, pack the filling into the peppers, stuffing as much as you can into each one.
5. Drizzle the peppers with the remaining olive oil, cover with foil, and bake for about 30 minutes, or until soft. Salt and pepper to taste.
6. Let cool for about 10 minutes before serving.

Yield: 6 servings

Variations

Substitute cooked millet, couscous, brown rice, or spelt for the barley.
Use green peppers instead of red, or try stuffing other veggies
like onions, mushrooms, tomatoes, zucchini, or pre-softened eggplant.
(Adjust the baking times accordingly.)

NOUVEAU POT AU FEU

This is a classic country French recipe that, over the years, became wildly popular among French city dwellers. Meat-laden versions grace the menus of countless restaurants all across France. I call my version "Nouveau Pot au Feu" because it imparts the traditional complexities of this slow-cooking stew with a new, meatless spin that also happens to be fat-free. Little bits of seitan add some texture, balancing out the tender autumnal vegetables.

When it comes to successful Pot au Feu, there are three secrets: good quality wine, good quality dark vegetable broth, and a long, slow simmer. This recipe is perfect to make when you are snowed in or have an entire day to just putter around the apartment and occasionally stir the pot. To be authentically French, serve with a dollop of mustard, a dish of cornichons (tiny French pickles), and crusty whole-grain bread for mopping up the complex broth.

1. In a large bowl, mix instant vital wheat gluten and 1 cup dark vegetable broth. Knead for 5 minutes. (Using your mixer's kneading blade is absolutely acceptable. I use my KitchenAid mixer.) Let rest for 5 minutes.
2. Meanwhile, pour about 2 tablespoons of wine into a very large pot and whisk in the cornstarch. Add the bouquet garni, all the vegetables, and the peppercorns, and cover with broth and wine. (Be careful not to splash yourself. The wine can stain.)
3. Now, using your hands, knead the seitan dough a few times. Cut into very small chunks (½ inch to 1 inch) and gently drop directly into the broth.
4. Bring to a boil, uncovered, and skim off any foam. Lower heat and simmer for about 3 hours, stirring occasionally. Then partially cover the pot and simmer for 1 more hour. Ideally, you want this to reduce ⅓ of the original liquid and without adding additional broth. Of course, if it looks like it's getting dry, add more broth in ½ cup increments, stirring very well after each addition.
5. On the other hand, if you prefer your vegetables firmer, then by all means, use a slotted spoon to scoop them out when they reach your desired texture, then return them to the pot about 20 minutes before serving.
6. When it's ready, the vegetables should be very soft, and the leeks and onions should be broken up. Season to taste with the salt. Serve mustard and cornichon on the side.

Yield: 8 servings

Seitan

1 cup instant vital wheat gluten

1 cup dark vegetable broth (I use Better Than Bouillon No Beef)

Stew

2 cups dry red wine (e.g., Merlot, Cabernet Sauvignon)

1 tablespoon cornstarch

1 bouquet garni (1 bay leaf, 1 thyme sprig, 6 or 7 parsley sprigs, and 1 celery leaf sprig tied together with cooking string)

1 onion, peeled and studded with 2 whole cloves

1 turnip, peeled and cut into 1-inch chunks

3 leeks, washed well and cut into 2-inch pieces (use white parts only; save the greens for other uses)

3 parsnips, peeled and cut into 2-inch chunks

2 large carrots, peeled and cut into 2-inch chunks

4 small organic potatoes, quartered

1 fennel bulb, cut into wedges

2 cloves garlic, crushed

1 teaspoon black peppercorns

6 cups dark vegetable broth (I use Better Than Bouillon No Beef)

½–1 teaspoon salt (to taste)

Dijon mustard (condiment)

Cornichons (condiment)

PANKO-CRUSTED TOFU WITH TAMARIND-RASPBERRY GLAZE

LF

1 pound extra-firm tofu, drained

Glaze

1 cup apple juice
½ cup water
1 tablespoon tamarind paste
   (available in Indian, Mexican, and
   Asian markets)
2 tablespoons raspberry jam
½ teaspoon cumin
Dash cayenne pepper
Salt to taste
½ teaspoon cornstarch

Panko coating

½ cup panko
½ teaspoon turmeric
Dash cayenne pepper

Other

1 tablespoon olive oil, plus about
   3 tablespoons for pan-frying
3–4 scallions, minced

Tamarind from India. Panko from Japan. Raspberry jam from France. This is fusion cuisine at its best, and I love the fact that, as a city dweller, I can buy all the ingredients, including organic tofu, within a 3-block radius. The glaze is a unique blend of sweet, sour, and earthy, and I like to think of it as one of my signature dishes.

1. Place a few paper towels on a large plate. Place tofu on towels and then top with a few more paper towels. Place another plate on top, and weigh down with two heavy books (dictionaries would do nicely). Let sit for 30 minutes, then flip, replace paper towels, and let sit for 30 more minutes. Cut in half lengthwise, and then cut on the diagonal, forming 4 triangles. Set aside.

2. In a small saucepan, whisk together all glaze ingredients, except for cornstarch. Cook on low until blended, about 5 minutes, then bring to a rolling boil.

3. Lower to a gentle boil and cook until sauce is reduced in half, about 10 to 15 minutes. When sauce has thickened, take about 2 to 3 tablespoons of sauce and place it in a bowl. Stir in the cornstarch to make a slurry, then return to the pot. Stir well, cook another minute or so, and remove from heat. Sauce will thicken slightly. It should be thin, but not watery. If too thin, cook a few more minutes.

4. Mix panko coating ingredients in a shallow bowl. Using a pastry brush, dab oil onto each piece of tofu. Dip each piece in the panko, and using a fork or your fingers, press the panko into the tofu so it's thickly coated.

5. Pour about 1 tablespoon of oil in a large sauté pan and heat to medium. Place breaded tofu triangles on pan, and let cook for about 5 minutes. Resist the urge to peek! Flip tofu, and add about 1 more tablespoon of oil to the pan. Cook 5 more minutes.

6. Divide the glaze between four plates, reserving ¼ cup for topping. Place the tofu triangles in the center of the glaze pools. Top with scallions.

Yield: 4 servings

VIDALIA ONION TART WITH PEAR-PEPPER CHUTNEY

This sweet onion tart and the Pear-Pepper Chutney (see page 194) go together like Minneapolis and St. Paul, like Buda and Pest, like . . . you get the picture. This dish is all about balance. The chutney is hot, sour, and sweet all at once, and adds an interesting layer of contrast to the smooth sweetness of the Vidalia onions, tofu, and buttery crust. This recipe is time-consuming, but is well worth the effort. To save time, make the chutney and crust the day before.

1. Preheat oven to 400°F. Grease a 10- or 11-inch tart pan.
2. Roll out dough and press into tart pan. Set aside.
3. In a food processor, blend together tofu, parsley, nutritional yeast, corn-starch, water, and nutmeg until creamy and smooth, scraping down the sides as needed.
4. In a large pan, heat oil over medium-low. Sauté onion and garlic until translucent, about 15 minutes, sprinkling with salt and freshly ground pepper a few minutes into cooking.
5. Stir in balsamic vinegar and turn heat to high. Cook until onion is slightly brown and no excess liquid remains, about 3 to 5 minutes. (Be careful not to brown onions. Onions should still remain moist.)
6. Pour tofu mixture into the prepared crust. Arrange onions on top and bake on third oven shelf from the top for 30 to 40 minutes, or until crust is golden brown and tofu is firm and no longer wobbly. Cover with foil if you find the tart browning too quickly.
7. Serve topped with Pear-Pepper Chutney.

Yield: 6–8 servings

1 Flaky Pie Crust (see page 160), made with 2 tablespoons nutritional yeast added to the flour
1 14-ounce aseptic box of extra-firm silken tofu (Do not use refrigerated tofu here; it isn't creamy enough.)
3 tablespoons fresh parsley, chopped
3 tablespoons nutritional yeast
2 teaspoons cornstarch
1 tablespoon water or broth
⅛ teaspoon nutmeg
3 tablespoons olive oil
3 medium Vidalia onions sliced (no substitutes)
3 cloves garlic, sliced
Sea salt
Freshly ground pepper
1 tablespoon balsamic vinegar
Pear-Pepper Chutney (see page 194)

Wine Pairing

Pinot Blanc from Alsace will sing right along with the sweet onions and the heat of the chutney.

PARSNIPS
ST. JACQUES

3 large parsnips, peeled and cut into ½-inch rounds (Save any smaller bits for another use. For this dish, pieces should be at least 1-inch in circumference.)

3–6 tablespoons flour

6 tablespoons Earth Balance

2 shallots, minced as finely as you can manage

4 large cloves garlic, minced as finely as you can manage

Sea salt

Freshly ground pepper

1¼ cups dry white wine

6 tablespoons parsley, finely chopped

Paprika

Parsnips as an entrée? Actually, once cooked, these humble, slightly gingery root vegetables are the perfect vehicle for this rich, wine-infused sauce. These buttery rounds are richer and more filling than anyone could imagine. Serve with a baked potato and simple frisee salad, dressed with Dijon Vinaigrette (see page 125).

1. Fill a medium saucepan with water and bring to a boil. Add parsnips and cook for 10 to 15 minutes, depending on size, until soft. Drain. Dredge in flour and set aside.

2. Over medium-low heat, melt Earth Balance in a large sauté pan. Sauté shallots and garlic until soft and clear, about 5 to 7 minutes. Season with salt and freshly ground pepper.

3. Turn heat to high. Add the wine and parsley. Cook for a minute or two on high, bringing mixture to a boil, stirring constantly.

4. Add the parsnips. Turn heat to medium-low. Cook about 5 minutes on each side. Sauce will reduce and will thicken up considerably.

5. Just before serving, sprinkle with salt, paprika, and additional ground pepper, if desired. Top with sauce. (A little goes a long way. This dish is rich.)

Yield: 2 servings as a main, 4 as a side

PORCINI RAVIOLI

Most new vegans think they will never again experience the joys of ravioli. Not so! The creamy porcini mushroom filling in these little gems will make you think you are dining in a hip little trattoria in Trastevere. Serve with John's Marinara Sauce (see page 193), Basil-Cream Sauce (see page 191), or the sauce from Fettucine Alfredo (see page 88). Any leftover porcini filling makes a great sandwich spread.

Ravioli are time-consuming to make, but if you like to cook, they're a fun diversion. You'll need a ravioli tray or cutter, which you can find online and in most kitchen shops.

1. Wrap tofu in several layers of paper towel. Put between two large plates and weigh down with two very large books (think dictionaries!). After 30 minutes, replace paper towels, and flip tofu. Do this a total of four times, letting the tofu press for 2 hours. It needs to be extra dry for the ravioli filling.

2. Bring a medium saucepan full of water to a boil. Add the porcini mushrooms. Let sit for 30 minutes, then drain, reserving the cooking liquid. Save at least a few tablespoons for this recipe. (If you want a really fabulous-tasting pasta, use this liquid when you make the pasta dough.)

3. In a food processor, mix drained mushrooms, tofu, salt, yeast, garlic, lemon juice, herbs, and olive oil until smooth. If mixture seems dry, add porcini liquid, about 1 tablespoon at a time. Finished consistency should resemble that of ricotta cheese.

4. Roll out dough according to your ravioli tray or cutter's instructions. If using a tray, place one sheet of pasta on the tray and fill each square with ⅓ to ½ teaspoon of filling, depending on the size of your tray. Cover with another sheet of pasta and gently use a rolling pin to seal the dough and cut the squares. Separate the pasta following the serrated grid. If using a cutter, lay one sheet of pasta down on a flat surface. Add about ½ teaspoon of filling in even internals, then cover with another sheet of pasta. Center the cutter over the mound created by the filling and push down to cut. Press the edges together lightly with your finger, sealing any open edges gently with a sprinkle of water. Cook in plenty of salted water. Don't overcook! These will float to the top when finished.

Yield: about 40 large ravioli

1 pound extra-firm tofu
1¾ cups dried porcini mushrooms
½ teaspoon salt
3 tablespoons nutritional yeast
3 cloves garlic, peeled and sliced
1½ teaspoons lemon juice
1 tablespoon dried parsley
1 tablespoon dried basil
1 tablespoon extra-virgin olive oil
Fresh Pasta (see page 94)

Wine Pairing

Soave Classico (white) or lighter, unoaked Barbera d'Asti (red). Both wines have the bright acidity needed to balance the creamy porcini filling.

RAVIOLI-MAKING TIPS

- Don't roll the dough out too thinly or the ravioli will break when you cook them.
- Don't overfill the ravioli or they will fall apart. Err on the side of skimping. My tray makes 12 ravioli, and I place about 1 teaspoon of filling into each cavity.
- Make sure no air pockets remain when you seal the two sheets of pasta together.

MARSALA MUSHROOM CREPES

Filling

2 tablespoons extra-virgin olive
oil

2 shallots, chopped finely

3 garlic cloves, minced

1 pound assorted mushrooms,
chopped (e.g., shiitake, oyster,
cremini)

3 tablespoons Marsala

2 tablespoons fresh parsley,
chopped, or 2 teaspoons dried

Salt and freshly ground pepper,
to taste

Crepes

1 cup flour (whole-wheat pastry
flour is fine)

1 cup plain soy milk

½ cup pure water

2 tablespoons soy flour

¼ teaspoon salt

2 tablespoons Earth Balance,
melted

If you want to create an entrée that provides a substantial wow factor for minimal effort, make like a Parisian and throw together these savory crepes. A shot of Marsala infuses the mushrooms and shallots with a distinctive, balancing sweetness.

1. In a large saucepan, heat oil over medium-low heat. Add shallots and garlic and cook gently until soft, about 5 minutes. Take care not to burn. Add mushrooms, then raise heat to medium and cook until soft, about 10 minutes.
2. Turn heat to high. Add Marsala and cook until it evaporates. Stir in parsley, salt, and pepper.
3. Whisk all crepes ingredients together in a medium bowl until smooth and no lumps remain. Batter should be thin—add a bit more soy milk, if necessary.
4. Heat pan over medium-high and spray with cooking oil spray. Pour about 2 tablespoons of batter onto pan and immediately twist the pan in one direction so that a thin layer of batter evenly coats the pan. Cook until bottom is golden. Set aside on a plate while you make the rest of the crepes.
5. Place a healthy tablespoon of filling into the center of each crepe. Fold into quarters and serve.

Yield: 10–12 crepes; allow 2–3 crepes per person as an entrée

Variations

Replace mushrooms with about 1 pound of finely chopped spinach. Omit Marsala. Instead, add 3 to 4 tablespoons vegetable broth, ½ cup toasted pine nuts and ¼ cup oil-soaked sun-dried tomatoes.

Wine Pairing

A light-bodied French red like Beaujolais-Villages is a classic pairing here. If you prefer white, Saint-Veran, a crisp, white Burgundy, would also be delicious.

JERK TEMPEH

This classy-looking, sassy-tasting main dish is especially magical during a steamy summer dinner party, especially when paired with your Damien Marley CDs. This version gives you all the flavors of Kingston, Jamaica, without the pricey airfare. If you want to get all Martha Stewart in your presentation, go ahead and serve it on a banana leaf. Enjoy it with a nice cold lager.

1. Steam the tempeh for 10 minutes, covered, and drain.
2. Process remaining ingredients in the food processor. Marinate tempeh in this mixture for at least 4 hours, or preferably overnight.
3. Grill on a medium-high grill pan for 5 to 10 minutes on each side, occasionally basting with more marinade as needed. Or bake in marinade in a 400°F oven for 15 to 20 minutes, checking every 5 minutes or so. Add water by the tablespoon if marinade cooks off too quickly.
4. Top with minced scallions and serve.

Yield: 4 servings

2 8-ounce packages of tempeh, cut into 8 triangles
3 teaspoons allspice
2 habañero peppers, seeded and minced (use gloves!)
8 scallions, minced, plus a few more for garnish
1 onion, chopped
10 cloves garlic, minced
1 3-inch piece ginger, peeled and chopped
4 tablespoons fresh thyme (or 4 teaspoons dried)
½ teaspoon nutmeg
½ teaspoon cinnamon
½ teaspoon freshly ground black pepper
½ teaspoon cumin
4 tablespoons lime juice
2 tablespoons rum, preferably Jamaican
Zest 1 lime
4 tablespoons olive oil
½ cup vegetable broth

Variation

Use pressed tofu instead of tempeh. (No need to steam it.)

COCONUT-CRUSTED TOFU WITH LEMONGRASS AND PEPPERS

Tofu

1 pound extra-firm tofu
Classic Marinade (see page 184)

Sauce

1½ tablespoons extra-virgin olive
   oil
6-8 scallions, thinly sliced, plus
   extra for garnish
4 cloves garlic, minced
2 red peppers, seeded and thinly
   sliced
½–1 hot pepper of your choice,
   seeded and minced finely (wear
   gloves!)
2 stalks lemongrass, with tough
   outside stalk removed, sliced as
   thinly as you can manage
3 tomatoes, seeded and chopped
½ cup coconut milk
1 tablespoon lime juice
1 teaspoon lime zest
Salt and pepper to taste
½ cup dried coconut flakes (or
   fresh grated coconut, if you're
   really ambitious!)
Lime wedges for garnish
   (optional)

City life has its ups and downs. The perks are great, and then there's the craziness, hustle and bustle, crime, long lines, and traffic jams. When I want to just get away from it all, and a vacation is impossible, I make this stress-free, island-inspired recipe.

This entrée is a snap to prepare, but the exotic flavors may fool your guests into thinking you spent all day in the kitchen. Marinate the tofu the night before if you can; it makes dinner-day prep even easier.

1. Press tofu for several hours. Cut into 8 triangles. Let it sit in marinade for at least 8 hours or overnight, turning occasionally.
2. Preheat oven to 400°F.
3. In a medium pan, heat oil over medium heat. Sauté scallions (reserving extra for garnish), garlic, peppers, and lemongrass until soft, about 5 to 7 minutes. Add tomatoes and coconut milk and bring to a boil. Lower the heat to a hearty simmer (medium-low) and cook until the sauce is reduced by half. Stir in the lime juice and zest. Adjust seasonings. Transfer to a blender or use an immersion blender to puree.
4. Pour coconut into a shallow dish. Dip each piece of tofu in the coconut, and using a fork or your fingers, press the coconut into the tofu so it's thickly coated. Place on a well-oiled cookie sheet and bake 15 to 20 minutes, checking every 5 minutes or so. Flip about halfway through. Serve immediately topped with sauce, sliced scallions, and a wedge or two of lime.

Yield: 4 servings

Variations
Use seitan steaks or steamed tempeh instead of tofu.

Wine Pairing
Riesling from Alsace or Germany, or a late-harvest version
from upstate New York

SEITAN STEAKS WITH TARRAGON-MUSTARD SAUCE

Most of us loved licorice as kids, but there's something so urbane and grown-up about the subtle anise flavor that tarragon imparts. This easy entrée will impress even the pickiest of dinner party guests. Get fresh tarragon if you can; it makes all the difference. This tastes wonderful paired with a comforting mound of mashed potatoes.

1. Preheat oven to 425°F.
2. Mix all ingredients except olive oil and seitan in a blender or food processor.
3. Brush bottom of a medium cookie sheet with olive oil. Place seitan steaks on sheet and season them with salt and pepper. Spoon sauce on top of each of the steaks and bake for about 7 to 8 minutes. (Don't spoon too much on! A few tablespoons ought to do it.)
4. Remove from oven, flip steaks, and spoon more sauce over the other side. Bake for an additional 7 to 8 minutes. Serve warm.

Yield: 4 servings

½ cup Vegenaise
5 tablespoons Dijon or brown mustard (make your own—see page 197)
6 tablespoons chopped fresh tarragon
4 garlic cloves, crushed
Juice ½ organic lemon
Zest 1 organic lemon
½ teaspoon salt
Pepper to taste
2 tablespoons agave nectar
1 tablespoon olive oil
Seitan (see page 104)

Wine Pairing

Chinon or Bourgeuil. These Cabernet Franc-based wines are terrific with garlicky bistro dishes.

PUMPKIN RISOTTO WITH SAGE AND SUN-DRIED TOMATOES

8 cups veggie stock

1 celery stalk

1 carrot

1 large onion, chopped

4 tablespoons plus 1 tablespoon Earth Balance

1½–2 cups pumpkin (either unsweetened canned or fresh, cubed and precooked)

⅓ cup oil-packed, sun-dried tomatoes, chopped

2 cups Arborio rice

1 cup dry Italian red wine

1 tablespoon dried rubbed sage (or about 36 fresh leaves, chopped)

3 tablespoons fresh parsley, chopped

5 tablespoons nutritional yeast

Salt and freshly ground pepper, to taste

Wine Pairing
Ribolla Gialla ("Zlata Rebula") from just over the northeastern Italian border in Slovenia.

In Rio de Janeiro, I visited Rochinha, one of the biggest favelas, or shanty-towns, that encrusts Rio's cliff like barnacles on a pier. Since they are the epicenter of the city's drug trafficking operations and crime, favela residents, by default, have gotten a bad reputation. This is unfortunate, because 99 percent of favela residents are not criminals; they are just poor. Most are hard-working people just trying to feed their families and realize their dreams. Sadly, most Cariocas (residents of Rio) have never crossed the invisible border to see how their less fortunate neighbors live. (For more information, visit www.favelatour.com.br.)

Like the favelas, this risotto isn't pretty. Owing to the combination of pumpkin, red wine, and sun-dried tomatoes, its color could be diplomatically described as "muddy." But sit down, pour yourself a glass of wine, and spend some time getting to know this comforting autumnal rice dish. Bite by bite, you'll uncover its playfulness and robust personality layer by layer—the sweetness of the dried tomatoes and pumpkin contrasting with the headiness of the sage, tied together with the subtle aromas of the wine.

What's the moral of the recipe? Peek behind the curtain. Try things you don't normally try. Talk to people you don't normally talk to. Go places you don't normally go. You might be pleasantly surprised.

1. Prepare your stock. Toss in the celery and carrot and heat to a simmer. Have a ladle ready.
2. Sauté the onion in 4 tablespoons of the Earth Balance. Add salt as needed, to slow down the cooking time.
3. When the onions are soft, toss in the pumpkin and tomatoes. Cook for 1 minute, then add the rice, stir to coat, and cook for 1 more minute. Turn the heat up to medium-high and pour in the wine and sage. Let it cook until the rice absorbs the wine.
4. Turn heat to medium-low (About 2.5 to 3 on your burner). Add broth, one ladle at a time. Allow rice to absorb broth. When it's at the point where it's almost sticking to the pan, add one more ladle of broth and then repeat until rice is al dente, about 40 minutes.
5. Add the parsley, yeast, and remaining 1 tablespoon of Earth Balance. Stir well, then close the lid and turn off the heat. After about a minute, mix again, add salt and pepper to taste. Serve with extra nutritional yeast or vegan Parmesan and a glass of the wine you used for cooking.

Yield: 6 servings

STAINED-GLASS SALAD

I've been lucky enough to have visited awe-inspiring stained-glass windows in cathedrals all throughout Europe. Of them, I would have to say that those in the cathedral in the French city of Chartres are the most spectacular and inspired. Those magnificent windows serve as the inspiration for this elegant, filling side salad. Its kaleidoscopic shards of color contrast randomly against the slivers of black wild rice—like deconstructed panes of stained glass. I hope that you find making it and eating it a spiritually moving experience.

1. Cook rice according to the package directions, except cook it in broth instead of water.
2. In a small bowl, whisk together all dressing ingredients. Make dressing while rice is cooking and let it sit so that flavors will meld.
3. In a large bowl, gently toss the rice with dressing and all remaining ingredients.
4. Serve at room temperature or chilled.

Yield: 8 servings

Variations

Replace grapefruit with organic orange (reduce agave nectar to 2 tablespoons); add a diced mango. Add a drained, rinsed 14-ounce can of beans in a contrasting color (e.g., pink or white beans).

Salad

1 cup dry wild rice, rinsed

3 cups vegetable broth

½ red onion, finely minced

1 stalk celery, diced

1 grapefruit, membranes and seeds removed, cut into ½-inch pieces

1 red pepper, diced

1 avocado, diced

3 tablespoons fresh parsley, chopped

2 tablespoons fresh cilantro, chopped

Salt and pepper, to taste

Dressing

4 tablespoons extra-virgin olive oil

3 tablespoons agave nectar

1 tablespoon soy sauce

2 garlic cloves, minced very finely

½ teaspoon fresh rosemary, chopped very finely

LEMON-SCENTED CARROTS WITH CAPERS AND CORIANDER

4–5 medium carrots, peeled and
    sliced about ⅛ inch thick
1 tablespoon extra-virgin olive oil
1½ tablespoons lemon juice
1 teaspoon ground coriander
1 teaspoon dried parsley
2 tablespoons capers, rinsed and
    chopped
¼ teaspoon cumin
½ teaspoon salt or more, to taste
Dash cinnamon

Because of their versatility and sweet crunchiness, the humble carrot is one of my favorite vegetables. Carrots always satisfy me, whether I snack on them or dress them up for a fancy dinner party side dish. In this dish, carrots are gussied up with exotic spices for a fabulous soirée. The sunny flavors might fool you into thinking you are supping in the Casbah in Tangiers.

1. Fill a medium saucepan with water and bring to a boil. Add carrots and cook until soft, about 10 minutes. Drain.
2. Add the remaining ingredients and mix well. Serve warm or at room temperature.

Yield: 4–6 servings as a side

Variation

For a raw salad, slice the carrots very thinly with a mandoline.

RESTAURANT SURVIVAL TIP

Most restaurants offer at least one vegan or vegan-possible item on their menu. It's always best to call in advance, tell them you're vegan, and explain what you will and will not eat. But this is not always possible. I've looked over many menus featuring meaty entrees with wonderful sides of veggies. I've simply asked them to "hold the steak" (and milk, butter, and cheese). It's a great ice-breaker and usually results in fabulous vegan fare.

LENTILS WITH RADICCHIO AND ONIONS

Sometimes city life is bittersweet. Yes, there are myriad advantages, like access to cultural events, nightlife, and a variety of vegan chow. Then there are the drawbacks: long lines, smaller living spaces, omnipresent traffic jams, and higher prices. But it all evens out somehow.

You could say these lentils are also somewhat bittersweet. They get a dose of bitterness from the radicchio, which is tempered by the sweetness of the onions and sweet-starchiness of the lentils.

2 cups vegetable stock
I bay leaf
I teaspoon dried thyme
I cup lentils, rinsed
I½ tablespoons olive oil
I medium Vidalia onion, diced
I clove garlic, sliced
¼ teaspoon salt
Freshly ground pepper
I large head radicchio, shredded or finely sliced
I½ tablespoons ume plum vinegar (available in most Asian groceries or in the Asian aisle at major supermarkets)
I tablespoon agave nectar

1. In a medium saucepan, bring stock to a boil. Toss in the bay leaf, thyme, and lentils, then cover and simmer for 40 minutes, until most of the liquid is absorbed. Drain well.
2. Heat oil over medium-low heat in a large sauté pan. Add the onions and garlic and sprinkle with the salt and freshly ground pepper. Sauté until translucent, about 10 minutes.
3. Add the radicchio. Let it wilt a bit and then stir into the onion mixture. Cook for an additional 20 minutes, stirring occasionally (tongs are helpful here). The radicchio will lose its trademark purple color and will "tan" to mushroom brown. The onions will also take on the brownish hue. This is normal. Remove from heat.
4. In a small bowl, whisk together the vinegar and agave nectar, then pour over the radicchio/onion mixture, tossing to combine. (The purple tint should now magically return!) Pour the lentils into a large serving bowl and then gently stir in the radicchio/onion mixture.
5. Serve warm, room temperature, or chilled.

Yield: 6–8 servings

SUNCHOKE SALAD

1 pound sunchokes, sliced about ⅛ inch thick (no need to peel)

3 tablespoons black oil-cured olives, chopped

1½ tablespoons extra-virgin olive oil

1 tablespoon fresh-squeezed lemon juice

½ teaspoon lemon zest (from an organic lemon)

½ cup roasted red peppers, chopped

½ teaspoon salt, or more, to taste

Freshly ground black pepper, to taste

It's a fact: Jerusalem is a world-class city, swarming with beautiful people, breathtaking historic and religious sites, and tons of great vegan food. But let's get one thing straight: The Jerusalem artichoke, aka sunchoke, does not come from Jerusalem. And although it may taste like an artichoke, it's actually a distant cousin of the sunflower. Go figure.

Whatever you call it, this tasty little tuber packs a significant flavor wallop for very little effort. Try it in this easy, elegant Mediterranean salad.

1. Fill a medium saucepan with water and bring to a boil. Boil sunchokes for about 10 minutes, or until soft. Drain.
2. In a large bowl, mix sunchokes with remaining ingredients. Allow to sit for at least 1 hour to let the flavors meld. Serve at room temperature.

Yield: 6 servings as a side

POMMES ANNA

If this recipe is made from just two ingredients, then why does it qualify as "haute cuisine"? Architecture, baby! This gorgeous little cake looks like the ornate trim you would find on the woodwork in the Louvre. Except in this case, it's built with concentric rings of potatoes, held together by an Earth Balance "mortar." Removing the cake from the pan is a bit unnerving; you might need to lie down for a few minutes after doing so. But the elegant end result is well worth any momentary stress. Just follow the directions exactly, and flip the dish quickly and confidently.

1 or 2 tablespoons plus 6 tablespoons Earth Balance, melted

About 2 pounds organic potatoes, peeled and sliced as thinly as possible (no thicker than ⅛ inch; using a mandoline makes this much easier)

Salt and pepper, to taste

About 2 teaspoons your favorite herbs (oregano, herbes de Provence, basil, etc.)

1. Preheat the oven to 450°F. Grease the bottoms and sides of an 8- or 9-inch cake pan or cast-iron skillet with 1 or 2 tablespoons of the Earth Balance.
2. Place the potatoes in the pan in concentric circles, in a snail-like pattern, making sure each piece overlaps the next by ¼ inch or so. After each layer, drizzle with about 1 tablespoon of the Earth Balance and season with salt, pepper, and any herbs you like.
3. Continue this pattern until you use up all the potatoes. Finish with one more drizzle of Earth Balance, then place a piece of oiled aluminum foil over the top. Weigh the cake down with a cast-iron skillet or other heavy skillet; the heavier, the better. Place the cake dish on a medium burner and cook for about 5 minutes. Then place in the heated oven and bake for about 25 to 30 minutes, or until potatoes are soft and top is golden and slightly crispy.
4. To remove, when the pan is cool enough to handle, remove the weighted pan. Slide a knife all around the edges of the pan. Place a larger dish over the top and quickly flip the pan. Tap the bottom and gently unmold.
5. Serve warm.

Yield: 6 servings as a side

Variations

Use sweet potatoes, yams, or sunchokes (Jerusalem artichokes)
instead of potatoes.

GREEN BEAN, MUSHROOM, AND TARRAGON SALAD

½ pound green beans, stems removed, and cut in two

1 tablespoon olive oil

2 cloves garlic, sliced

6 ounces cremini or shiitake mushrooms, thinly sliced

½ cup plain soy yogurt

1 tablespoon lemon juice

Zest of 1 organic lemon

1 teaspoon fresh minced tarragon

1–2 teaspoons mustard, preferably Dijon

Salt and pepper, to taste

In haute cuisine and haute couture, simplicity is a consistent key to success. Here, green beans and mushrooms are paired with a creamy, tarragon-infused dressing. Simple? Yes. Elegant? *Bien sûr!*

1. Cook beans in a large pot of salted water until tender-crisp, about 5 minutes. Drain and rinse with cold water to stop cooking. Drain again and cool.
2. In a small sauté pan, heat oil over medium heat. Cook garlic until it softens, about 3 minutes, then add the mushrooms and cook until soft. Set aside and let cool.
3. Whisk together yogurt, lemon juice, zest, tarragon, and mustard. Gently toss with beans and mushrooms. Season with salt and pepper to taste.

Yield: 4 servings as a side

JUST DESSERTS

Living in a city is both a blessing and a curse for vegan dessert lovers. The good news is that a proliferation of vegan sweets and treats are available. The better news is that you can make vegan treats yourself whenever your sweet tooth makes itself known.

FLAKY PIE CRUST

½ cup whole-wheat pastry flour
¾ cup unbleached white flour
Scant ¼ teaspoon salt
¼ cup nonhydrogenated
  shortening
¼ cup Earth Balance
2–4 tablespoons ice water

Perfectionists, consider yourselves warned. The secret to a flaky pie crust is simply to resist the urge to overmix. By leaving your crust dough a bit on the primitive side, you are actually creating little air pockets that will make a delectable base for your pies.

1. Mix dry ingredients.
2. Cut in shortening and Earth Balance. Don't overmix!
3. Add enough water to make dough stick together when you squeeze it, then let the dough chill in the fridge for 30 minutes.
4. Roll into one disk on a lightly floured surface.

Yield: I crust for a 9-inch pie

PUNKA' PIE

Crust
I Flaky Pie Crust (see above)

Filling
I 14–16-ounce can unsweetened
  pumpkin
2 12.3-ounce boxes firm Mori
  Nu tofu (Don't use refrigerated
  tofu! It will be too grainy)
¾ cup sugar
⅛ teaspoon salt
I½ teaspoons cinnamon
I teaspoon ginger
¼ teaspoon cloves
¼ teaspoon nutmeg
I tablespoon egg replacer or I
  tablespoon soy flour, plus
  4 tablespoons water

Fool all your friends and tell them you've given up veganism because you missed cream too much. Then feed them this pie, and spill the beans, or rather, the tofu.

This pie is creamy and pumpkiny. It's autumn in a pie.

1. Preheat the oven to 425°F degrees.
2. Roll out dough and place into greased pie pan. Flute edges as desired.
3. Mix filling ingredients in a food processor until creamy.
4. Pour in the batter, leaving ¼ inch of headspace between filling and crust edge. Bake for 15 minutes, then lower heat to 350°F and bake for 35 minutes. Top will be golden and perhaps just ever-so-slightly cracked when done.
5. Refrigerate pie for several hours before slicing.
6. If you have leftover pie filling, bake it in a greased dish for 30 minutes at 350°F, and voilà—punka' pudding!

Yield: 8 servings

URBAN
APPLE PIE

When the weather turns cold in autumn, making an apple pie is right up there with pulling out your boots and sweaters and getting your Halloween costume together. This one's easy. Really.

1. Preheat oven to 450°F.
2. Combine filling ingredients and spoon into prepared crust. Top with the second crust and crimp edges as desired. Sprinkle with sugar.
3. Put the pie on a cookie sheet (to avoid nasty cleanup later) and bake for 15 minutes. Turn down heat to 350°F and bake for 45 more minutes until the top is golden. If crust seems to brown too quickly, cover the pie with aluminum foil.
4. Allow to cool completely before slicing.

Yield: 8 servings

Crust

Double the Flaky Pie Crust recipe (see page 160), divided and roll into two disks

Filling

5 large organic Granny Smith apples, peeled and chopped

2 tablespoons flour

1 cup sugar

¼ teaspoon nutmeg

½ teaspoon cinnamon

¼ teaspoon salt

1 tablespoon vanilla

⅔ cup soy half and half (or vanilla soy milk)

Demerara sugar, to sprinkle on top (optional)

CRANBERRY UPSIDE-DOWN CAKE

½ cup Earth Balance, softened, divided in 2

¾ cup vegan brown sugar

1 12-ounce bag cranberries

1½ cups flour (I use half whole-wheat pastry flour, half white spelt)

1 cup vegan sugar

1 tablespoon baking powder

1 tablespoon soy flour

1 cup soy milk

1 teaspoon vanilla

¼ teaspoon lemon oil or 1 tablespoon organic lemon zest, chopped very fine

During a recent October, the Northeastern autumn was unseasonably warm. On several days, temperatures reached 80 degrees and I wore sandals to work. People gleefully ate their dinners al fresco at sidewalk tables across the city. It felt, at the same time, wonderful—yet a bit wrong.

But even unseasonably warm weather could not stop me from craving seasonal delights like cranberries. Cranberry Upside-Down Cake to the rescue. A shot of lemon oil tempers the cranberries' tartness—my homage to summer's magnificent swan song.

1. Preheat oven to 350°F. Grease a 9-inch round cake pan.
2. In a small saucepan over medium heat, melt together ¼ cup of the Earth Balance and all the brown sugar. Pour into oiled cake pan and arrange cranberries evenly on top.
3. In a large bowl, mix flour, granulated sugar, baking powder, and soy flour. In a medium bowl, mix milk, vanilla, lemon oil or zest, and remaining ¼ cup Earth Balance). Using a mixer, blend the wet ingredients into the dry ingredients and mix well.
4. Spoon the cake batter over the cranberry mixture and bake for about 45 minutes or until knife inserted in center comes out clean. Remove cake and run a knife along the circumference of the pan to separate the cake from the pan's edge.
5. Allow cake to cool for at least 15 minutes—ideally 30 minutes. Place plate on top of cake and quickly invert and remove pan.

Yield: 8 servings

CHOCOLATE-SWIRL CHEESECAKE

This is my go-to, New York-style, "I'm going to impress an omnivore" dessert. No one can believe it's vegan. Including me.

1. Preheat oven to 325°F.
2. In food processor, mix crust ingredients. Press into lightly oiled 9-inch springform pan.
3. Mix cake ingredients in food processor until very smooth (don't be afraid of overmixing), then pour on top of crust in pan.
4. Melt chocolate in microwave at 50 percent (about 3 minutes). Gently swirl this into the cheesecake mixture with a knife.
5. Bake for 75 minutes. Cool completely, then refrigerate overnight. Slide a knife around the cake before removing the springform from the pan base.

Yield: 8 large or 10 reasonable servings

Crust

1½ cups vegan chocolate wafer cookies (or vanilla)
4 tablespoons vegan sugar
4 tablespoons Earth Balance

Cake

2 8-ounce containers soy cream cheese (nonhydrogenated variety)
2 12-ounce aseptic packages silken firm tofu
1 teaspoon vanilla
1 tablespoon vanilla pudding mix (optional)
¼ cup white flour
1 cup vegan sugar

Swirl

½ cup best quality dark chocolate (buttons are easiest to melt)

HAVE A SWEET TOOTH? WHITE SUGAR ALTERNATIVES

- **Agave nectar:** Agave nectar comes from the agave plant, the same plant used to make tequila. It's a wonderful substitute for honey or to use in coffee, tea, or other drinks. Besides having no aftertaste, it also has a low glycemic index, so you won't feel the intense lows that you'd get from sugar.
- **Maple syrup:** Especially lovely in baked goods.
- **Brown rice syrup:** Since it's not quite as sweet as sugar or other sweeteners, I consider this an acquired taste. It's less refined than many other sweeteners and works especially well in baking.

LF

1 pound extra-firm tofu
2 tablespoons confectioners'
    sugar
1 tablespoon canola oil
Pinch salt
1 10–16-ounce jar of any jam

SWEET FRENCH TERRINE

Mais oui. You can impress your friends with this creamy terrine. Serve with fruit for breakfast or dessert. (This dish might remind you of a popular Italian dessert—ricotta cheese with jam.)

1. Wrap tofu in clean tea towels or paper towels. Place on a dish, cover with another dish, and then press between two large books, such as dictionaries. Let sit for 30 minutes. Replace towels and let sit for another 30 minutes. With paper towels still swaddling tofu, gently squeeze out as much water as possible. Please don't skimp on these steps—they are crucial to the success of the recipe.
2. Meanwhile, spray a mini loaf pan (or other suitable rectangular mold) with cooking spray. Line with plastic wrap, making sure there is some overhang. Smooth out any wrinkles and spray with cooking oil. Set aside.
3. After the tofu has been sufficiently pressed, use your hands to break it into cottage cheese–size crumbles. Work in confectioners' sugar, oil, and salt.
4. Using your knuckles, mash this mixture until it is absolutely smooth and creamy. Using a spatula, spoon a layer into the prepared pan and tamp it down well to ensure that it's firm and even. It should be about ½ inch thick. Follow with a layer of jam. This layer should be about ⅛ inch thick, give or take. Follow with a layer of tofu. Continue in this manner, lasagna-style, ending with a tofu layer. You can use just one filling or several different ones—it's up to you.
5. Cover terrine with plastic-wrap overhang. Refrigerate for at least 4 hours or preferably overnight. Slice with a very sharp knife.

Yield: 6–8 servings

Variations

You can also substitute fresh fruit, very thinly sliced, for all or part of the jam. Add citrus zest, spices, or essences to the tofu base. If you want a richer—and more expensive—terrine, use store-bought vegan cream cheese. Tofu is just the beginning—many French terrines are made with agar-based concoctions, bread whites, etc. Explore!

EASY PASSION FRUIT MOUSSE

I first became a die-hard passion fruit addict in Rio de Janeiro, after sampling passion fruit *sucos* (smoothies) at many of the city's many famous corner juice bars. I then bought fresh passion fruit pulp for pennies at practically every farmer's market and grocery store I visited. I was in heaven!

Unfortunately, whole passion fruits are not indigenous to the United States, which means they are very expensive. Luckily, the frozen pulp is affordable. If you're a passion fruit fan like me or are simply craving a light dessert, try this simple recipe. It's puckery, yet sweet. We enjoy this mousse for breakfast, or as a refreshing palate cleanser after a spicy Indian or Caribbean meal.

14 ounces passion fruit pulp (I use Goya brand)
¾ cup vegan sugar
1 tablespoon agar-agar flakes
1 12-ounce aseptic box of silken firm tofu (do not use refrigerated tofu—it will create a grainy mousse)
Strawberries or raspberries and/or soy whipped topping for garnish

1. Pour fruit pulp and sugar into a saucepan. Sprinkle in agar-agar, mix, and let sit for 10 minutes. Meanwhile, open the box of tofu and pour it into the food processor.
2. Slowly bring the fruit-agar mixture to a boil, stirring every now and again. Boil gently for about 1 minute, then remove it from the heat and let it sit for another minute.
3. Carefully pour the hot mixture into the food processor with the tofu. Blend well, being careful of the hot liquid!, until the mixture is absolutely smooth, scraping down the sides as needed. This takes about 3 to 5 minutes. Pour into dishes or glasses and chill until firm and cool, about an hour. Garnish and serve.

Yield: 6–8 small servings

RED JUMBLE CRUMBLE

Fruit Bottom

5 medium stalks rhubarb, chopped into ½-inch pieces

1 cup organic strawberries, fresh or frozen, chopped in half

1 cup cranberries, fresh or frozen

Zest 1 organic lemon

Juice ½ organic lemon

2 tablespoons flour

2 tablespoons cornstarch

½ teaspoon baking soda

¾ cup sugar

Crumble

1 cup instant oats

½ cup flour (whole wheat or spelt)

½ cup maple syrup

½ cup chopped pecans

¼ cup canola oil

2 tablespoons uncooked amaranth

1 teaspoon cinnamon

Pinch each cloves and allspice

When I spot the first blushing stalks of rhubarb, pertly lined up for sale at my neighborhood produce market, I can giddily exhale, knowing I survived another dismal Northeastern winter. For me, it's a sure sign that my favorite season, spring—and its spirit of rebirth and renewal—has firmly taken hold.

Tart rhubarb practically begs you to make it into a crisp or crumble. Problem is that, this time of year, a jumble of different fruits, both fresh and frozen, are simultaneously competing for my attention. This ruby red phytochemical-laden crumble is the perfect seasonal transition. The lemon zest brightens the flavor. Amaranth diversifies the topping's crunch level. Serve this crumble warm, with a scoop of vanilla soy ice cream. Or you can enjoy it as I do, straight out of the baking dish.

1. Preheat oven to 425°F.
2. In a medium ovenproof 8 x 8-inch square or 10-inch round baking dish, combine all fruit bottom ingredients until well mixed.
3. In a large bowl, mix all crumble ingredients until well combined. If mixture seems wet, add additional flour a tablespoon at a time.
4. Using your fingers or a spoon, crumble topping evenly over the fruit. Bake uncovered for 25 minutes, and then cover with foil or a lid and bake an additional 10 to 15 minutes, or until rhubarb is soft.

Yield: 6 restrained or 4 indulgent servings

SUPER-SONIC SUNFLOWER SQUARES

City dwellers need lots of energy to navigate crowds, traffic, and all the little surprises that urban life throws your way. Boost your energy by eating these semi-healthy cookies, instead of a sugary alternative.

1. Heat oven to 375°F. Spray a 9 x 9-inch pan with cooking spray.
2. Mix the first six ingredients together in a medium bowl. Make sure everything is well combined. Use a spatula sprayed with cooking spray to spread this mixture into the pan, then bake for 15 to 18 minutes, or until the top is just beginning to turn golden.
3. Remove from oven and sprinkle the cookie crust with chocolate buttons. Cover this pan with a cookie sheet and let it sit 5 minutes to melt the chocolate. Remove pan and then spread the melted chocolate evenly over the cookies. Cool in the refrigerator, then cut into 16 squares.

Yield: 16 cookies

5 tablespoons maple syrup
1 tablespoon agave nectar
5 tablespoons tahini
¾ cup instant oats
¼ cup sunflower seeds
¼ cup unsweetened coconut flakes
½ cup best-quality dark chocolate buttons

VEGAN CUT-OUT COOKIES

Over the years, I've amassed quite a collection of cookie cutters. I especially like to make these cookies for specific holidays, like Christmas and Easter, using appropriate, or better yet, inappropriate shapes. But the best thing to do is to make a bunch of these—vividly decorated and brightly colored—to finish off a formal dinner party. You'll feel like a kid again.

Cookies

⅔ cup Earth Balance

¾ cup sugar

1 teaspoon baking powder

¼ teaspoon salt

2 tablespoons vanilla soy milk

1 teaspoon vanilla

1 cup white flour

1 cup whole-wheat flour

1 heaping tablespoon soy flour

Icing (optional, recipe follows)

Decorations (optional)

Natural food coloring (optional)

1. Preheat oven to 375°F.
2. With an electric mixer, cream Earth Balance, sugar, baking powder, and salt. Add liquid ingredients, and then flours, a bit at a time. Start mixing by hand when necessary. Cover and chill dough for about an hour until it's easy to handle. Divide the dough.
3. Roll half on a lightly floured surface to about ⅛ inch thick, then using cookie cutters, cut out shapes.
4. Place 1 inch apart on a greased cookie sheet and bake for about 7 to 8 minutes. Let cool on a wire rack completely before decorating.

Yield: 3 dozen cookies

Icing

2 cups vegan confectioners' sugar

2 tablespoons soy milk

1 teaspoon vanilla extract
(or almond, but use only ¼ teaspoon)

Icing

1. Mix sugar and soy milk until it is creamy enough to spread. Add more milk if needed, 1 teaspoon at a time. Stir in vanilla extract.
2. Divide the frosting and color it with food coloring, preferably all natural. Adorn wet icing with sprinkles, candy, nonpareils, and colored sugars. Your imagination is the only limit. Let cookies dry completely before storing.

ORANGE-SCENTED CRANBERRY-ALMOND BISCOTTI

I created these cookies in preparation for Thanksgiving—a holiday when even ascetics have been known to overindulge in rich foods. One or two of these cookies, dipped in Grand Marnier, sufficiently cleanse the palate after a heavy holiday meal—and they won't leave you reaching for the bicarbonate. Dipped in tea, they also make a light-but-inspired Black Friday breakfast.

If you're a lemon fan, substitute lemon oil, zest, or extract for the orange oil.

¼ cup Earth Balance
¾ cup vegan sugar
¼ cup nonhydrogenated shortening
1 teaspoon vanilla extract
1 teaspoon almond extract
¼ teaspoon orange oil
3 heaping tablespoons soy flour
2 teaspoons baking powder
½–¾ teaspoon salt
1½ cups whole-wheat pastry flour
1½ cups white spelt flour
Up to ¼ cup water
1 cup dried cranberries
½ cup slivered almonds (optional)

1. Preheat the oven to 375°F, and line a large cookie sheet or two with parchment.
2. In a large bowl, cream together the Earth Balance, sugar, shortening, extracts, and orange oil. Blend until smooth. Add the dry ingredients, about a half-cup at a time, and blend until the dough sticks together and is easy to handle. (If dough is too dry, add water, 1 tablespoon at a time.) Finally, mix in cranberries and almonds, if using.
3. Divide the dough into 3 even balls and place on cookie sheet(s). Using your fingers, form balls into rectangles. Flatten dough until it's about ¾ to 1 inch thick, and tuck in the edges to smooth.
4. Bake for 20 minutes or until golden brown. Remove and let sit at room temperate for about 30 minutes. Turn the oven down to 325°F.
5. When cookies are cool, use a bread knife to carefully slice the "logs" into biscotti; they should be between ½ and ¾ inch thick. (Aside: the cookies are rather crumbly at this point, and you will inevitably have to sacrifice one or two to the Biscotti Gods.) Turn them on their sides and let them "tan" in the oven for about 25 minutes. Remove from the oven, flip, and let the other side "tan" for about 25 minutes.
6. Remove. Cool completely before serving. I recommend making these a day or two ahead, so they can sufficiently dry out.

Yield: about 3 dozen cookies

CHOCO-COCO-OAT BARS

With the exorbitant price of seeing a movie these days, and the lack of vegan candies available at the theater, I usually make a few of these to bring along to the show and share. The texture of these bars reminds me of a candy bar—but yet they're healthy—not exactly fat-free, mind you, but fairly healthy nevertheless.

Bottom

1½ cups oatmeal
5 tablespoons coconut oil
¼ cup agave nectar

Top

1 cup dark chocolate buttons
(you can use chips, but buttons
give you better chocolate
coverage)
½ cup walnuts
1 cup dried coconut
¼ cup maple syrup
1 teaspoon vanilla, maple, or
coconut extract
Optional additions: 2 tablespoons
dried raisins, cranberries,
cherries, or cacao nibs

1. Preheat oven to 350°F. Mix bottom ingredients and press into oiled 9 x 9-inch pan.
2. Mix top ingredients and spread atop crust.
3. Bake for about 20 minutes or until golden. Let cool and then cut into squares.

Yield: 9 large or 18 mini bars

SOGNI D'ORO ("SWEET DREAMS")

City life can be overstimulating. There's so much to do, so many interesting people to talk to, and so much to see, that sometimes, winding down before bed can be hard. One or two of these cookies with a glass of ice-cold rice milk make the perfect pre-bed snack. I call them "Sogni D'Oro," or "sweet dreams" in Italian. The phrase literally translates out to "golden" dreams—the exact color of these rich, slightly chewy cookies.

½ cup Earth Balance
1 cup vegan brown sugar
4 tablespoons soy milk
1 teaspoon vanilla extract
1 teaspoon rum extract (you may
substitute vanilla)
2 cups flour (I use half spelt and
half whole-wheat pastry flour)
2 teaspoons baking powder
½ teaspoon baking soda
1 tablespoon soy flour
1 teaspoon cinnamon
¼ teaspoon salt
1 10-ounce bag vegan white
chocolate chips

1. Preheat oven to 375°F. Cream together Earth Balance, brown sugar, soy milk, and extracts.
2. In a large bowl, mix dry ingredients except for chips. Gradually add dry ingredients (except chips) to the cream mixture, blending well. Scrape down the sides of the bowl with a spatula as needed. Fold in the chips. Drop by tablespoon onto a greased cookie sheet and flatten slightly with a spatula. Space well apart.
3. Bake for about 8 to 10 minutes or until golden. Cool on a wire rack.

Yield: 28–32 cookies

STICKY TOFFEE PUDDING CAKE WITH CARAMEL SAUCE

I first tasted sticky toffee pudding years ago in a crowded restaurant in Covent Garden in London during my pre-vegan days. Unctuous, creamy, and the mother of all sugar highs (and then lows), I was not able to get it out of my head until I created this dessert.

Both kids and adults will dive right into its gooey decadence. The dates, turbinado sugar, and caramel sauce infuse the moist cake with an extravagant, musty sweetness. Although it's rich enough as is, you can boost the hedonism quotient by topping it with a scoop of soy vanilla or dulce de leche ice cream, or a dollop of whipped soy or coconut cream.

1. Heat oven to 375°F. Grease a 9 x 9-inch ovenproof dish or baking pan.
2. To make cake, mix all wet ingredients in a small bowl. Mix all dry ingredients, except dates, in a large bowl. Mix wet and dry ingredients until just combined and moistened. Fold in dates.
3. Pour warm water into an ovenproof vessel and place on the top rack of the heated oven. (This will help keep the cake moist as it bakes.) Pour batter into greased pan and bake, on middle rack, for 40 minutes, or until top is golden brown and springs back when you touch it.

Important! For your safety, remove the cake but allow water to cool completely in oven before removing the water pan.

4. Let cake cool on a rack about 10 minutes.
5. To make caramel sauce, dissolve kudzu root or cornstarch in soy milk. Pour milk mixture and remaining ingredients in a medium saucepan and slowly heat to boiling, whisking constantly, watching it carefully. When mixture comes to a full, rolling boil, turn heat down to medium and boil gently, whisking continually (every minute or so) for about 8 minutes.
6. Remove from heat and set aside to cool for about 15 minutes.
7. Poke top of cake with tines of a fork. Pour sauce over cake, coating evenly. Cut and serve as is, warm or room temperature.

Yield: 9 belly-busting servings (or 18 reasonable servings)

Cake

1 cup plain soy milk
1 teaspoon vanilla
1 tablespoon rum
2 tablespoons Earth Balance, melted
½ cup whole-wheat pastry flour
½ cup unbleached white flour
2 teaspoons baking powder
2 heaping tablespoons soy flour
¾ cup turbinado sugar
Healthy pinch salt
2 cups pitted dates, roughly chopped
2 cups warm water

Sauce

2 teaspoons kudzu root or cornstarch
2 cups plain soy milk
1½ cups vegan sugar
4 tablespoons Earth Balance, melted

LAYER CAKE
(FOR SPECIAL OCCASIONS)

Cake

1½ sticks (12 tablespoons) Earth Balance, softened

2 cups sugar

1½ tablespoons baking powder

½ teaspoon salt

4 tablespoons–½ cup your favorite liqueur (choose from Kahlua, Cointreau, rum, brandy, cherry brandy, Chambord, or Framboise)

1 teaspoon vanilla or almond extract

2¾ cups flour

¼ cup soy flour

1½ cups plain soy yogurt

Frosting

½ cup dark chocolate chips or buttons

1 stick (8 tablespoons) Earth Balance, softened

4 tablespoons vegan shortening, softened

2 tablespoons cocoa powder

3 cups confectioners' sugar

3 tablespoons rice or soy milk

1–2 tablespoons same liqueur you used in the cake

Pinch salt

Optional: Jam to spread between the layers. Use a flavor that complements your liqueur choice. For example, if using Framboise, consider using raspberry jam. Kahlua would go nicely with a chestnut puree, and Cointreau and orange marmalade is a match made in heaven!

This very tall, very decadent cake is perfect for special occasions like birthdays, anniversaries, and holiday parties. Or if you've had a really, really bad day, you can just make a cake for yourself.

1. Preheat oven to 350°F. Grease and flour two 8 x 8- or 9 x 9-inch round cake pans.
2. To make cake, cream together Earth Balance, sugar, baking powder, salt, liqueur, and extract, mixing until well blended, occasionally scraping down the sides of the bowl.
3. Alternate adding flours and yogurt, occasionally scraping down the sides of the bowl.
4. With an electric mixer, mix on medium until very well blended—about 5 minutes. Batter will be thick, but liquid. At this point, you'll need to taste batter to determine if you need to add more liqueur.
5. Divide batter between the two cake pans and bake for 25 to 35 minutes or until a knife inserted in center comes out clean. Cover with foil if you find edges are browning too quickly
6. Cool on racks for 10 minutes. Then run a knife along the sides and carefully remove cakes (since the batter is very moist, the cakes are very heavy for their size). Allow to cool completely on racks before frosting, ideally for a few hours.
7. For frosting, use microwave to melt chocolate. Nuke at 50 percent power for 2 to 2½ minutes.
8. Cream together Earth Balance and shortening until fluffy. Stir in the chocolate, and then the cocoa and salt, occasionally scraping down the sides of the bowl. Alternate adding the confectioners' sugar and the milk, 1 tablespoon at a time, again scraping down the bowl as needed.
9. Finally, add liqueur, 1 tablespoon at a time, tasting after each addition to determine the right proportion.
10. If using jam, spread on top of bottom layer, then frost the cake. Serve with coffee, spiked with a shot of the liqueur used in the cake—and plenty of water!

Yield: 1 large, decadent layer cake

Variation

Teetotaler? Skip the booze. Just bump up the vanilla extract to 1 tablespoon. Add 4 tablespoons rice or soy milk to the batter and 1 to 2 tablespoons rice or soy milk to the frosting.

NINJA GINGA' BREAD

Think all gingerbread tastes the same? This sophisticated gingerbread packs an intense flavor punch—hence its name—and is not for the faint of heart.

Being a city girl, I chose to ignore gingerbread conventions and start a few trends of my own. While most gingerbread recipes rely on light, dainty molasses, I used blackstrap molasses, since I adore its deep, damp muskiness. I also don't think that white flour has any business going anywhere near a gingerbread batter. But on the other hand, adding a helping of nutty teff flour to the spelt flour-based batter complements the spectrum of spices. Best-quality Dutch cocoa powder, espresso powder, and a splash of best-quality balsamic vinegar further round out the heady flavors of this seasonal favorite. It's delicious as is, better when slightly warmed, and through-the-roof good when served slightly warmed with a large scoop of vanilla soy ice cream or vegan whipped cream, which helps to balance the intense flavors.

1. Preheat the oven to 350°F. Grease a 9 x 9-inch baking pan.
2. In a large bowl, with electric mixer, cream together oil, applesauce, brown sugar, corn syrup, molasses, vinegar, extracts, and orange oil until smooth. (Depending on the temperature, the coconut oil may not totally dissolve. This is normal.)
3. In another large bowl, sift together the dry ingredients. Slowly add the dry ingredients to the wet, about a cup at a time, mixing each time until smooth. Pour the batter into the pan and bake for 30 to 40 minutes, or until a knife inserted in the center comes out clean.
4. When cool, dust with confectioners' sugar.

Yield: 9 servings

¼ cup coconut oil
⅓ cup unsweetened applesauce
½ cup brown sugar, packed
¼ cup dark corn syrup
½ cup blackstrap molasses
½ teaspoon balsamic vinegar
1 teaspoon vanilla extract
1 teaspoon rum extract (optional, but wonderful)
Few drops orange oil
1½ cups spelt flour
¼ cup teff flour
2 heaping tablespoons soy flour
2 tablespoons Dutch cocoa powder
2 teaspoons espresso powder
1 tablespoon baking powder
1 tablespoon powdered ginger
1 teaspoon cinnamon
¼ teaspoon cloves
¼ teaspoon salt
Confectioners' sugar, for dusting

½ cup Earth Balance, softened
¾ cup sugar
1 teaspoon baking powder
½ teaspoon baking soda
¼ teaspoon salt
1 teaspoon vanilla
2 heaping tablespoons soy flour
1 cup flour

Icing (optional)
1½ cups powdered sugar
1½ tablespoons soy or rice milk
  or water
1 teaspoon extract (vanilla,
  almond, rum, or orange)

ALL-PURPOSE
SUGAR COOKIES

This versatile recipe is a must for urban vegans. These chewy cookies are delicious as is, dipped in an ice-cold glass of rice milk. Frost them with a powdered sugar icing or decorate them with colored sugars (e.g., red and green for Christmas, or orange and black for Halloween), and you have an instant holiday dessert. They're also wonderful crumbled on top of a scoop of soy ice cream, or used as a crust in the Def-Jam Bars (see page 8).

1. Preheat oven to 300°F.
2. Using an electric mixer, cream together Earth Balance and sugar. Add baking powder, baking soda, and salt. Mix until smooth. Add vanilla. Beat in flours, about ¼ cup at a time. (Switch to a spoon if batter becomes too thick.)
3. Using your hands, knead the dough until smooth. Dough will be slightly dry. Shape into 1-inch balls and place on lightly greased cookie sheet. (Do not flatten them.) Bake for about 15 minutes. Be careful not to let edges brown. Cool on racks and enjoy.
4. For optional icing, mix ingredients. Add a few drops of food coloring, preferably all-natural, if desired.

Yield: about 30 cookies

Variations

For cinnamon-sugar cookies, add 1 teaspoon cinnamon to the batter. Replace the vanilla extract with almond, rum, maple, lemon, orange, or coconut extract. Add ½ cup of very finely chopped nuts, or almond meal, to the batter.

CHOCOLATE MOUSSE

This recipe is decadent enough to appeal to your harshest vegan critics, and easy enough to appease the most kitchen-phobic. This is the closest thing to real French mousse that I've ever tasted, and the irony is that it does not contain a drop of cream.

1 cup best-quality dark chocolate buttons
½ cup sugar
1 12-ounce aseptic container of soft tofu (not refrigerated, block tofu—that would give you a grainy texture)
2 teaspoons Cointreau or other liqueur

1. Melt dark chocolate buttons in the microwave at 50 percent power (about 3 to 5 minutes). Blend chocolate in food processor along with sugar and tofu. Process until smooth and creamy. HINT: Better to over-process than to underprocess. Add liqueur.
2. Pour into individual serving dishes and garnish with a chocolate-covered espresso bean, fresh raspberry, chocolate button, chocolate slivers, or organic orange zest. Refrigerate for a few hours before serving.

Yield: 4 normal or 6 restrained servings

Variations

Depending on your taste and your liquor stash, instead of Cointreau, you could substitute Kahlua, Grand Marnier, Amaretto, or Frangelico.
If you don't drink, you could simply eat the mousse plain, or add espresso, espresso powder, or raspberry or orange marmalade.

1½ cups sugar
½ cup light corn syrup
Pinch salt
¼ cup water
2–2½ cups peanuts
1 teaspoon vanilla
1 teaspoon baking soda

Variations

Substitute any other kind of nut
for the peanuts, e.g., almonds,
slivered almonds, hazelnuts,
pecans, walnuts, or pine nuts.
Substitute almond or rum
extract for the vanilla
(especially nice with almonds).

PEANUT BRITTLE

Making candy is easy. No candy thermometer required! (This is how I learned to make candy as a little girl.) Just set aside 20 minutes when you're sure you won't be interrupted, since you need to keep a close eye on the mixture as it boils. Package in cellophane bags with a fancy ribbon, and voilà! You have an inexpensive, creative holiday gift. Plus you won't have to navigate all those crazed shoppers clogging the city streets.

1. Spray a 9 x 13-inch rimmed cookie sheet and a spatula with cooking spray. Fill a short glass with cold water and set it next to your stovetop.
2. Mix sugar, corn syrup, and salt in a saucepan with ¼ cup water. Over medium heat, bring this mixture to a boil, stirring constantly until the sugar dissolves. Continue to boil, stirring constantly. After about 8 to 9 minutes, complete Soft Ball Test (see below for details), about once a minute, as many times as needed, until you reach the soft ball stage. It usually takes about 10 to 12 minutes, but results can vary depending on many different factors, so just pay close attention.
    Soft Ball Test: Drip some of the boiling sugar mixture into the glass of water. The mixture should attain the texture of taffy—not hard, but not watery, a little sticky, but gummy enough so that you could fish it out and eat it. This is called the "soft ball" stage. When liquid reaches this stage, the quality of the bubbles will change from being far apart to closer together. The bubbles will also appear lighter in color than the rest of the liquid.
3. Toss in the nuts. Continue to mix constantly so the nuts don't burn. Once this mixture turns a medium brown, in about 7 to 9 more minutes, turn heat to low. You will smell the sugar starting to caramelize (aka "burn"), so pay attention.
4. Now it's time to test for the hard ball stage. Drop a bit of the mixture into the water. Pull it out with your fingers or a spoon and taste it. Your teeth should detect the "glassy" quality of the brittle. If not, then it's still not done; continue to cook over medium-low until done, checking every 20 to 30 seconds.
5. Stir in vanilla and baking soda. BE CAREFUL! The mixture will probably foam up slightly at this point. It's normal; just take care.
6. Spread onto the greased cookie sheet using your oiled spatula. Work quickly. The layer should be about ⅓ to ½ inch thick.
7. Let this cool for about an hour, then break in into pieces.

Yield: about 2 cups

TIRA MI SU, PERFECTED

Tira Mi Su means "pick me up" in Italian. The name probably alludes to the caffeine-wallop of coffee used in the recipe. Although making Tira Mi Su might sound mysterious, it's basically just a simple trifle: a sponge base soaked with a creamy, liquor-infused topping. Much debate remains over which liquor to use to flavor the topping. Some use cognac, others use rum or Amaretto, while others swear by rum. I prefer the elegance of brandy here, with cognac coming in second.

I've found 99 percent of the vegan Tira Mi Sus I've tried to be either grainy, healthy tasting, or just plain "off." So I experimented until I came up with a version I liked. It's important to use the best ingredients possible. (Avoid American coffee or instant espresso, for example, and generic cocoa powder.) This is my very favorite dessert recipe and is one of my proudest accomplishments as a vegan cook. I find it's better if you make it the day before serving it, so the sponge can properly soak up the liquid.

1. Preheat oven to 350°F. Grease an 8 x 8- or 9 x 9-inch square pan. Set aside an 11 x 7-inch baking dish or other small, rectangular dish.
2. Pour all dry cake ingredients into food processor. Whiz around to mix. Add softened Earth Balance. Again, whiz around until well combined. Add vanilla, then drizzle in soy milk, ½ cup at first, then 1 tablespoon at a time, until batter is very smooth. It should be extremely thick, but thin enough to drop into the pan.
3. Drop batter into pan. Smooth top with spatula and bake for 25 to 30 minutes, or until a cake tester inserted in center comes out clean and top is golden brown. Set on rack and cool for at least 15 minutes.
4. Cut into 20 squares. Remove from pan. Don't worry if they're not perfect or if they fall apart a bit.
5. Whip Soya Too according to package directions.
6. In a large bowl, whip together cream cheese, liquor, and sugar until smooth. Fold in Soya Too.
7. Dip each cake square into the espresso. Cake should be soaked, but not dripping. Lay each piece into the baking dish. The entire dish should be covered with the coffee-soaked sponge. Use your fingers to press down slightly and even layer.
8. Using a spatula, top sponge with filling. Smooth out. Then sift top with cocoa powder. If you can manage, let it sit overnight before serving.

Yield: 9 servings

Sponge Cake

1⅓ cups flour, sifted
2 teaspoons baking powder
½ cup sugar
1 tablespoon cornstarch
Pinch salt
½ cup Earth Balance, softened
1½ teaspoons vanilla
½–¾ cup soy milk

Topping

1 cup Soya Too Soy Whip (Sorry, there is no substitute! This is available in many Whole Foods stores or online at www.veganessentials.com)
8 ounces vegan, nonhydrogenated cream cheese
2 tablespoons brandy, cognac, rum, Amaretto, or Kahlua (listed in my order of preference)
½ cup sugar
1½ cups freshly brewed espresso
2 tablespoons Dutch-process cocoa

CLASSIC CRÈME BRÛLÉE

1 10.4-ounce container Soya
   Too Whip (sorry, there is no
   substitute as of yet)
1 cup full-fat soy milk
1 vanilla bean, split lengthwise
¼–⅓ cup sugar, to taste
1½ tablespoons agar flakes or
   1½ teaspoons agar powder
1 teaspoon best-quality vanilla
   extract
Pinch salt
Pinch turmeric, for color
Sugar for topping (about 1
   teaspoon per serving, more or
   less to taste)

Ah, crème brûlée. Never thought you'd have it again, did you? My version gets its luscious creaminess from Soya Too Whip, a soy product with the exact texture and flavor of heavy whipping cream. A real vanilla bean and best-quality vanilla extract add a smooth but powerful vanilla one-two punch.

Crème Brûlée means "burnt cream" in French. It gets its moniker from its burnt sugar topping. Using a small chef's blowtorch is, by far, the most effective way to brown the sugar. But if you're cheap . . . er . . . frugal like me, and can't justify spending $60 on a tool you'll use maybe twice a year, just buy a matchless lighter at the dollar store. You'll need to keep it lit above each section for about 20 to 30 seconds to brown the sugar. (Do not put this dish under the broiler. It will undo the custard.) Your fingers will be sore, but the rewards will be sweet.

On the other hand, you can also skip the burnt sugar topping and simply enjoy the vanilla crème sans brulée topping. This creamy vanilla-infused custard tastes great either way.

1. Lightly spray six ramekins with cooking spray.
2. In a large saucepan, whisk together Soya Too and soy milk. Scrape the seeds from the vanilla bean and add them to the liquid, along with the bean, sugar, agar flakes, and extract. Allow to sit for 15 minutes. Slowly bring to a boil, stirring occasionally. It should take about 10 minute to reach the boiling stage.
3. Boil for 1 minute, watching carefully and stirring occasionally. If mixture foams up, reduce heat slightly.
4. Remove from heat. Add salt and turmeric and stir. Strain into ramekins. (I suggest first pouring the mixture into a Pyrex beaker to avoid spilling it.) Put in refrigerator and let set for at least an hour.
5. Just before serving, sprinkle sugar over each serving. Brown sugar using a blowtorch or a matchless lighter. Eat immediately.

Yield: 6 servings

ARROZ CON LECHE

I was never a big fan of rice pudding . . . until I visited Madrid. The Spanish infuse their rice pudding with lemon zest, which makes this dessert taste as sunny as the Costa del Sol. Using a real vanilla bean makes a huge impact on the flavor. But if you don't have one, good-quality vanilla extract is a fine substitute.

2 cups full-fat soy milk
1 cinnamon stick
Zest 1 organic lemon, chopped as finely as you can manage
1 vanilla bean, split, or 1½ teaspoons vanilla extract
½ cup white rice
½ cup sugar
3 tablespoons Earth Balance
½ teaspoon ground cinnamon, more or less, to taste

1. In a medium saucepan, combine milk, cinnamon stick, and lemon. Add the vanilla bean (or vanilla), making sure to scrape out most of the seeds and mix them into the milk. Slowly bring to a boil. Add the rice, then lower to a simmer and cook until the rice is tender, about 15 to 20 minutes.
2. Stir in the sugar and Earth Balance and continue to cook until pudding reaches your desired consistency.
3. Sprinkle with cinnamon and serve.

Yield: 4 servings

MAKE YOUR OWN VANILLA EXTRACT

Split two or three vanilla beans lengthwise to release the seeds. Fill a small to medium glass bottle with vodka. Insert the beans and seeds, close bottle, and shake gently. Store in a cool, dark place for about six weeks.

As you use up the vanilla, you can continue to add vanilla beans and paste left over from other baking projects. Top off the vodka when the level runs below the beans.

The longer this sits, the sweeter and more fragrant it becomes. Homemade vanilla makes an excellent gift, especially when accompanied by a cute, homemade label.

MICHELE'S PEANUT BUTTER-GRAHAM BALLS

16 vegan graham crackers
1 cup natural, smooth peanut butter
⅔ cup agave nectar or maple syrup
½ cup brown rice flour
Instant oats, chopped nuts, coconut flakes, cinnamon, cocoa powder, or any other topping

Michele is quite a baker and chef. So when she created this veganized version of one of her favorite healthy snacks, I knew it would be superb. And I was right. This recipe is especially great for kids.

1. Crush graham crackers in food processor. Place crumbs in medium bowl and add peanut butter, agave nectar, and rice flour. Mix until smooth and well blended.
2. Using hands, shape mixture into balls. Roll in your coating of choice.

Yield: 18–24 balls

CLAFOUTI

2 tablespoons Earth Balance, melted
1¾ cups full-fat soy milk
½ cup sugar
⅔ cup flour
2 tablespoons soy flour
2 teaspoons vanilla
Pinch salt
3 cups cherries, pitted (or canned cherries, drained well)
Powdered sugar, for dusting

Clafouti is on virtually every other dessert menu in major cities all across France. And no wonder: It's a classic French dessert. Reminds me of a cross between a pancake and a pudding. Although Clafouti is almost always made with cherries, feel free to experiment with other fruits.

1. Preheat oven to 350°F and grease a pie pan. Pour melted Earth Balance on bottom of pie plate.
2. In a large bowl, mix milk, sugar, flours, vanilla, and salt until combined.
3. Arrange cherries on the bottom of the pie plate, and gently pour the batter over it. Bake for 45 to 55 minutes or until golden.
4. Cool on a wire rack for at least an hour. Before serving, sprinkle with powdered sugar.

Yield: 6 servings

Variations

Substitute other fruits (e.g., blueberries, cut-up peaches, red grapes) for the cherries.

LEMON-SCENTED KIWI SORBET

Some days you win, and some days you lose. I really won big when I found seven organic kiwis for $1 at the farmers' market. They inspired this recipe. Although dessert is the logical sorbet choice, you can also serve a palate-cleansing, melon-ball scoop to your dinner party guests between courses.

6–7 kiwis, peeled and cut into
  small pieces
1¼ cups sugar
Juice 1 large organic lemon
2 tablespoons brown rice syrup
2 cups water
½ cup Limoncello (see page 204)

1. In a large glass bowl, mix kiwis, sugar, lemon juice, and brown rice syrup. Allow to macerate for at least 1 to 2 hours in the refrigerator or overnight.
2. Remove and mash, using a potato masher (for a chunkier texture) or immersion blender (for a smoother texture). Add water and Limoncello and mix well.
3. Process in an ice cream maker per the manufacturer's directions.

Yield: 4 servings

¼ cup crushed Wasa Crispbread
(about 2 crispbreads)*
2 teaspoons ground cinnamon
2 teaspoons Dutch-process cocoa
2 cups your favorite vanilla soy or
rice ice cream**
Slivered almonds, for topping
Agave nectar, for drizzling
Soy whipped cream for topping,
optional

* Substitute or augment with any
combination of the following:
your favorite ground nuts,
ground corn flakes, ground bran
flakes, ground cookies, or panko

** Substitute any of the following
soy or rice ice cream flavors:
dulce de leche, chocolate, or
coconut

UN-FRIED ICE CREAM

I'm not a big fan of deep-fried foods. But during my pre-vegan days, I had a serious thing for Mexican fried ice cream. I love Mexico, and my trips "south of the border" inspired me to create Un-fried Ice Cream, an enlightened interpretation of this popular, belly-busting dessert. Un-fried Ice Cream tastes mucho better than the high-fat, labor-intensive version. It's also much easier and less messy to make, and it won't bust your diet—or your belly. Did I happen to mention that it's vegan, too?

Un-fried Ice Cream is a surprisingly light finish to heavy Mexican entrees like enchiladas, taquitos, and guacamole. It's a snap to assemble and a surefire dinner party hit. Plus, you can easily change the recipe to suit your personal preferences.

1. In a small bowl, using a mortar and pestle, crush together crispbread (or variations), cinnamon, and cocoa. Mix together well with a spoon. Line a pan with plastic wrap.
2. Scoop out 4 healthy servings of ice cream. Use your hands to smooth into "snowballs." Cover lightly with plastic and freeze for at least 30 minutes.
3. After 30 minutes, roll each of your snowballs into the coating mixture. Use your fingers to press mixture into the snowballs. Make sure there are no "bald" patches.
4. Return coated snowballs to the pan and freeze, covered lightly with plastic wrap, for at least 30 more minutes, ideally longer.
5. Just before serving, transfer each snowball to a serving dish. Top with a few slivered almonds and a healthy drizzle of agave nectar and soy whipped cream, if desired.

Yield: 4 servings

SAUCY VEGAN

Knowing how to make a few standby sauces and condiments—both plain and fancy—can elevate many dishes from mundane to urbane. My theory is that if you have some sauce in the fridge, then you have an easy, healthful dinner waiting to be enjoyed. They help stretch your recipe repertoire and your culinary imagination.

Most people equate sauces with pastas and over proteins, but they're much more versatile than that. Drizzled over vegetables, various sauces will tease out the produce's inherent taste. Some, like the Pear-Pepper Chutney, make intriguing sandwich spreads while others, like Sun-Dried Tomato Pesto, can help give your soups and stews an extreme but simple taste makeover.

So go ahead, get saucy.

CLASSIC MARINADE FOR TOFU OR SEITAN

6 tablespoons best-quality extra-virgin olive oil (Please don't skimp. This is the mortar that holds all the flavors together.)
Splash balsamic vinegar
Splash mirin
1 tablespoon ketchup
½ teaspoon garlic powder or 1 clove garlic, minced
1 teaspoon oregano
½ teaspoon sage
1 tablespoon nutritional yeast
Pinch red pepper flakes
1 bay leaf
Salt and pepper, to taste

When life's obligations leave me crazy-busy, this is my classic, go-to meal centerpiece (this, and ordering takeout from our favorite Malaysian restaurant). You need only enough foresight to marinade your protein of choice overnight or before you leave for work in the morning—and you can alter the recipe depending on what you have on-hand.

1. Mix all ingredients together in a shallow pan. Douse your protein of choice in this culinary bath, cover with plastic, and let it rest in the fridge until dinner time. (If using tofu, cut into 4 steaks, and cover with marinade.)
2. Grill tofu or seitan over medium heat, brushing occasionally with extra marinade. Or bake, as is, in a 375°F oven for 25 minutes, basting occasionally with marinade.

Yield: enough to marinate 1 pound of extra-firm tofu, 1 pound of seitan, or 1 pound tempeh (steam tempeh for 10 minutes before marinating to remove any lingering bitterness)

SUN-DRIED TOMATO PESTO

1 cup sun-dried tomatoes packed in olive oil
5–7 cloves garlic (more or less, to taste. I recommend more.)
¼ cup pine nuts
¼ cup walnuts
1 tablespoon flaxseeds
¼–½ teaspoon salt
Zest 1 large organic lemon, finely chopped
Freshly ground pepper, to taste
Up to 1 cup best-quality extra-virgin olive oil

I freshen up this easy Ligurian classic with finely grated lemon zest, mild flaxseeds, and a vampire-chasing amount of raw garlic. Toss it—ideally—with a pound of homemade strascinate. (Farfalle or orecchiette make fine substitutes.) I recommend cooking the pasta al dente, tossing it with the pesto, and then—gasp!—letting it sit overnight before serving. This allows the pasta to drink in the pesto's sweet, earthy essence. To reheat, just nuke in the microwave for a few minutes, then serve with a drizzle of olive oil and a sprinkling of vegan Parmesan or nutritional yeast. This pesto also makes an intriguing pizza topping or sandwich spread, paired with hummus, peanut butter, or vegan cheese slices.

1. Process everything but the olive oil in a food processor until thick and pasty.
2. Drizzle in the oil until the pesto reaches a smooth but spreadable consistency. Freeze what you will not use within the next 2 weeks.

Yield: enough for 1 pound of pasta

WINTER PESTO

One of my all-time favorite foods is pesto, made with fresh basil and pine nuts that I've just toted home from the farmer's market. What's a girl to do in mid-February when she's experiencing a powerful pesto craving, but there's no fresh basil to be had? Make winter pesto, of course. Though it's not quite as pungent as licorice-scented basil, organic spinach makes a wonderful substitute and base for a creamy sauce. (Arugula also works well.) Toss winter pesto with gnocchi or pasta, or use it as a sandwich condiment in place of mayonnaise. A dollop or two is also a divine addition to soups.

Did I mention how ridiculously simple this is to make?

Place all ingredients in food processor. Process until smooth, scraping sides of processor as needed.

Yield: about 1½ cups

3 cups fresh organic spinach* or arugula, packed

½ cup plus 1 tablespoon extra-virgin olive oil

6 cloves garlic

½ cup pine nuts or walnuts, or a mixture

¼ teaspoon salt and freshly ground pepper, to taste

* Non-organic spinach is usually rife with chemicals. Spinach is one vegetable you should always buy organic.

BASIL-FENNEL CREAM

This rich, northern-Italian-inspired sauce is versatile and simple to prepare. You can use it in place of mayo on a sandwich, as a rich salad dressing, or to top the Oven Roasted Potatoes on page 129.

1. Whisk all ingredients together in a bowl until smooth.
2. Let sit in refrigerator for at least an hour; overnight is even better.
3. Drizzle with extra-virgin olive oil, if desired.

Yield: about ½ cup

4 tablespoons Vegenaise (There is no substitute. This product is simply the best.)

1 tablespoon extra-virgin olive oil

2 tablespoons dry white wine

2 tablespoons dried or fresh basil

1 tablespoon dried fennel seeds

Salt and sweet paprika to taste

EASY
TAHINI SAUCE

4 tablespoons tahini
4 tablespoons plain soy yogurt
3 tablespoons lemon juice
1 tablespoon water (for a thinner
    sauce, add more water, 1
    tablespoon at a time)
3 cloves garlic, crushed
1/4 teaspoon salt and freshly
    ground pepper, to taste

Optional additions:
cayenne pepper,
mint
fresh parsley
a few dashes of sumac

Think of this sauce as an extreme makeover tool for typically boring foods. It can take salads, steamed veggies, and baked potatoes from drab to fab in 5 minutes. When you're serving Middle Eastern food, this sauce is also a must. Drizzle it over veggie kabobs. Use it as a dip for pita bread—or as a sandwich spread. I really enjoy a few spoonfuls drizzled over the Moroccan Millet Timbales (see page 73).

Mix all ingredients in a small bowl until well combined.

Yield: about 1 cup

CREAMY
CILANTRO-LIME SAUCE

1 12.3-ounce aseptic box of silken
    tofu (Do not use refrigerated
    tofu—it's too grainy for this
    sauce.)
1/4 cup chopped fresh cilantro
    (leaves only)
1 tablespoon lime juice
Healthy dash of white pepper,
    about 1/8 teaspoon
Healthy dash of salt

These days, more Mexican restaurants will now top their entrees with soy sour cream on request. When you're at home, you can easily use store-bought soy sour cream. But why not kick it up a notch and make your own thick, cilantro-scented sauce?

This is heavenly served atop chili or burritos. You can also use it to "Mexi-fy" a burger or to accompany any Southwestern or Mexican dish. If you really love cilantro like I do, try it as a soup base, watered down with a bit of vegetable broth and adorned with scallions and slices of fresh avocado.

Using an immersion blender or food processor, mix all ingredients in a small bowl until smooth.

Yield: about 1 1/2 cups

MICROWAVE SATAY SAUCE

This sauce is the perfect dinner rescue for busy urbanites. It uses basic ingredients you already have in your pantry, and it only takes—get this—about 5 minutes to make.

Serve it as a dipping sauce for seitan (see page 104) or dry-fried tofu, or use it to top steamed vegetables or a baked potatoes. You could also use it as a traditional curry sauce; just simmer your vegetables and/or legumes of choice in the sauce for about 30 to 45 minutes, or until everything is cooked. Then serve over rice.

¼ cup peanut butter
1 cup coconut milk (light is fine)
1½ teaspoons red curry paste
(More or less, to taste. I suggest starting with ½ teaspoon and working your way up in ½ teaspoon increments.)

1. In a medium bowl, whisk everything together until smooth.
2. Microwave on high for 1½ to 2 minutes. Or heat in a saucepan, stirring occasionally, over medium-low heat until warm, about 5 minutes.

Yield: about 1½ cups

Variation

Substitute cashew butter for peanut butter.

WASABI-MISO DIPPING SAUCE

1 teaspoon white miso
½ teaspoon wasabi paste
½ teaspoon dark sesame oil
2 teaspoons ume vinegar
3 tablespoons warm water
1 tablespoon brown rice syrup or agave nectar

Sometimes, you want a little Japanese flavor without spending a bankroll on sushi. This dipping sauce combines the heat of wasabi with miso's balancing mellowness. Use it as a dip for vegetables, cold noodles, fried tofu, or the Mini–Rice Croquettes (see page 102).

Mix all ingredients well. Allow to come to room temperature before serving.

Yield: ½ cup sauce

HARISSA

18 small dried bird chili peppers
3–4 garlic cloves, peeled
1 tablespoon organic lemon juice
½ teaspoon organic lemon zest
1 teaspoon cumin
½ teaspoon fennel seeds
About ¼ cup olive oil

Harissa is a hot sauce commonly used in North African cuisine. It's the kind of ingredient that, when used prudently, will make your guests wonder, "What's that flavor?" It adds a mysterious kick to pasta, couscous, or any dish that likes a bit of spice. They say every region has their own harissa recipe. Tunisian harissa, for example, usually contains caraway or coriander seeds. My harissa includes cumin, lemon juice, lemon zest, and fennel seeds.

   The most tedious part of making harissa is removing the fiery seeds. Remember not to touch your eyes afterward—like I always manage to do. Better yet, wear rubber gloves while handling these little fireballs.

1. Remove the seeds from the chilis and discard.
2. Soak chilis until they soften, about 30 minutes. Once they're soft, toss them in the food processor with the spices and enough olive oil to make a paste—or if you're feeling particularly traditional, grind with a mortar and pestle.
3. Let the harissa sit overnight before serving to allow the flavors to get to know each other. Store in the refrigerator for several weeks in a glass jar.

Yield: a healthy cup

PIRI-PIRI SAUCE

I fell in love with piquant Piri-Piri Sauce in Lisbon, where you'll find a bottle gracing every restaurant table. I love bathing steamed tempeh with Piri-Piri. It's also amazing over extra-firm tofu that's been pressed, marinated, and grilled.

If you're a fan of heat, you need to make a large jar of this zesty little sauce; it keeps for a month or two, but it won't last that long, since you'll find yourself drizzling it on everything, Plus, "piri-piri"—the name of the African hot pepper—is just fun to say.

Instead of writing out a traditional recipe, I thought I'd give it to you in parts. This way, you can easily make any quantity you like, depending on the kind of jars you have on hand and your affinity for heat. (I make my batches in a quart mason jar!)

I part vinegar
2 parts olive oil
½ part small, red hot dried chili peppers (If you're lucky and/or persistent, you can find the piri-piris online or in a gourmet shop.)
I whole clove of garlic for every "part"
I bay leaf
Splash lemon juice
Splash whiskey (optional, but wonderful)
Coarse sea salt, to taste

Place the whole peppers in a glass jar or bottle. Add remaining ingredients. Close tightly and shake vigorously. Place in a dark place and let sit for 2 weeks.

Yield: ½ cup to I quart

QUINCE-CRANBERRY SAUCE

2 quinces, peeled

2½ cups water

1 pint cranberries (about 2 cups)

1 cup sugar

Juice ½ lemon

½ teaspoon orange extract

2 tablespoons Cointreau or Triple Sec

Unfortunately, quinces are underused in American cooking. Every autumn, I see them in the farmer's markets, largely ignored while shoppers snatch up flashier seasonal fruits like pomegranates and persimmons. I am on a mission to bring the quince back into the mainstream American kitchen. These fragrant celadon fruits smell like a cross between a very sweet apple, orange, and lemon. As they sit in your fruit bowl, they will infuse your kitchen with a sweet aroma that no synthetic candle can match. (Back in medieval times, people used whole quinces to scent their wardrobes.) They pair perfectly with cranberries in this Thanksgiving-friendly sauce.

1. Core the quinces and slice them into cranberry-size chunks. Put them in a medium saucepan and cover them with water. Cook, partially covered, over medium heat for about 1 hour until soft.
2. Add the cranberries, sugar, lemon juice, extract, and liquor, and bring to a boil. Boil gently for 15 to 20 minutes until thick. Remove from heat and let cool. Sauce will thicken.

Yield: 6 servings

Variations

Substitute any of the following liquors: Calvados, Poire William, or Limoncello.

BASIL-CREAM SAUCE

This creamy, slightly sweet sauce adds a rich sophistication to everything from steamed vegetables to baked potatoes and pasta. But it is especially good when paired with the Sweet Potato Gnocchi (see page 136).

1. In medium saucepan, melt Earth Balance. Sprinkle in flour and stir with a wire whisk to make a roux. Slowly pour in soy milk, whisking constantly. Sprinkle in the nutritional yeast flakes and miso, again whisking until smooth. Turn heat down to low.
2. Chiffonade the basil and add to the cream sauce. Mix then season with with salt and pepper.

Yield: about 1¼ cups

1 tablespoon Earth Balance
1 tablespoon flour
1 cup soy milk
1 cup nutritional yeast flakes
1 teaspoon miso paste
¼ cup basil leaves, minced
Salt, pepper to taste

Variation

Use 2 tablespoons sage leaves instead of basil.

WALNUT SAUCE

¾ cup walnuts, chopped

4 tablespoons bread crumbs

3 cloves garlic, sliced

½ teaspoon red pepper flakes

½ teaspoon dried oregano

¼ cup extra-virgin olive oil, or
 more, to taste

¼ cup nutritional yeast

¼–⅓ cup chopped Italian parsley

This decadent, earthy sauce is a nice one to stow in your culinary bag of tricks. It's a no-brainer over spaghetti when you're too tired to cook after a long day in cubicle-land, and it makes an easy-to-prep midnight snack over gnocchi after a night of dancing and pub crawling. I especially love it generously smudged over grilled tofu, seitan, or tempeh (steam tempeh 10 minutes before topping).

Mix everything in a food processor until it forms a paste. Add more oil if the sauce is too sticky.

Yield: about 1 cup

Variations

Use other nut varieties. Good options include almonds, hazelnuts, and pistachios.
Omit the oregano and add leaves from about 8 sprigs of fresh rosemary.

Wine Pairing

Nosiola, a dry white varietal from the Alto-Adige region of Italy; citrusy acidity and a nutty character that's unique for northerly whites will play beautifully off the walnuts and herbs.

JOHN'S MARINARA SAUCE

Six tablespoons of oil? An entire bulb of garlic? This sauce is packed with attitude—and flavor, and you don't have to travel all the way to Napoli to taste it. Of course, if you're garlic- or fat-phobic, you can alter the proportions to suit your preferences. But trust me, you have to try it exactly as is at least once. I mean, there's a reason we devour this sauce at least once a week. It's great on whole-wheat pasta, white pasta, and lasagna.

1. In a large soup pan, heat oil over medium–low heat. Sauté onion until soft, about 5 minutes. Add garlic, freshly ground pepper, and hot pepper flakes, if using, Sauté until garlic is soft, about another 5 minutes, being very careful not to burn it. (Turn down heat and/or remove from heat and sprinkle with salt to draw out moisture if you find it browning too quickly.)
2. Add red wine. Stir well. Add tomatoes, herbs, salt, and sugar.
3. Cook uncovered over medium heat about 45 minutes to 1 hour. If sauce thickens too quickly or if you prefer a thinner sauce, add vegetable broth, about ¼ cup at a time, until sauce reaches the desired consistency.

Yield: a large pot, enough for 1½ pounds of pasta or a pan of lasagna. Recipe is easily doubled or even tripled. Make once and freeze the rest for easy weeknight dinners.

6 tablespoons olive oil
1 medium onion, finely chopped
1 bulb garlic, sliced (about 15 cloves; no, this is not a typo)
Freshly ground pepper
⅛–¼ teaspoon red pepper flakes (optional, for arrabiata sauce)
2 tablespoons dry red wine
40 ounces canned or packaged chopped tomatoes (I recommend Pomi, an Italian brand that comes in an aseptic box)
2 tablespoons plus 1 teaspoon fresh chopped basil
1 tablespoon dried parsley
½ teaspoon dried oregano
1–1½ teaspoons salt
¼ teaspoon sugar
Vegetable stock (only needed if you want a thinner sauce or if sauce thickens too quickly)

Variation

Marinara Arrabiata (Arrabiata means "angry" in Italian):
When sautéing the onions in the oil, toss in ⅛ to ¼ teaspoon cayenne pepper flakes. The heat will infuse into the oil.

PEAR-PEPPER CHUTNEY

1 red pepper, diced
1 small onion, diced
8 dried apricots, chopped
1 ripe pear (any variety), peeled
    and diced
1 Thai hot chili pepper, deseeded
    and finely minced
1 tablespoon lime juice
½ cup water
½ cup apple cider vinegar
¼ cup sugar
1 teaspoon cumin
¼ teaspoon salt

One sad fact of city life is that you often pay more for things than your suburban peers. Housing, gas, food, you name it. I was incensed, for example, to see a jar of chutney on sale for $6 at a trendy, overpriced city gourmet shop. This little chutney is my protest condiment. It's tasty, uses common ingredients, and costs under $1 to make.

The obvious use for this chutney is as a condiment for spicy Indian food. But it's also yin to the Vidalia Onion Tart's yang, (see page 145) and is the shining star of the Elegant Lunch Sandwich (see page 45).

1. Mix all ingredients in a large saucepan. Bring to a boil, lower heat, and simmer for 30 to 40 minutes until thickened.
2. Once cool, transfer to a jar and refrigerate. Wait at least 2 hours before serving to allow the flavors to meld. Will keep for a few days in a tightly sealed jar in the refrigerator.

Yield: about 1½ cups

PASSION FRUIT–CILANTRO SAUCE

1 cup passion fruit pulp (available
    in the frozen food sections of
    many Spanish or larger grocery
    stores)
1 small onion, chopped
3 garlic cloves, pressed
2–4 tablespoons fresh cilantro,
    chopped
2 tablespoons agave nectar
1 tablespoon ketchup
¼ teaspoon salt, or more, to taste

Sweet and puckery. Tangy and hot. Passion fruit and cilantro go together like Portland and vegans. Like Philly and vegan cheese steaks. Like Bethlehem and Vegan Treats pastries. You get the picture.

Try this sauce as a topper for your favorite Mexican dishes (I love it drizzled on the Bean and Bulgur Tacos, along with avocados and vegan sour cream; see page 83). It also makes a great marinade for tofu. Skip the ketchup and use fresh passion fruit juice for a refreshing and puckery raw soup.

Put everything in a jar. Seal and shake until blended. Will keep for a few days in a tightly sealed jar in the refrigerator.

Yield: about 1¼ cups

TAMARIND BARBECUE SAUCE

Since tamarind is sweet and sour, I consider it a must in barbecue sauces. It adds a mysterious complexity and packs a powerful flavor wallop for very little effort. Tamarind paste is inexpensive and keeps for a long time. You can find a small jar for a dollar or two at your local Indian grocery. Careful: it's addictive.

Try this sauce over grilled seitan or baked tofu or tempeh. It's also heaven drizzled on a baked sweet potato or over fried plantains. I also like to use it as a condiment over store-bought veggie burgers.

1. In a medium saucepan, heat oil over medium-low heat. Toss in the onions, garlic, and spices. Sprinkle with salt and sauté until onions are soft, about 10 minutes. Take your time and sauté slowly and methodically, so the tiny bits of spice have time to infuse the oil with their heat and sweetness. This will really help to flavor the sauce.
2. Stir in the tomato paste, and cook for 1 minute. Add the remaining ingredients. Mix well and bring to a boil.
3. Reduce heat to low, and cook uncovered until reduced to about half, or until sauce reaches your desired consistency, about 15 to 20 minutes.
4. Will keep in refrigerator, covered, for a few days. You can also freeze this sauce in a well-sealed container for up to a month.

Yield: about 1½ cups

1½ tablespoons canola oil
1 small onion, very finely minced
2 garlic cloves, very finely minced
⅛ teaspoon paprika
⅛ teaspoon chili powder
⅛ teaspoon cinnamon
Dash of allspice
Dash of salt
1 6-ounce can tomato paste
2 tablespoons apple cider vinegar
1 tablespoon blackstrap molasses
4 packed tablespoons brown sugar
1 teaspoon soy sauce or tamari
1½ teaspoons tamarind concentrate
¼ teaspoon liquid smoke
2 cans water (use the tomato paste can) or 1¼ cups water

BÉCHAMEL SAUCE

$

6 tablespoons Earth Balance

3 tablespoons flour

½ cup nutritional yeast

3 cups soy or rice milk

½ teaspoon nutmeg

1 teaspoon salt

Dash turmeric, for color
  (optional)

Freshly ground pepper

What could be more urbane than creamy Béchamel sauce? It can transform the humblest of vegetables into an haute cuisine side dish. It's also a wonderful base for white lasagnas and the foundation for Pastitsio (see page 115).

1. In a medium saucepan, melt Earth Balance over medium heat. Whisk in flour and nutritional yeast to make a roux. Let mixture brown, stirring constantly, for about 5 minutes. Slowly whisk in the milk a little at a time, whisking frequently; mixture should be smooth. (Using a flat whisk helps.)
2. After all the milk has been added, add nutmeg, salt, turmeric, if using, and pepper. Bring to a boil, whisking constantly, and cook for about 1 minute. Lower heat and simmer on low, whisking frequently, until thickened slightly.
3. Set aside to cool. Skim off any "skin" that forms on top of the sauce.

Yield: about 3 cups; recipe is easily halved or doubled

BÉARNAISE SAUCE

$

2 tablespoons white wine vinegar

2 tablespoons water or stock

1 shallot, very finely minced

1 handful fresh tarragon sprigs
  plus 1 tablespoon chopped fresh
  tarragon

4 whole black peppercorns

1 bay leaf

8 tablespoons Earth Balance

3 tablespoons flour

½ cup soy or rice milk

½ cup vegetable stock

Salt and freshly ground pepper,
  to taste

Oh là là. You don't have to be a Parisian vegan to enjoy this French classic. It jazzes up grilled tofu and tempeh and also transforms steamed veggies and baked potatoes from drab to fab.

1. In a medium saucepan, place vinegar, water, shallot, tarragon sprigs, peppercorns, and bay leaf. Simmer until liquid is reduced by half. Strain and set aside until it's at room temperature.
2. In a medium saucepan, cream Earth Balance until soft and fluffy. Put this over medium heat and melt Earth Balance. Whisk in flour and make a roux. Let it cook and brown for a minute, then turn heat to low and very slowly whisk in milk, vinegar mixture, and additional stock. Season with salt and pepper. Mixture should be very smooth. Cook until reduced by half. Add chopped tarragon. Serve warm.

Yield: about 1 cup

Variations

Substitute other fresh herbs, such as parsley, basil, oregano,
or dill, for the tarragon.

RED PEPPER SAUCE

This sassy red sauce will make you think you are eating in an outdoor tapas bar on the Ramblas in Barcelona. I especially love it over pressed, marinated tofu, but you can spread it on slices of French bread, topped with a few sliced black olives, use it as a dipping sauce for crudités, or drop a few tablespoons into soups and stews for added flavor. It also makes a surprisingly tasty sandwich condiment.

Mix everything in the food processor.

Yield: about 1 cup

1 ripe tomato, roughly chopped
⅔ cup oil-packed, roasted red peppers, drained
1–2 cloves garlic, chopped
2 tablespoons almonds or walnuts
1 teaspoon red wine vinegar
Pinch red pepper flakes
2 tablespoons fresh parsley
Salt and pepper, to taste

GRAINY HOMEMADE MUSTARD

Whenever I visit Paris, I return home with a small stockpile of real Dijon mustard, even though I know it means I'll have to check my bag—something every city girl tries to avoid at all costs. Fortunately, you don't have to travel all the way to France to get good mustard (although I highly recommend you do, at least once!). Making your own is pathetically easy and fun. It's not Dijon by any means. But like many city dwellers, it's loud and will make its tart and spicy presence known on sandwiches, vegan hot dogs, and in sauces. Better than that, you can smugly tell all your friends that you made it yourself.

1. In a small bowl, mix the seeds together.
2. In a very clean coffee grinder or dedicated spice grinder, process about half the seeds to a powder. Pour into a large jar.
3. Process the other half only part way, so that some seeds remain intact. Pour into the jar with the rest of the ingredients. Using a spoon, mix very well to form a thick paste.
4. If you prefer a thinner mustard, add more water, 1 teaspoon at a time.
5. You can consume this right away, but I think it tastes much better and calms down a bit if you let it sit in the fridge for about a week. Store tightly sealed in refrigerator. Should keep for several weeks, if it lasts that long.

Yield: about 1 cup

1 tablespoon black mustard seeds
7 tablespoons yellow mustard seeds
Dash turmeric
½ teaspoon salt
¼ cup dry white wine *
1 tablespoon white vinegar *
3 tablespoons water *
1 teaspoon agave nectar (optional; this is a strong mustard, and some might prefer to temper it with some sweetness)

* Play around with the proportions of these ingredients to achieve the taste you like best.

CLASSIC AIOLI

1 garlic clove, peeled and crushed

¾ cup Vegenaise

2 tablespoons fresh lemon juice

2 tablespoons extra-virgin olive oil

1 pinch saffron dissolved in 1 tablespoon water

Salt and pepper to taste

Living in the city, you see many rags-to-riches stories, and aioli is one of them. Here, mayonnaise, or in this case Vegenaise, gets an extreme makeover: from humble sandwich condiment to sophisticated, haute cuisine sauce.

Typically used in French cuisine, think of aioli as mayonnaise with an Ivy-League degree. It's wonderful dabbed onto soups and stews or slathered on sandwiches. It's also nice drizzled on steamed veggies like broccoli, cauliflower, and roasted red peppers.

1. Mix everything in a food processor until just blended. Do not over-blend.
2. Adjust seasonings. Let sit for about an hour before serving to allow the flavors to meld. Best served at room temperature, but store in the refrigerator before serving.

Yield: a scant cup

Variations

Add up to 2 teaspoons of any of the following—
smoked paprika, cumin, or fresh minced herbs.

CARAMEL SAUCE

2 teaspoons kudzu root or cornstarch

2 cups plain soy milk

1½ cups vegan sugar

4 tablespoons Earth Balance, melted

Call me the devil incarnate, but given the choice between chocolate and caramel, I'll choose caramel every time. This sauce is incredible over ice cream or drizzled in your latte, but the best way to enjoy it is to drizzle it over the Sticky Toffee Pudding Cake (see page 171).

1. Dissolve kudzu root or cornstarch in soy milk. Pour milk mixture and remaining ingredients in a medium saucepan and slowly heat to boiling, whisking constantly, watching it carefully. When mixture comes to a full, rolling boil, turn heat down to medium and boil gently, whisking continually (every minute or so) for about 8 minutes.
2. Remove from heat and set aside to cool for about 15 minutes. Mixture will thicken when you refrigerate it. Store in the refrigerator for up to 1 week.

Yield: about 1¾ cups

SABAYON SAUCE

This classic sauce will transform an ordinary pound cake or dish of soy ice cream into a sophisticated, haute cuisine dessert. And it's a breeze to make, since you don't have to worry about separating any eggs! Try it drizzled over the fruit salad on page 42. It's an especially nice dip for apples. If you're only planning on using it to dress fruit, this recipe is easily halved. On the other hand, if you want to make a proper English trifle, double or even triple the recipe.

Blend all ingredients in a food processor until creamy. Don't be afraid to overprocess! Smooth is the operative word. Chilling this in the refrigerator for a few hours will help it thicken up.

Yield: about 2 cups

1 12-ounce container firm tofu (not refrigerated tofu, which would give you a grainy texture)

⅓–⅔ cup Marsala or sweet white wine, like Sauterne

1–1½ cups confectioners' sugar

Zest 1 organic lemon, very finely grated

Juice ½ lemon

Pinch salt

MACHO FUDGE SAUCE

¼ cup Dutch-process cocoa
½ cup brown sugar
3 tablespoons corn syrup
½ cup vegan half and half (I prefer Soya Whip, but any brand should work here)
½ cup dark chocolate buttons
Pinch salt
3 tablespoons Earth Balance, melted
1½ teaspoons best-quality vanilla extract

Nowadays in city restaurants, the "food styling" way to finish a dessert is to drizzle it with delicate swirls of chocolate sauce—barely enough to get your dessert wet. This in-your-face sauce is the proud antithesis of the dainty fudge drizzle.

With a decadent fudge sauce recipe in your repertoire, you can dress up the most mundane desserts, or take special treats to new, ecstatic levels of culinary ecstasy. This sauce is thick, rich, and deliciously overbearing. Serve it with abandon over nondairy ice cream. Dollop it unabashedly on cakes and cookies, or just eat it right out of the bowl. A tablespoon of this sauce is a dessert in itself.

1. In a medium saucepan over low heat, mix together cocoa, sugar, corn syrup, half and half, chocolate, salt, and Earth Balance, stirring occasionally until the chocolate is melted. Bring very gently and slowly to a boil, stirring occasionally. Boil gently for about 3 minutes.
2. Remove from heat and stir in vanilla.

Yield: about 2 cups

Variations

Add 1 tablespoon of your favorite compatible liqueur (e.g., Cointreau, Kahlua, Framboise); for a mocha sauce, add 1 tablespoon espresso powder as you melt the chocolate. For a nuttier sauce, replace vanilla extract with almond extract (especially good on sundaes).

HAPPY HOUR

Happy hour is an important cultural phenomenon here in U.S. cities. It helps us overworked, overstressed Americans wind down, lighten up, and ease the transition from our professional lives to our personal lives. It also helps whet our palates for dinner, provided that we don't overindulge.

Many people assume that, because I am vegan, I don't drink. Nothing could be further from the truth. When I go out, I enjoy ordering mixed drinks as much as the next person. I enjoy vegan wine almost every night with my dinner and enjoy seeking out wines that pair well with the foods I cook. (My friend Susan Crawshaw works at Moore Brothers Wine Company, a renowned wine boutique near Philadelphia. You'll find her excellent wine pairing recommendations throughout the book.)

Whether you enjoy a daily tipple or an occasional indulgence, these drink recipes will help you get the most from your liquor stash. (Please drink in moderation, and never drink if you are pregnant.)

1 lime, cut into eighths
2 tablespoons vegan sugar
1½ jiggers cachaca
Ice cubes

JOHN'S COPACABANA CAIPIRINHA

On a hot summer night, what could be more refreshing than this hot little drink from Brazil? I fell in love with its sweet-n-sour charm the first time we visited Rio de Janeiro, a very vegan-friendly and physically gifted city. It's made with cachaca (sugar cane alcohol). Careful: It's pretty potent stuff. You could use vodka if you don't happen to have any on hand, but cachaca is much more authentic and sweet.

1. Put lime wedges into tall glass.
2. Using a pestle, muddle the sugar and limes.
3. Add the cachaca and mix until the sugar dissolves completely.
4. Fill the glass with ice cubes and enjoy.

Yield: 1 serving

DID YOU KNOW?

Caipirinha means "little peasant girl." To me, this drink more aptly brings to mind the "Girl from Ipanema," a sophisticated yet refreshingly simple lady.

1¼ liters vegan red wine (I suggest a Poggio or Rioja)
4 peaches, peeled and cut into chunks
2 plums, peeled and cut into chunks
1 organic orange, peeled and cut into chunks
Juice ½ organic lemon
Rind ½ organic lemon
6 strawberries, sliced
3 tablespoons vegan sugar or agave nectar

JOHN'S SUMMER SANGRIA

Just close your eyes and think of Ibiza. When it's hot and sticky outside, sangria cools you off quicker than any air conditioner. Interestingly, this version tastes subtly spiced, even though no spices are used in the recipe; the acidity of the various fruits actually coaxes out the wine's earthy and zesty notes.

1. Mix everything in a pitcher. Chill well to allow the flavors to merge. Overnight is ideal.
2. To serve, spoon some wine-soaked fruit into a clear glass along with 3 ice cubes. Top with sangria and a few frozen green grapes.

Yield: 1 pitcher—about 4–6 servings

Variation
Use white Rioja instead of red.

MONACO

Stroll the Right Bank during summertime, and you'll see chic Frenchies languishing in outdoor cafes over an impossibly pink frou-frou drink. It's called the Monaco (pronounced "Moon"-a-co, if you're in France). The juxtaposition of unlikely ingredients initially requires a leap of faith. But once you taste this refreshing libation, you'll find yourself making it again and again.

Splash grenadine syrup (about 4
   tablespoons, or to taste)
1 bottle vegan lager
1 can lemon-lime soda

1. Pour enough grenadine syrup to line the bottoms of two glasses—about 4 tablespoons, total, 2 tablespoons per glass.
2. Divide the bottle of beer between the two glasses. Then divide the soda between the two glasses. *À votre santé!*

Yield: 2 drinks

MAKE YOUR OWN GRENADINE SYRUP

Besides being the foundation flavor of the Monaco, grenadine syrup is also nice with a little sparkling water or drizzled over vanilla soy ice cream. Keeps refrigerated for a few weeks.

1. In a medium saucepan, bring 2 cups pomegranate juice to a boil.
2. Stir in 1 cup sugar and lower to a simmer.
3. Simmer until liquid is reduced by half. Cool and use in a Monaco or other drinks.

1 glass iced tea (unsweetened, without lemon)
1 shot glass Limoncello (store-bought, or make your own—see below)
Scoop lemon sorbet, optional
Extra sugar, optional

SORRENTO ICED TEA

Limoncello is my favorite digestivo. It comes from the Sorrento region of Italy. Since it's so delicious, I can't just limit it to "after dinner" status. Iced tea and lemon go together like Sophia Loren and Marcello Mastroianni, so I say, why not add a little spirit to your iced tea?

1. Pour iced tea into a tall glass.
2. Add shot of Limoncello and sorbet and/or sugar, if desired.

Yield: 1 drink

12 organic lemons, washed well and dried (Please use organic only; other citrus fruit are ridden with pesticides.)
1 750-milliliter bottle vodka
3 cups sugar
4 cups water

LIMONCELLO

When life gives you organic lemons, make Limoncello. If you love lemons, this is the drink for you. Limoncello is a wonderful digestivo, refreshing after a heavy meal, especially during summer. Store it in the freezer; it gets rather milky and the colder it is, the better. Serve it in tiny vodka glasses while you spin all your Laura Pausini and Eros Ramazotti CDs.

While it's delicious on its own, Limoncello also serves as the base for many other drinks and is a nice liqueur to add to many baked goods and desserts. Sure, you can buy an imported bottle for $20. Or you can keep it local and make your own. (Hint: Homemade Limoncello—with a homemade label—makes a special holiday gift.)

1. Peel the rind from the lemons, being very careful to avoid the bitter pith. (Using a vegetable peeler helps.) Put rinds in a large glass pitcher or bowl, and cover them with the vodka. (Save the lemon sections for another use; I suggest juicing them. You can freeze the juice in ice cube trays or make lemonade.)
2. Cover with plastic wrap and let sit for 1 week at room temperature. Strain. Toss the peels down the garbage disposal; it will freshen up its scent.
3. Make a simple syrup with the sugar and water: Stir them together in a large saucepan over medium-low to medium heat until the sugar dissolves. Let this mixture sit for an hour or so until it cools to room temperature.
4. Add the simple syrup to the vodka mixture and stir well. Store in the freezer for a few hours until very cold. Then it's ready to sip or to use in recipes. It keeps in the freezer for a few months—if it lasts that long.

Yield: 750 milliliters or about ¾ quart

Variation
Make Arancello (Orane-cello) by substituting oranges for the lemons.

LEMON DROP

Did you get the feeling that I love lemon? Nothing—and I mean nothing—is more refreshing on a steamy summer night than looking at the skyline from your penthouse patio, while listening to Keith Jarrett and nursing an ice-cold Lemon Drop. (In my case, it's more like looking out my fourth-floor window. And I don't have a skyline view.) I love the contrast of a deep red berry for garnish, instead of the more expected lemon slice.

1. Divide the lemons between two large glasses.
2. Process remaining ingredients in a blender until slushy and smooth. Pour over lemons. Top off with a berry or three and enjoy.

Yield: 2 drinks

2 organic lemons, peeled and cut into eight wedges
4 tablespoons vodka (lemon-flavored, if you have it)
6 tablespoons Limoncello (see page 204)
2 tablespoons sugar or simple syrup (2 parts water and 1 part syrup, cooked briefly to dissolve the sugar; good to have on hand if you mix drinks often)
6 ice cubes
Fresh raspberries or sliced strawberries

MINTY MOJITOS

Straight from Havana, with an extra blast of cooling mint. Of course, Mojitos are inherently minty, but mine benefit from a little extra refreshment via a splash of peppermint extract. It really makes a difference—and so does playing "Buena Vista Social Club" while you imbibe (strongly suggested!).

1. Using a pestle, muddle the mint leaves together with the sugar.
2. Fill two medium glasses with ice and divide mint mixture between the two glasses.
3. Mix together rum, lime juice, and extract and divide between the two glasses.
4. Top off with seltzer water and an extra sprig of mint for garnish, if desired.

Yield: 2 drinks

4 sprigs fresh peppermint leaves
3–4 teaspoons sugar
Ice
3 ounces rum
Juice 2 fresh limes
⅛ teaspoon peppermint extract
Seltzer water

BAJAN RUM PUNCH

3 tablespoons freshly squeezed
  lime juice (sour)
6 tablespoons sugar (sweet)
9 tablespoons rum, preferably
  from Barbados (strong)
12 tablespoons water (weak)
A healthy dash of Angostura
  bitters
Freshly grated nutmeg or
  powdered nutmeg
Maraschino cherry for garnish
  (optional)
Ice

Citizens of Barbados call themselves Bajans, and you can't visit their capital city of Bridgetown without trying their refreshing rum punch, while you listen to a magical chorus of whistling frogs. Making it is as easy as 1, 2, 3, 4, as you'll learn from the little poem that graces practically every souvenir T-shirt and dishtowel. I kept the measurements in tablespoons so you could better see the formula.

> One of sour,
> Two of sweet,
> Three of strong,
> Four of weak.

1. Mix lime juice, sugar, rum, and water in a medium saucepan. Heat to medium-low and cook for about 3 minutes, until sugar is dissolved. Transfer to a glass container and chill for a few hours.
2. Fill four glasses with ice. Divide punch between glasses. Finish each with a splash of Angostura bitters and a grate of fresh nutmeg or a dash of powdered. Top with a cherry, if desired.

Yield: 4 drinks

KIR

4 tablespoons cassis (black
  currant liqueur)
4 small glasses of dry white wine

The purpose of an aperitif is to stimulate the appetite. But so many before-dinner drinks are either so heavy that you end up losing your appetite, or so alcoholic that you throw all inhibitions to the wind and end up eating everything in sight. This lovely Parisian drink is simple, sophisticated, and perfectly whets your palate for a fabulous dinner to be savored—slowly.

Pour about 1 tablespoon cassis into each of four wineglasses. Top off with wine.

Yield: 4 drinks

Variation

Kir Royale, for special occasions. Substitute champagne for the wine.

SPIKED AND SPICED CIDER

Tart and tangy, apple cider is perfectly fine on its own. But when you heat it up and add a few spices and some brandy, this humble country drink is transformed into a va-va-voom city slicker. It's especially wonderful to sip on during winter, while you stand before the biggest window in your apartment and watch the snow fall like powdered sugar onto the street below.

1. In a large pot, heat all ingredients, except liquor and cinnamon sticks, until hot but not boiling. Simmer for 10 minutes.
2. Strain and pour into mugs. Add an equal amount of liquor to each mug. Garnish with a cinnamon stick.

Yield: 6 servings

I quart apple cider, preferably organic
¼ cup orange or lemon juice, or a combination
¼ cup agave nectar
I teaspoon whole cloves
½ teaspoon cinnamon
¼ teaspoon nutmeg
Dash allspice
I cup brandy, calvados, or dark rum
6 cinnamon sticks for serving

PROSECCO SPRITZER

Prosecco is an aperitif that's often served at city dinner parties. But I find this Italian bubbly a tad too sweet for my taste, so I temper its cloy with a shot of slightly sour cranberry juice. Toss a few ruby-red cranberries into the glass, and you have a luxurious drink that will elegantly whet your guests' appetites.

Place about 3 cranberries in a champagne flute, and pour in the cranberry juice. Finish off with the Prosecco.

Yield: I serving

Fresh cranberries, for garnish
2 ounces unsweetened cranberry juice
6 ounces Prosecco

OPINIONATED COSMO

1–2 tablespoons vodka, depending on how bad your week has been

1½ teaspoons Cointreau, Grand Marnier, or Triple Sec

1½ teaspoons fresh lime juice

2 tablespoons cranberry juice

Fresh cranberries, for a girly-girl garnish

Anyone who's seen at least one episode of *Sex in the City* knows this pink and pretty drink is the urban girls' quintessential imbibement of choice. I often order one when I'm out, but I rarely make Cosmopolitans at home. It's a pity, because it's so easy.

I am always amused when bartenders ask me what kind of vodka I want in my Cosmo. Honestly, I think they all taste pretty much the same, especially with the influence of the other ingredients. That said, I usually go for the house vodka. (I can feel some of you cringing.)

On the other hand, I wish bartenders would start asking me if I'd prefer Cointreau, Grand Marnier, or Triple Sec in my Cosmo. I would choose the orange blast of Cointreau without hesitation, but you can make yours with whatever you'd like.

Shake all ingredients with ice in a cocktail mixer. Strain into a martini glass.

Yield: I drink

SNOBBY MARGARITA

Salt or sugar for rim (optional)

1½–2 tablespoons tequila

2 teaspoons Cointreau

2–3 tablespoons fresh squeezed lime juice

Ice

I confess: I am a margarita snob. The sickeningly sweet, pre-made, food-coloring-laden versions commonly served at American happy hours are no match for a scratch-made 'rita sipped in a bar in Mexico City.

I take my margarita snobbism one step further by replacing the more usual Triple Sec with the more flavor-packed Cointreau. I take it two steps further by listening to Lila Downs while I sip.

Dip margarita glasses in salt or sugar, if desired. Shake liquors and lime juice with ice in a cocktail shaker and strain into margarita glass.

Yield: I drink

RICO SUAVE

He's a street-wise city slicker and smooth talker, dressed from head to toe in chocolate brown. He might come across as slightly insouciant, but give him a chance: He's also got a very sweet side. And he's vegan.

Ice
4 ounces Kahlua
4 ounces chocolate soy milk
Dollop vegan whipped cream
and dusting of cocoa powder
(optional)

Fill a tumbler with ice, pour in the Kahlua and then the soy milk. Top with whipped cream, if desired, and dust with cocoa. Serve with a swizzle stick.

Yield: 1 drink

Variation

You can also serve this drink without the ice, in a mug, gently heated.

SPIKED BANANA SMOOTHIE

Why should happy hour be restricted to early evening? Surprise your Sunday brunch guests by serving this rum-spiked smoothie instead of the more traditional mimosa.

2 frozen very ripe bananas
2 cups vanilla soy milk
1 teaspoon vanilla
3 tablespoons rum
¼ teaspoon nutmeg

Process everything in the blender until smooth, If you like a thicker smoothie, add another banana or a few ice cubes. Prefer a thinner smoothie? Add more milk—or rum!

Yield: 2 large or 4 small smoothies

Tip

As bananas turn too black to use, unpeel them and freeze them in ziplock bags. This way, you'll always have bananas on hand for smoothies or muffins.

Variation

Use chocolate milk instead of vanilla. Replace nutmeg with cinnamon.

3 tablespoons vodka
1–2 tablespoons lime juice
1–2 tablespoons agave nectar
Dash of bitters

SWEET GIMLET

Since I have a sweet tooth, I've always found traditional gimlets a bit dour. A dash of agave nectar sure does the trick.

Shake all ingredients with ice in a cocktail mixer. Pour, along with ice, into a martini or cosmo glass.

Yield: 1 gimlet

3 tablespoons gin
3 tablespoons grenadine syrup
3 tablespoons sweet vermouth
3 tablespoons pomegranate juice

THOROUGHLY MODERN POM-GRONI

The Negroni has been around since the '30s. I've given it an urban update by adding a shot of pomegranate juice and by replacing nonvegan Campari with grenadine. Not only do they add splashes of pretty color, but they also provide at least a dash of antioxidants to counter all that alcohol!

Stir all ingredients with ice. Strain into a chilled glass.

Yield: 1 drink

Variation

If you're a traditionalist and want the original Negroni, substitute Campari for the pomegranate juice. Make sure you're using new Campari. It used to contain carmine, but no longer does.

MEXICAN-IRISH COFFEE

These days, most large cities are microcosms of the larger world. You stroll through ethnic neighborhoods, hear languages you don't understand, and taste foods from every nation: hence the birth of fusion cuisine. I think it's time for some fusion bartending.

Pour coffee in a tall glass or Irish coffee mug. Add Kahlua and top with a healthy dollop of vegan whipped cream. Garnish with a sprinkling of dark cocoa powder.

Yield: 1 drink

¾ cup strong, black coffee
4 tablespoons Kahlua
Vegan whipped cream
Dark cocoa powder for garnish

ZESTY BLOODY MARY

The Bloody Mary is the quintessential urban American aperitif: slick, smooth, and a little spicy. I add lemon zest to mine to give it a refreshing citrus kick.

Mix everything (except the celery stick!) in a cocktail shaker filled with ice. Strain into an iced glass. Use the celery stick as a stirrer/garnish.

Yield: 1 drink

3–4 tablespoons vodka
8 ounces tomato juice
1½ tablespoons lemon juice
1 teaspoon organic lemon zest
½ teaspoon soy sauce or vegan Worcestershire sauce
Freshly ground pepper
Hot sauce, to taste
Celery stick, for garnish

MIMOSA

⅓ cup champagne

3–4 tablespoons freshly squeezed orange juice

Dash Cointreau

¼ teaspoon organic orange zest per person

Light, bubbly, and citrus-scented, mimosas are classic brunch drinks. They reek of sophistication, yet they're surprisingly easy to make. If champagne is not within your budget, do as I do, and substitute Cava, a much cheaper Spanish dry bubbly. No one will be the wiser.

Fill a champagne flute ⅔ full with champagne. Top off with orange juice and a splash of Cointreau. Garnish with zest.

Yield: 1 drink

THANK YOU!

First, thanks to John Gatti, for his love, support, creativity, and patience.

Thanks to my friends and family, who have encouraged me, provided me with honest feedback and recipe ideas, and have just generally been there for me: Babs Byorick, Debbie Post, Regina Grunwalski, Genia Shea, Clara Gatti, Mark Gatti, Michele Gatti, Mike Gatti, Karen Gatti, Darice Colbert, Pam Sweeney, Karen Pearlman, Valerie Oula, Violet Phillips, Nadine Gorson, Cathy Rohland, and Leonard Streckfus. A special thanks also to my lawyer and good friend, Noah Gorson and to the folks at Café Lift, where I consumed endless cups of ginger-lemon tea while completing this manuscript.

Thanks to my agent, Clare Pelino, for her sage advice, enthusiasm, and positivity. A big shout out to my fabulous testing squad, who patiently edited, tested, and retested my recipes. Thank you, Cherie Anderson, Nicole Carpenter, Becca Cleaver, Ed Coffin, Jessica De Noto, Cynthia Eng, Sarah Gatti, Jennifer Hambach, Vicki Hodge, Carrie Bagnell Horsburgh, Jessica Ledbetter, Nadège Loucheux, Romina Martucci, Dianne Mayer, Jenni Mischel, Beth Morrow, Tami Noyes, Carrie Price, Theresa Petray, Sara Reynolds, Lisa Harrington Seaman, Beth Serafin, Mary Worrell, Bahar Zaker, and Guilia Zanchi. Also, cheers to my sommelier and friend, Susan Crawshaw of Moore Brothers Wine Company, who provided the excellent wine pairings.

A big thanks to two of the founding mothers of vegan cuisine, Isa Chandra Moskowitz and Dreena Burton, for their generous advice and enthusiastic encouragement.

Finally, thank you to the folks at The Globe Pequot Press for believing in this book and in me.

Metric Conversion Tables

Approximate U.S. Metric Equivalents

Liquid Ingredients

U.S. MEASURES	METRIC	U.S. MEASURES	METRIC
¼ TSP.	1.23 ML	2 TBSP.	29.57 ML
½ TSP.	2.36 ML	3 TBSP.	44.36 ML
¾ TSP.	3.70 ML	¼ CUP	59.15 ML
1 TSP.	4.93 ML	½ CUP	118.30 ML
1¼ TSP.	6.16 ML	1 CUP	236.59 ML
1½ TSP.	7.39 ML	2 CUPS OR 1 PT.	473.18 ML
1¾ TSP.	8.63 ML	3 CUPS	709.77 ML
2 TSP.	9.86 ML	4 CUPS OR 1 QT.	946.36 ML
1 TBSP.	14.79 ML	4 QTS. OR 1 GAL.	3.79 L

Dry Ingredients

U.S. MEASURES	METRIC	U.S. MEASURES		METRIC
1/16 OZ.	2 (1.8) G	2⅘ OZ.		80 G
⅛ OZ.	3½ (3.5) G	3 OZ.		85 (84.9) G
¼ OZ.	7 (7.1) G	3½ OZ.		100 G
½ OZ.	15 (14.2) G	4 OZ.		115 (113.2) G
¾ OZ.	21 (21.3) G	4½ OZ.		125 G
⅞ OZ.	25 G	5¼ OZ.		150 G
1 OZ.	30 (28.3) G	8⅞ OZ.		250 G
1¾ OZ.	50 G	16 OZ.	1 LB.	454 G
2 OZ.	60 (56.6) G	17⅗ OZ.	1 LIVRE	500 G

Animal Rights Resources

Alley Cat Allies
alleycat.org

An Animal-Friendly Life
http://ananimalfriendlylife.com

Farm Sanctuary
FarmSanctuary.org

Peta
Peta.org

Physicians' Committee for Responsible Medicine
http://pcrm.org

Vegan Action
http://vegan.org

VeganFreaks
http://veganfreaks.com

Vegan Outreach
veganoutreach.org

Menu Ideas

BRAZIL

Feijoada
Easy Passion Fruit Mousse
Caipirinhas

CARIBBEAN

Island Gumbo
Gobhi Aloo
Coconut-Lime Bars
Bajan Rum Punch

CUBAN

Havana Beans and Rice
Pan-Fried Plantains
Minty Mojitos

FRENCH: PROVENÇAL

Tapenade with French Bread
Salade Niçoise
Poivrons Farçis

FRENCH: CLASSIC

Kir
Pot au Feu
Side Salad with Dijon Vinaigrette
Chocolate Mousse

INDIAN

Pumpkin-Dal Soup
Spicy Indian Eggplant
Chai

ITALIAN 1

Italian Wedding Soup
Risotto Milanese
Tira Mi Su

ITALIAN 2

Bruschetta
Farfalle with Fennel Saltimboca
Fresh fruit

MEDITERRANEAN

Granada Paella
Spinach with Pine Nuts and Raisins
Orange-Scented Cranberry-Almond Biscotti

MEXICAN

Guacamole with Corn Chips
Jicama Salad
Portobello Burritos
Un-fried Ice Cream

MOROCCAN

Moroccan Millet Timbales
Easy Tahini Sauce
Cauliflower-Chickpea Tagine

SOUTHEAST ASIAN

Nasi Goreng Soup
Satay Seitan
Spicy Udon Noodles
Green Papaya Salad

BOUNTIFUL BRUNCH

Orange Poppy Seed Waffles
Pecan-Streusel Coffee Cake
Fruit Salad with Sabayon Sauce
Mimosa

FANCY SCHMANCY

Green Goddess Soup
Sweet Potato Gnocchi with Basil-Fennel
  Cream
Cranberry Upside-Down Cake

FAST

Philly Portobello Cheesesteak
Easy Roasted Asparagus
Monaco

KID-FRIENDLY

Grilled Cheese and Banana Sandwiches
Seitan with Satay Sauce
Raw-klava

OMNIVORE IMPRESSER

Balsamic-Roasted Vegetables
Spaghetti Carbonara
Chocolate Swirl Cheesecake

SATURDAY BREAKFAST

Easy Cornmeal Scrapple
Better than Buttermilk Pancakes
Zesty Bloody Mary

SPRING LUNCH

Chilled Zucchini Soup with Dill
Pan Bagnat
Brownie Bites

SUMMER PARTY

Arty Farty Party Nuts
Fruit Salad with Sabayon Sauce
Wrap Artistry
Summer Sangria

AUTUMN COMFORT

Potatoes with 40 Cloves of Garlic
Acorn Squash with Pecan-Cherry Stuffing
Red Jumble Crumble

WINTER WARMER

Hearty Adzuki Bean Soup
Curried Wheat Berry Salad
Balsamic-Roasted Veggies

WOW YOUR DATE

Prosecco Spritzer
Spinach-Fennel Salad
Panko-Crusted Tofu with Raspberry-Tamarind
  Glaze
Tricolor Quinoa
Crème Brulée

Glossary

Achiote: Also known as annatto, the ground pulp found around the seeds of the annatto tree, often used in Latin American cooking. Used as both a dye and to impart a slightly earthy flavoring to foods.

Agar-agar: Agar-agar is a versatile, neutral-tasting seaweed. A kinder, less processed thickening agent than gelatin, which is made from cows' hooves, agar is commonly used in Asian desserts. The name comes from the Malay word "agar," which means "jelly." In Japan, agar is known as "kanten."

To use: You need to dissolve agar in hot or boiling liquid for at least 1–2 minutes to unleash its powerful gelling properties. I let agar flakes sit in the liquid, usually fruit juice or soy milk, at room temperature for about 10 minutes before bringing the liquid to a boil to ensure everything is thoroughly mixed.

- You can substitute powdered agar for equal amounts of gelatin.
- If you're using agar flakes, you'll need to up the quantity 3:1; for example, 3 teaspoons agar flakes = 1 teaspoon agar powder.
- Generally speaking, for a "jello-like" texture, you'll need about 2 teaspoons of powder or 2 tablespoons flakes added to about 2 cups of liquid. Use less for mousses, more for "jigglers."
- With highly acidic fruits like strawberries, you'll need to add more agar.
- Certain fresh fruits, including pineapple, kiwi, mango, and peaches, actually disable agar's gelling properties. You can still use these fruits—you just need to cook them first.

While all these factoids might sound complicated, in reality, using agar is easy. The most common mistakes are not adding enough agar, or not ensuring it's properly dissolved before molding.

Saving money on agar-agar:

Buying agar powder or flakes in a health food store is agar-vatingly expensive—usually about $6 for about 6 tablespoons. To save money, I buy large packets of whole agar in an Asian grocery, and then gently pulse it into flakes in the food processor. The result? A few years' supply for only about $1.40.

Agave nectar: Sweetener made from the agave plant. Excellent substitute for honey.

Brown rice syrup: Mild sweetener made from brown rice and sprouted barley.

Cacao nibs: The slightly bitter, edible portion of a cocoa bean after harvesting, drying, and fermenting.

Fiori di Sicilia: Flavoring traditionally used in pannettone, with vanilla and citrus notes.

Instant wheat gluten: Pure protein extracted from the wheat kernel. Used to make seitan and to help bread rise.

Miso: Fermented soybean paste often used in Asian food.

Nutritional yeast: Cheesy, nutty-tasting yeast prized for its nutrition.

Seitan: "Wheat meat" made from wheat gluten. Very chewy and absorbs marinades and sauces well.

Sumac: A lemony spice often used in Middle Eastern cooking. Comes from the berries of sumac trees.

Tahini: Sesame seed butter, typically used in Middle Eastern foods.

Tempeh: Fermented soybean cakes common in Indonesian food.

Tofu: Pressed soybean "cheese." Neutral flavor; absorbs whatever flavoring you impart it with.

ADDITIONAL RESOURCES

Vegan Online Shops
Food Fight
foodfightgrocery.com

Moo Shoes
mooshoes.com

Vegan Essentials
http://veganessentials.com

Vegan Worldwide Restaurant Locator
Happy Cow
happycow.net

Vegan Alcohol Check
Barnivore
barnivore.com

INDEX

ABOUT THE AUTHOR

Dynise Balcavage has been cooking since age seven. The author of eleven books for young readers, she recently published recipes in *Herbivore* magazine and *Végétariens* magazine (France's first vegetarian magazine) and is a contributor to *VegNews*. She has appeared in the *New York Times* and *International Herald Tribune*. Dynise volunteers for Philly PAWS (Philadelphia Animal Welfare Society). When she is not globe-trotting, she calls Philadelphia home. She blogs at urbanvegan.net.